P9-DXI-975

An Infinity of Little Hours

An Infinity of Little Hours

FIVE YOUNG MEN AND
THEIR TRIAL OF FAITH
IN THE WESTERN WORLD'S
MOST AUSTERE
MONASTIC ORDER

NANCY KLEIN MAGUIRE

PUBLICAFFAIRS
NEW YORK

Published in the United States by PublicAffairs™,
a member of the Perseus Books Group.

The author is grateful to the Carthusian order for their generous permission to use photographs from their archives. Many ex-Carthusians gave pictures taken by their parents and siblings. Manfred Hassemer-Tiedeken and the author took the more recent photographs.

Printed in the United States of America.

Book design by Janet Tingey

Library of Congress Cataloging-in-Publication Data
Maguire, Nancy Klein.
An infinity of little hours : five young men and their trial of faith in the Western world's most austere monastic order / Nancy Klein Maguire.–1st ed.
p. cm.
Includes index.
ISBN-13: 978-1-58648-327-2
ISBN-10: 1-58648-327-7
1. St. Hugh's Charterhouse(West Sussex, England) 2. Carthusians—England—West Sussex. I. Title.
BX2596.S74M34 2006
271'.71042264—dc22
2005052955

First Edition

10 9 8 7 6 5 4 3 2 1

. . . When will I come and see the face of God?

—Psalm 42:3, quoted by St. Bruno

Give up all else that you may be a man of prayer. Leave the common people on the plain and with Moses climb the mountain to pray to God.

—Dom Bonaventure, Prior

Of this there is no doubt, our age and Protestantism in general may need the monastery again, or wish it were there. The "monastery" is an essential dialectical element in Christianity. We therefore need it out there like a navigation buoy at sea in order to see where we are, even though I myself would not enter it. But if there really is true Christianity in every generation, there must also be individuals who have this need . . .

—Søren Kierkegaard

CONTENTS

⊕

LIST OF ILLUSTRATIONS

ACKNOWLEDGMENTS

I am indebted to the generosity of nearly thirty Carthusians for sharing their experience. Clearly, this is their book. One of these ex-monks is my husband, which made the task possible. Twelve other monks have vetted *An Infinity of Little Hours.*

Dom Ignatius was essential to the project, providing encouragement and information from the beginning to the publication of the book. His journal and copies of Dom Joseph's sermons were an essential resource, providing the spine of the book. Brother Peter, the current Procurator of Parkminster, continually gave prompt and generous responses to arcane requests. My friend and fellow author Tom Cody gave me invaluable suggestions and encouragement throughout the six-year process. Professor Kent Cartwright of the University of Maryland's English department encouraged the initial effort and made thoughtful comments on an early draft, as did Professor Marshall Grossman on the final draft. Many friends from various professions read drafts of the book carefully and insightfully, including Lawrence Zippin, Gretchen Gehrett, Dr. Elizabeth Rosdeitcher, and Dr. Patricia Hammick. Fr. Michael Holleran read a late draft, providing unique information and encouragement, and Dr. Robert Gerwin provided support throughout the process. Professor James Hogg, the editor of *Analecta Cartusiana,* and foremost authority on matters Carthusian, kindly read several drafts of the book with great care and answered innumerable queries.

Betsy Walsh of the Folger Shakespeare Library was, as always, unfailingly helpful. David Kelly of the Library of Congress, Father Joseph Tylenda of the Woodstock Theological Library at Georgetown, and Bruce Miller of the Catholic University Library answered numerous queries. Jeannette Robinson of the Bath County Public Library in Warm Springs, Virginia, located a copy of *Pontificale Romanum*, as well as other elusive books such as the privately published eight-volume *Aux sources de la vie cartusienne.*

My agent, Martha Kaplan, took a chance on an unusual book, as well as introducing me to Ralph Eubanks, author and the director of publishing at the Library of Congress. Ralph's enthusiasm and friendship kept me going throughout the marketing process. Martha also introduced me to a very demanding editor, Clive Priddle, editorial director of Public Affairs. I am indebted to Clive for the final shape of this book, and for many hours of encouragement.

Introduction

In the year 1084, on about June 24, Bruno of Cologne and six companions reached the top of a mountain wilderness in the French Alps. In this hostile environment, known for heavy snows and extreme cold, they built individual hermit huts for themselves. It was here, over time, that the intimidating and awesome buildings of the Grande Chartreuse would develop, yet the initial principle of the individual monk pursuing God in his solitary cell would never change. From 1084 until the reforms of the second Vatican Council (1962–1965), the hermit life initiated by Bruno remained constant, a remnant of life in the eleventh century. The group has always boasted, "Cartusia nunquam reformata quia nunquam deformata," a statement reflecting the Carthusians' great pride that their order was never reformed—because it was never deformed. The eleventh-century Carthusians survived the Avignon schism, Martin Luther's ninety-five theses, the Reformation, the Council of Trent, the Enlightenment, and secularism, without changes or concessions to modern developments. In this radical religious order, or cult, as some would describe it, we have a living, breathing organism direct from the eleventh century, with all its culture newly laid bare.

Today the elderly members of the order, those who entered before 1965, provide the last opportunity to revisit the life of the eleventh-century Carthusians. The equivalent of a lost tribe will disappear from recorded history with their deaths. In fact, very few people know that the Carthusians exist—they function like the characters in Thomas Pynchon's *The Crying of Lot 49*. In Catholic schools, various religious orders recruit young Catholics on days set aside each year to encourage religious vocations; Carthusians are not present. Even informed Catholics confuse them with the Cistercians, a very different religious order. Yet some kind of homing instinct brought young men to a place where they could practice a radical form of religion—to seek God alone. By various indirect means, they found their lost tribe.

When Bruno and his followers first gathered, life was perhaps more turbulent than usual. In 1054, a schism separated the Roman Catholic Church from what we now know as the Eastern Orthodox Church. In these stormy times, on March 12, 1088, the College of Cardinals unanimously elected one of Bruno's French pupils as Pope. Eudes of Châtillon took the name of Urban II and in 1090 called Bruno to be his adviser. In 1096, Urban II eloquently preached the message of the First Crusade, deploring the killing of Eastern Christians by Muslims and the captivity of Jerusalem. He promised that devout Crusaders would go to Heaven immediately; he also designated their lands as sacred and untouchable. The crowds shouted, *"Deus vult!"* and the First Crusade began with a well-organized plan to meet at Constantinople. On their way to the Holy Land, the Crusaders massacred thousands of Jews, whom they declared "murderers of Christ." Against all odds, the Christians captured Jerusalem in 1100, and they would wage war against the Muslims in Palestine until 1291.

But Bruno saw none of that. After spending less than a year in the center of power, he successfully begged to return to his hermit life. Long before Urban's Crusaders set out, Bruno was back in the solitude of a new Carthusian monastery in Calabria, Italy. He had reached the Pope's side because his parents decided to send him from Cologne to the superb schools in Rheims, the most important archdiocese in France, where he excelled as both student and teacher. For about twenty years, Bruno taught at Rheims; the papal legate even invested him with the distinguished title of "Teacher of the Church of Rheims." After being promoted to chancellor of Rheims, Bruno resigned, protesting the abuses and the internecine struggles in the Church. As with many of us, he was looking for a new way of being religious. Perhaps like today's Fundamentalists, he felt that the bureaucracy threatened his most sacred values. His idea of becoming a hermit was certainly not new. Humans have always shown an urge for religious experience, a need to transcend themselves. Perhaps this urge, which is now metaphorically referred to as the "God gene," is hardwired. In every country, in every generation, some humans will have the God gene to such an extent that they surrender to it totally. An early Carthusian monk, Guigo II (1150), compares this appetite to the claret freely dispensed by a taverner. God gives the prospective seekers a taste of Himself, with the result that:

> *They drink all night, they drink all day:*
> *And the more they drink, the more they may.*
> *Such liking they have of that drink*
> *That of none other wine they think.*
> *But only for to drink their fill*
> *And to have of this drink all their will.*

Guigo suggests that those who have tasted the sweetness of God give everything they have to obtain more of Him.

God seekers have been around for a long time. In the second century B.C., a Jewish brotherhood of men and women, called the Essenes, lived an essentially monastic life along the west coast of the Dead Sea. In about 270 A.D., St. Antony, one of the earliest of the Desert Fathers, left his home in Egypt when he was twenty years old to seek God in the desert. By the middle of the fourth century, thousands of male and female Christians went to the deserts of Egypt, Syria, and Asia Minor in the expectation that they would find God. They were called "hermits," a term derived from the Greek word for "desert." The father of Western monasticism, St. Benedict (480–543), also became a hermit but later established twelve monasteries with twelve monks in each monastery. His monastic rule influenced every succeeding order of monks and spawned other orders. In 1012, St. Romuald reformed the Benedictines, creating a new order, the Camaldolese, which later experienced many rifts and resettlements. In the twelfth century, St. Bernard of Clairvaux hugely advanced a reform of the Benedictine order called the Cistercians. In the seventeenth century, the Abbot de Rancé reformed the Cistercians to create what we now call the Trappists. But Bruno's order was different. Once founded, it never reformed. There is no comparable continuity among Christian religious orders.

⊕

As a scholar of the seventeenth century, more than anything, I would have wanted to be on the scaffold when Charles I, king of England, was executed in 1649, an event that changed Western history. What was it really like? Was Charles really fearless? How large was the crowd? How did they smell? What was the emotional climate? Of course I could never have witnessed this seminal event, but with the possibility of writing this book, I saw an opportunity to look through a high-powered telescope at men perched high on a mountaintop since 1084. The possibility of getting inside an occult group of monks that had retained the customs of the eleventh century seemed an amazing opportunity.

What was it like to enter a Charterhouse? How does the life within change men? Who comes? Who leaves? Why? What do monks think? What do they feel? What happens to men following a routine that they believe will never change? To answer questions of this sort, I unearthed old periodicals, turn-of-the-century French sources, and a few books on Carthusians in England. I didn't find much. My ex-Carthusian husband dried up very quickly, especially since he thought no one could capture the texture of the Charterhouse. But he led me to another ex-monk and soon, although an outsider, I had some insider access to the pre-1965 Carthusian order, my portal to the eleventh century.

Finally, I learned that the Prior of Parkminster, the Charterhouse in West Sussex, England, was a classmate of my sources. So, I telephoned him. The answering machine requested that all communication be faxed. After endless revisions, I sent an introductory letter. To my utter amazement, the Prior responded the next day, extending an invitation to visit. I had hoped, at best, for a very formal hour of conversation. Yet the Prior had suggested that if I were discreet, I could use the library on the grounds of being "a professional person in the execution of her duties." I was very nervous. I wasn't sure what discreet meant, but I cut my hair short, wore a gray-hooded baggy sweater, baggy slacks, no jewelry, and no makeup. The Prior was a quick study; he sized me up immediately. I knew that in some sense, he had accepted me into the tribe. Only when all the monks were in their cells did the Prior's chosen representative lead me into the Charterhouse through a side entrance. Out of my mind with excitement, bogged down with cameras, two tape recorders, hours of tape and film, I entered another world, another century. I rather surreptitiously took pictures as rapidly as I could on the longest possible route to the library. During this visit, instead of the expected formal hour, I talked to the Prior and another monk from the 1960–1965 class for about twenty hours. I was awestruck, not only by the beauty of the Charterhouse but by the beauty of the life. As I left the grounds, I became aware that what was missing in the Charterhouse was anxiety. I had felt very safe.

When I returned to the United States, I wrote nonstop for four months in isolation, trying to capture this slice of history that had been frozen in time for nearly 1,000 years and was now about to drop into oblivion. I determined, whatever it took, to find other pre-1965 monks of this religious order, now in their sixties and seventies, and persuade them to tell me how they had fared when they tried to live in another era, to travel back in time. I had never before encountered this sort of challenge.

Carthusians are hermits by instinct, and even ex-Carthusians are difficult to trace. Using telephone, Internet, and word-of-mouth clues, I located twenty ex-Carthusians, from Berlin, Germany, to Perth, Australia, who had been in the order between 1960 and 1965 and ten others who had entered at other times. Because Carthusians are like the U.S. Marines—once a Carthusian, always a Carthusian—I treated the ex-monks the same as those who had stayed. Initially, the men were cautious in communicating with me. But after several years, especially after personal interviews with eight of the European monks in 2003 and a return visit to Parkminster, any doubts vanished. One of them even said, "You *are* a Carthusian." The entire cadre of ex-monks shared the excitement whenever I located another of their number. One of them suggested that the CIA should hire me. Yet during the course of writing this book, except for two monks, one of whom the order put in touch with the other when he departed after a breakdown, the monks did not communicate with each other until they met in 2003.

As the remaining eyewitnesses were dying off, I considered it important to reconstruct, as accurately as possible, the pre-1965 Carthusian way of life. All the monks generously gave me lengthy interviews: by telephone, fax, in person, and some in nearly daily e-mail exchanges for over five years. Because I usually only found the monks who were willing to be found, I cannot guarantee that my collection of monks is unbiased. But even those monks who left under the most unfavorable circumstances responded to my introductory letter immediately, and positively. They were shocked to learn of the changes since Vatican II: One of the ex-monks wrote, "To be undertaking a study of pre-Vatican II Parkminster tells me there must be a post-Vatican II Carthusian order. This horrifies me."

The information the monks gave has all the merits and defects of oral history—moreover, oral history compiled forty years after the events. Yet a rigorously conservative, factual account, garnered from the statutes of the order, for example, could not pick up the psychological register of the Charterhouse. So, men in their sixties and seventies recounted the highly charged and, at times, very stressful events of their youth. Not surprisingly, they frequently remembered different things; sometimes they contradicted each other. Selective memory occurred. I learned, for example, of a post-Christmas celebration from letters written in the mid-1960s. Although three monks insisted that the celebration never happened, others remembered it in great detail. One of the three, when confronted with the detailed descriptions, was then able to remember the event. The other two still insist that the celebration never happened—although, in this case, the records of the order prove it did. Sometimes the monks just got it wrong. More often, though, several monks would remember the same events. When three or more monks agreed on something, I concluded that their collective memory was probably accurate. When in doubt, I used information from other sources, mostly other Charterhouses, as verification. To aid the reader, I have included a glossary of sometimes arcane religious and monastic terms at the end of this book.

The monks gave me letters, notes, pictures, sermons, books, manuscripts, and various other documents. Sometimes, these are personal accounts of events, which have the same validity as, for example, *The Diary of Samuel Pepys*, where events are seen through the filter of Pepys. The documents record the reactions and transactions of the monks; if nothing else, and perhaps most significantly, they record their mindset. The detailed information about the monks' thoughts, actions, and feelings comes from this material, including the information about their Novice Master. The monks gave me many letters that he had written. I have also used all the available printed material recording Carthusian life; thanks to the monks, this material includes books recording the liturgy of the Carthusians, specifically, their breviary, diurnal, and missal, as well as books containing other rituals and statutes. Parkminster also allowed me access to its "Annals," an in-house manuscript journal of events. From these bits and pieces of information, a mosaic of the monk's life emerged. Sometimes I have used the current opinions and sentiments of the monk as a guide to his earlier character or have used my own personal response to him. Occasionally, I draw from the reflections of one of the monks, written many years later and published by the order in 1998. I have recorded as many monk voices as feasible within the scope of this book.

The monks remain reclusive, and to preserve their anonymity, I've changed the last names of those still living and the religious names of those still in the order. I have included nothing that could not have happened, but I have not bound myself to reproducing an exact chronology. To create a sense of the texture of life within the Charterhouse, I have chosen illustrative calendar days throughout these five years. The story that follows reveals the transition of the newcomers as they become attuned to the rhythms and rigors of the Carthusian life. The process of becoming a Carthusian can be likened to the painful, arduous journey to the summit of Mt. Everest, the most challenging and rigorous of all adventures; the monks' spiritual marathon, however, lasted five years instead of forty-some days. As the monks progress in their journey, the chapters become more explicit about their inner life. The real struggle, the mental and psychological hurdles, began after they had acclimated to the eleventh century. They then began to move from base camp into more rarefied air.

An Infinity of Little Hours documents the journeys of five Carthusian novices, those seeking permanent admission to the order, as they travel toward inner space within the confines of their solitary cells. I draw a portrait of these rare but perennial men, seen from various perspectives. The reader witnesses them adjusting or failing to adjust to the Carthusian regime. While acclimating to eleventh-century life, the novices also had to adapt to the most rigorous monastic regime in the Western world; by modern standards, the early monk founders appear to have designed the regime for the purpose of discomforting and disrupting. From the founders' perspective, however, they created customs designed to encourage a life of prayer and meditation. The newcomer learned the route with difficulty, surmounting physical, emotional, and intellectual hurdles. For the first two years, the novice learned how to adapt to the external life of the order; then, if the solemnly professed monks, or the "solemns" as the novices called them, voted him into the order, he was allowed to make a three-year commitment, known as simple profession, as a "junior." Then, while continuing to live in the novitiate, he assimilated the interior life of the Carthusian monk. Before making solemn profession, he had to convince the solemns that he would be able to persevere until he died.

Carthusians mark time not by decades, years, hours, or days, but by the liturgical year, the seasons of the Church. Their time is out of time, directed not by business opportunities, not by social engagements, but by the tolling of the immense church bell. Its deep and continuing resonance gives structure to monastic days and nights. Time moves slowly and predictably, in measured instants of the Latin "now": *nunc, nunc, nunc.* For the monk, there is no future and no past, merely a series of "nows." Moment by moment, breath by breath; like a heartbeat. Time slows down; by secular standards, the monks move in slow motion. The life-support system of the Charterhouse allows the monks to function at a slower pace, diving deeper and still deeper into the silence. Hazily and distantly, the monks mark the time by their progress in the order: the novitiate, the time when the newcomer enters and gets acclimated; the juniorate, the time when he gets enough votes to permit him to continue and to make simple profession; and finally, solemn profession, the time when he is or is not permitted to bind himself to the order for life.

In the microcosm of his cell, the novice observes the changes of the natural year in his garden, secluded from any other view. After the dead of winter, he sees shoots springing up in the garden, and he digs, plants, and weeds. During the few hot spells in summer, he carries buckets of water from his cell to keep the garden alive. In December, he watches the last rose in his garden fade and crumple. The novice strains to hear the silence. A bird flies overhead, a cricket chirps, he drops a hoe, his boots squeak as he walks around his garden, a pear drops from the espaliered tree, he hears the scurry of a mouse . . .

CHAPTER 1

Arrivals (July 1960–March 1961)

JULY 13, 1960

Once more Paddy O'Connell thought to himself, "If God exists, being a Carthusian makes sense, is rigorously coherent. If God does not exist, then I am a fool, a victim of a self-destroying illusion. Everything hangs on this one question." Then, taking a deep breath, he took hold of the bell rope of the Gatehouse of St. Hugh's Charterhouse.

He hesitated. Why not get a look at the outside of the building complex before ringing the bell? Paddy, a Dubliner, was twenty-seven years old. Inside the white and black habit of a Trappist novice, his wiry body moved with endlessly restless energy. He found it hard to stand still for any length of time. Even at this crucial moment, there was a twinkle in his eye. From the drive, he had seen the rather forbidding front of the Charterhouse, with its gray-brown stone and iron-barred windows, for the first time. The massive Charterhouse looked much like an English estate or an Oxford college. He walked around the Charterhouse to the right of the Gatehouse. He saw beehives, lots of apple trees, and more rabbits than vegetables in the gardens. He retraced his steps and walked to the left of the Gatehouse. He could just see over the walls from this angle and saw what he thought were the monks' cells—their modest two-story dwellings. From here, he could see a lot more of the church; he clearly saw the bell tower, close to the front steeple; then, on top of the steeple, he saw a curious wrought-iron cross with a circle around the intersecting lines and a four-foot finial with four curling ornaments. He also saw buildings that branched out from the church. He smelled and heard sheep in a meadow right behind the cells. Then he heard the boom of the bell as it rang the Angelus, resonating across the countryside.

Before joining the Trappists in January 1959, Paddy O'Connell had lived with his parents and his two older brothers and a sister in Kimmage, a suburb about three miles from the center of Dublin. His mother shopped every day for food in small grocery stores; there were no supermarkets, and refrigerators were still uncommon. His father had died when he was fourteen. His family lived next door to a Passionist monastery and he served there as an altar boy, although not a very good one because he couldn't keep a straight face. He was boisterous and good at every kind of sport; the only time he really sat still was when he was in a corner totally absorbed in reading a book while his family made all kinds of noise around him. He went to school with the Christian Brothers on Synge Street, but he was not a pious teenager; he never got involved with parish activities. Yet the church was the center of Dublin social life. In a lively city, about 95 percent Catholic, Paddy had a very good time and had frequent romantic encounters. He was a natural flirt; he couldn't help himself.

While having a grand time with sports and girls, Paddy received scholarships throughout college and graduated with honors in economics and commerce from University College, Dublin. He was frequently elected to offices; he had, for example, been president of the debating society, and he had an entrepreneurial streak. After graduation, he joined the civil service, where he rose to fairly high levels early in his career. His boss called him an "absolute genius" in administration. He more or less ignored the Marian Year in 1954, but he paid attention to Ireland joining the United Nations in 1955 and to Ronnie Delaney taking a gold for Dublin in the 1956 Melbourne Olympics, the high point of Irish middle distance running. Although the Irish economy was bad in the 1950s, Dublin did well; in fact, its population increased by 5 percent during the 1950s. Paddy thoroughly enjoyed life in Dublin. He felt great: "On a beautiful summer's day, I walked along the canal, feeling fit, savoring life, smiling at the girls, everything was going fine." But at the same time, Paddy kept trying to comprehend *everything* in one idea, or as a young man taught in Catholic schools would say, in one synthetic vision. Going to work, he would sit on the upper deck of a green Dublin bus reading a concise presentation of St. Thomas Aquinas.

When he was twenty-six, he broke his leg playing rugby. He spent six or more weeks in the Mater Hospital. He witnessed all the dramas of suffering and death in a big city accident ward. Immobilized on a hard plank, without television, radio, sports, or girls, he came face-to-face with himself and thought critically about his very pleasant life, which suddenly seemed hollow. The Catholic alternative, of course, was religious life. Paddy could hardly see himself as "a dignified priest leading the ladies' sodality." He suspected that he was not virtuous enough. He read *The Seven Storey Mountain* by the Trappist Thomas Merton, then a British citizen, in which he discovered the ideal of seeking God, an expression of the elusive synthetic vision. After that, Paddy visited various monasteries in Ireland and then chose what he considered the worst one from the point of view of buildings and singing—the Trappist Abbey's of Mellifont. Established in 1140, Henry VIII confiscated the abbey in 1539, evicting 150 monks and seizing the abbey's treasure. In 1938, the Trappists purchased 1,000 acres of the old Mellifont Abbey's land and started to rebuild. Paddy wanted a challenging life, and perhaps he also wanted to help rebuild the ancient abbey.

"God help me," he thought, "I am bloodthirsty." As most young men drawn to monasticism, he felt he needed a very strict ascetic life. He realized what a hard life he was choosing for himself, but he knew he needed something physically rough. He felt that he needed to sweat out his conversion, and sweat he did. The Trappists perform hard agricultural labor mostly by hand. He got one clean shirt a month, and he slept in his habit; his living space was a curtained cubicle in a large dormitory. The Trappists did not speak, and he deliberately did not learn their sign language. After a year and a half, Paddy discovered a desire for more solitude and more direct contact with God. Then, during mealtime, the lector for the week read from a book on monasticism in England, and, for the first time, Paddy discovered the existence of the Carthusian order. Was this what he wanted? His Trappist Novice Master suggested that he make a one-month retreat at Parkminster. The solitude of the Charterhouse tempts many Trappists, and a brief exposure to the real thing usually turns them off. The Novice Master fully expected that Paddy would return.

The Abbot approved but, of course, did not want this trial retreat to be too public. So Paddy's brother Brendan came and picked him up at the crack of dawn before anyone was about. He drove him to Dublin's airport, bought him a huge ice-cream cone (at seven o'clock in the morning), and sent him on his way to London. As he was walking awkwardly through the city center to Victoria Station in his white and black Trappist habit and displaying his shaved head, two girls came toward him on the sidewalk and looked casually at him. He felt chagrined as he blushed deep red. The girls burst out laughing and went by nudging one another. "Well," he reflected, "I have been in a monastery for eighteen months. I guess I've lost my touch."

JULY 14, 1960

Hans Klein's family were prominent and well-to-do members of a small East German town outside Berlin. During World War II, his father served in the German army. When the Russians were attacking from the East, Hans's invincible mother had taken her three boys to the river Elbe so that the Americans would transport them to the West. Because the first boats only took the fleeing German soldiers, the Americans told the civilians to come back the next day. Hans and his family spent the night in a deserted castle, sleeping on precious carpets. They still have a silver spoon that they took as a souvenir. During the night the Russians unexpectedly arrived, and Hans and his family lost their chance to cross the river. The Russians ordered them to return home within three days or forfeit all their property.

After the war, when East was divided from West, Hans could go back and forth to his school in West Berlin quite easily. But in 1953, when Hans was fifteen, his life changed radically. The border guards caught his father smuggling margarine for his family into East Berlin. The guards told his father to report to the police station the next day. Hans's mother called a Catholic soldier, and the soldier assured her that her husband faced imprisonment, if not worse. She telephoned Hans at school and told him to come home immediately. That night, wearing all the clothes they could put on, Hans and his entire family fled to the West, leaving their assets and properties behind, including a very large and elegant summer home by the Kalksee in Woltersdorf near Berlin. The five members of Hans's family lived in one room in an aunt's house until they could recover financially.

Hans continued his studies at the college of St. Peter Canisius, whose teachers were the erudite Jesuits. A militant religious society (somewhat aligned with the guilds) founded by St. Ignatius Loyola in 1534, the Jesuits officially included teaching in their Constitutions and excluded chanting the Divine Office. While Hans studied, his parents made a new start. His father got a job in a grocery store, and after a while his mother rented a shop that she ran, and then they were able to get an apartment of their own. As the oldest of the three boys, and absolutely responsible, Hans helped in the shop, weighing produce and packing groceries. At school, he read books about religious contemplatives, such as *The Song at the Scaffold* by Gertrud von Le Fort and *Le Dialogue des Carmélites* by Georges Bernanos. He also read Merton's *Seven Storey Mountain.* But instead of joining a contemplative order, he decided to become a missionary. In 1957, he joined the White Fathers, a religious order dedicated to African missionary work. After two years, using his West German passport, Hans went to the White Fathers' London College in Totteridge, North London, where he studied theology for a year. He spoke Greek, Latin, French, English, and German and was part of a lively international community of about 120 young men.

Although Hans was very happy with the White Fathers, when he was in his third year, he came across Pope Pius XI's 1924 letter, "Umbratilem." In this letter, Pius XI had written to the Carthusian order insisting that contemplatives contribute *"multum plus"* to the growth of the Church—more than those who worked as parish priests or even missionaries. This impressed Hans. About the same time, the Pope made St. Thérèse of Lisieux, a Carmelite contemplative nun, the patron saint of missionaries. This patronage and the letter persuaded Hans that he was called to the contemplative life. He thought that he would help the missions more by prayer than by missionary work. Geographically, Parkminster was the closest contemplative monastery.

Hans visited the Charterhouse in early May, and on July 14, 1960, Dom Bonaventure, the Prior, wrote to him, "I received your letter of May 16th and agree to your proposal to try our vocation in a cell. Generally we believe that a month just suffices to try the aptness of an aspirant with us: is that all right with you?" All Carthusian monks refer to themselves as "Dom," which is an abbreviation for the Latin *dominus,* meaning "master"—in modern use, the word would mean "Mr." Hans left Totteridge the next morning. He took the bus to High Barnet tube station and went from there to Victoria and by rail to Horsham.

As he rode the bus from Horsham, he could hear the noontime Angelus from the Charterhouse, and when he got off the bus, he could make out a small sign, which seemed to be trying to hide itself, on the right side of the road: below the Carthusian cross and orb, the sign read, in diminutive lettering, "St. Hugh's Charterhouse." He saw what appeared to be a lodge by the entrance to the Charterhouse. He walked the winding road of about 200 yards carrying a few essential items: razor, toothbrush, casual clothes, underwear, socks, and sturdy shoes. Dom Bonaventure had instructed him to wear secular clothes and to bring supplies for a fortnight. When he saw the façade of the Gatehouse emerging through the winding, oak-sheltered drive, he felt his stomach plunge.

He suddenly glimpsed what looked to him like the yellowish haze of a huge building complex at the end of the drive. Then, all at once, Hans was in front of the Gatehouse with its grilles on the windows and formidable, heavy, double-oak doors, set back from the façade by three tiers of columns. Heavy black steel hinges reinforced the double doors. He noted the three tiers of barbed wire above the eight-foot walls. He shivered a bit, but grabbed the bell rope next to the door.

OCTOBER 1960

The night before Bernie Shea left for Parkminster, he had had the time of his life, reveling under the bright lights of Manhattan. He'd gone to a little jazz bar on Broadway where he'd heard a fantastic drummer, Gene Krupa. He had luxuriated in the music.

Both of Bernie's parents were children of Irish immigrants, and they were strict Catholics. Bernie was the middle child—in a family of two boys and three girls. His older brother was very conservative and religious, but Bernie was a troublemaker. The nuns in Bernie's Irish-Italian school in Brooklyn would not have chosen Bernie for a monk. He started smoking at age twelve, fought willingly with older boys, and really liked the girls. Every Friday night he went to the school dance, but instead of learning how to dance, he preferred standing on the side looking like a tough guy. He loved rock and roll. But in spite of being a troublemaker, he was an altar boy and went to daily mass. His parents kept his enthusiasm for girls in check—he wasn't even allowed to date until after graduating from high school.

To finance his lifestyle, Bernie worked hard: paper route, delivery boy, and cleaning in the local butcher shop. When he was fifteen, he cheered on Senator Joe McCarthy as he watched the afternoon Senate inquiries on television. He and his friends were sure McCarthy was the good guy fighting the "Reds." At sixteen, he spent the summer ushering at Brooklyn's Paramount Theater. He was built like a block of granite and liked breaking up fights. But during that summer, he read what he thought would be an adventure story, a book by Thomas Merton called *The Seven Storey Mountain.* Once he finished it, Bernie suddenly stopped being a troublemaker.

Bernie graduated from high school in 1957, the year the Soviet Union launched the first satellite, *Sputnik I,* which circled the earth in ninety-five minutes. Bernie liked math and science, and the United States needed engineers to catch up with the Russians. He decided to study engineering in college—a lucrative career at the time. He quit after a year. Monetary success just didn't appeal to him. The more rebellious act seemed to be to join a monastery, making a truly alternative statement. So Bernie quit college and joined the Trappists in Spencer, Massachusetts. He thought the Trappists had a marvelously balanced life; he had almost everything he wanted. Yet he could not suppress a desire for greater solitude, and after nearly two years, he decided to join the Carthusians. His Novice Master counseled against it, but Bernie believed he was called to be a Carthusian. Following his intuition, and not the counsel of a man he considered a good and holy monk, frightened him. But he persisted, and in 1959, he made a retreat at the one-monk Carthusian foundation in Vermont, manned by Dom Stephen Boylan. At that time, 420 American applicants had tested their vocation in Vermont; only fourteen wanted to continue. Bernie was one of them.

He returned home to New York, where he attended the City College of New York for a year in order to study Latin at no cost to anyone. During the summer, he worked on a construction site to earn passage to England by boat. In late September 1960, he boarded the *Mauretania* from the docks on the East River. On the ship, he enjoyed the new *Ocean's Eleven* movie with Dean Martin and Frank Sinatra. The Irishmen on the boat were very excited about the possible election of a

Catholic president—John F. Kennedy—but Bernie was not interested in politics. When another passenger asked him why he was going to a monastery, he said, "I must be about my Father's business." In some mysterious way, that summed it up for Bernie. But he had not abandoned all worldly interests. During the Atlantic crossing, he met and fell in love with a glorious young woman. He was in conflict. He had made a promise to God to enter the Charterhouse, but God had presented him with this dazzling woman. What did God want him to do? He let it simmer and stew in his head, but when the boat docked in Liverpool, instead of going to the Charterhouse, he accompanied the young woman to her home in Manchester. Still dazzled, he took her to a movie theater and arrived there in time for the last of the commercials that preceded the feature film. The ad showed a line of Carthusian monks on their way to church. With monastic chant in the background, the ad went on to promote green Chartreuse liqueur. Bernie didn't need any more signs. He got up immediately, said goodbye to the young lady, and set off for London and then on to Sussex.

He reached Parkminster early in the morning, long before dawn—the bus driver knew where to let him off. He saw a light in the little lodge by the road, knocked on the door, and met an elderly couple, Eddie and his wife. They told him that the monks would be asleep at 4:00 AM, but they gave him a flashlight. He walked up to the castle-like gate and fumbled in search of an electric doorbell. Instead, he finally found the bell rope. The entire environment was surreal. After much confusion and hesitation, he pulled the rope, which produced an eerie clang. There was no reply, so he returned to the cottage to enjoy the warmth of the gatekeepers' hospitality until morning. They gave him a good breakfast. At daybreak, he gave them all the money he had left and went down the road again. He gratefully noticed a white statue of the Blessed Virgin above the entrance and St. Bruno and John the Baptist standing guard on either side. He studied the order's coat of arms, a cross and orb with seven stars above the orb, carved in stone above the double doors. Without any hesitation this time, he grasped the bell rope.

DECEMBER 2, 1960

Chuck Henley really didn't have a clue where he was going. He didn't realize how early the sun set in December, and it was dark by the time he found himself standing at the end of the drive. There were no streetlights, so he might as well have been in the middle of the woods. He slowly stumbled along the winding path before finally glimpsing a huge building hovering in the darkness. After what seemed about a quarter of a mile, past the last bend, the Charterhouse loomed like a fortress. At night, the front of the Charterhouse was huge, black, and undifferentiated, with no light whatsoever. As Chuck reached for the door handle, his whole world was reduced to the vast black wall and the bell rope.

Chuck had grown up in a town outside Philadelphia where the parish church was built in honor of, and named for, his great-great-grandfather, the son of an Irish immigrant. His great-great-grandfather laid more miles of railroad track than anyone in America; his estate was valued at $5,000,000 at the time of his death in 1895. Chuck once asked his father what had happened to all that money. His father had said cryptically, "Shirtsleeves to shirtsleeves in three generations." Chuck's father was the town doctor, who, with the parish priest, held the town together.

Chuck's entire family—parents, siblings, and grandparents—took part in his Carthusian adventure. Chuck knew that he was adding a new honor to the family name and that he would be successful at being a monk. His grandmother, Aunt Rita, and Uncle Frank sent a telegram from Chicago that he received onboard ship. Aunt Rita, who taught at Loyola University in Chicago, had written the message: "Bon voyage, Charles. A bargain is a bargain. Prayers here for prayers there. Take care. Love. Grandma, Rita, and Frank." The *Maasdam*, a Holland America ship, departed Hoboken, New Jersey, on November 21, 1960.

Chuck's trip to England was uneventful, inasmuch as crossing the stormy North Atlantic with forty-mile-an-hour winds in a small ocean liner can be said to be uneventful. Few passengers made the crossing. "Stateroom" proved an ironic name for his tiny cabin, big enough to hold two bunk beds, and very close to the boiler room on a very low deck. Except for sleeping, Chuck lived in the gym. The gym featured a Ping-Pong table, with only about three feet on either side of the table, and ten feet on each end. Besides the table, the only other things in the gym were miscellaneous items of marine gear strewn on the floor at the ends of the room, whose purpose seemed to be to test the footwork of the players. The high point of the trip was a tournament, which, to Chuck's disappointment, he did not win. But Ping-Pong spurred a friendship with a worldly-wise-beyond-his-years Australian named Kent. He was serious, thoughtful, and, although completely secular, seemed to be on his own journey of discovery. To Chuck he was a "living, breathing exemplar of Western Man's striving for who knows what," restlessly searching and interrogating the world along the way.

Toward the end of the voyage, Chuck felt that he wanted to tell Kent that he was about to join a monastery. At first, Kent said nothing, then he finally asked, "Have you read Steinbeck and Hemingway?" Chuck said no, smiling to himself, because the usual question people wanted to ask him was, "Have you screwed any girls?" Kent replied, "I might have become a monk when I was twenty," and there the conversation ended. Without ever saying so, Chuck felt that Kent had indicated that he thought the monastery a terrible idea, even though he respected Chuck for his decision.

Chuck didn't try to explain, although he would later tell the other novices in considerable detail of how he had come to the decision. Since he was sixteen, he had walked the beach every night, trying to figure out his life. By the summer of 1960, he was hopelessly conflicted. The conflict ended on a day when he was sitting by himself in the vast cavern of an old church and started thinking about prayer. Instantly, he realized: "If prayer is real, then why would anyone not want to spend their time praying?" During his junior year in college, he told the chaplain: "This is what I want to do. Are there any religious orders that do this?" The chaplain gave him a slim book on the three contemplative orders—Camaldolese, Trappist, and Carthusian—but advised Chuck to join the Carthusians. Chuck never questioned his subsequent decision.

The *Maasdam* docked at Southampton on Tuesday, November 29, and Chuck sent a telegram to his parents. A boat train took the passengers to London but arrived too late for Chuck to continue to Parkminster. He and Kent found a hotel, the Francia Private Hotel on Gillingham Street, and planned a tour of the capital. They started off on foot from near the Catholic Westminster Cathedral in the late afternoon, and they managed quite a respectable tour of London in what turned out to be a four-hour hike. A week later, Chuck would be taking a four-hour hike with the monks in the Sussex countryside.

MARCH 4, 1961

Dave Lynch had never taken a transatlantic flight before, and he was frayed by the ordeal by the time he reached Heathrow. In a hurry to get to the Charterhouse, he ignored his jet lag and took a bus directly to Victoria Station. He didn't even look at the sights of London. He pushed into the swarms of people trying to get tickets. No one seemed to have a clue where they were going. He found a timetable and discovered that he would have to wait a while for the train to Horsham; he checked his bag at Left Luggage and went to see Westminster Cathedral. By the time he boarded the 10:33 AM to Horsham, a squalid commuter train, he was exhausted. As the train drew out of Victoria, he noticed the run-down shanty-type houses on either side of the track, which reminded him of Chicago. Thirty minutes later, he was gazing at the passing countryside, thinking about nothing in particular as the train moved through the slightly rolling hills with tidy fields separated by trees and bushes.

Dave had studied maps of the area and could see the North Downs, a ridge of chalk hills, from the train. Hedgerows crisscrossed the fields, and he enjoyed the sight of black-and-white cows, familiar to him from the Midwest. After Holmwood, the ground seemed to be sloping more. Some villages with old timber-frame houses appeared. After a little over an hour of travel, he got off the train. Horsham station was beyond shabby. He was intrigued. Chicago had no equivalent to a down-at-the-heels, nineteenth-century small market town with a miserable train station. Horsham began as a Saxon village, and by 1961 had a population of about 25,000. During World War II, the Germans bombed Horsham, about fifteen miles from Parkminster, several times, despite the nationwide wartime blackout, which caused the monks not to ring their bells for Night Office from August 31, 1939, until December 16, 1944. During World War I, a German plane flew over the Charterhouse on August 26, 1916, at night, and from that time on, the monks kept black hangings over the church windows. The monks removed the hangings and started ringing the bells again after the Armistice on November 11, 1918.

Dave found a men's room at the end of the platform and then walked up the steps to street level. He found his bus stop to the right of the train station. He liked finding his way around new places and learned that bus 107 went by the Charterhouse. He had missed a bus by ten minutes. There was a slight drizzle, and he waited under the overhang by the bus stop, thinking idly about his twenty-third birthday celebration the day before. The next bus eventually came, occupied by seven people. As the bus went through a dense wooded area, almost a tunnel, he became concerned, wondering where he was, but soon enough, the driver said, with a grin, "Monastery coming up." With increased nervousness, Dave got off the bus and started walking down the drive. He looked at his watch. On the other side of the Charterhouse wall—inside the church whose spire he saw from the road—he knew the monks were praying Vespers.

When he got to the Gatehouse, Dave pulled the bell rope, then jerked back at the volume of sound that assaulted his ears. Almost immediately, he heard the rasp of a wooden partition being drawn back behind a small grated window, perhaps fifteen inches square. Dave felt an unseen presence looking at him.

CHAPTER 2

The Order (1084–1965)

When Paddy, Hans, Bernie, Chuck, and Dave decided to become Carthusian monks, they left the secular world, or other less austere religious orders, and entered a Charterhouse, an enclosed world where men live alone with God. The Charterhouse supports a unique way of life, one that allows, even forces, total attention to God alone. The order carries the battle cry *"Soli Deo"* (God Alone). The Camaldolese, the Cistercians, and the Trappists, reforms of the sixth-century Benedictines, also focus entirely on God, but the Catholic Church recognizes the Carthusians as the most contemplative, the most completely devoted to God alone. In the letter to the Carthusians that Hans had read, Pope Pius XI noted, "God who is ever attentive to the needs and well being of his Church, chose Bruno, a man of eminent sanctity, for the work of bringing the contemplative life back to the glory of its original integrity."

The Carthusian order actually happened by accident, or as Pope Pius XI would probably have said, "by Divine Providence." In 1081–1083, Bruno, already chancellor of the archdiocese in Rheims, France, gave up a probable appointment as archbishop to escape the corruptions of the contemporary Catholic Church and live a life devoted to God alone. In 1084, he and six companions headed for a mountain wilderness in the French Alps called the Chartreuse, known for heavy snows and extreme cold. In a dream, God had alerted the local bishop, Hugh of Grenoble, a pupil of Bruno's, that they were coming, and Hugh led them to the Chartreuse, where they climbed to the top, to the very end of the gorge, fourteen miles north of Grenoble. The Carthusians believe that day was the feast of St. John the Baptist; he and the Blessed Virgin are the order's patrons. Bruno and his companions climbed high into the mountainous region, building individual huts for themselves at 4,268 feet above sea level. Of Bruno's original group of six companions, two were lay brothers who did the manual labor. Hugh then persuaded the owner of the land to deed it to the prospective Carthusian hermits. The Latin word for "chartreuse" is *cartusia*; hence the name "Carthusian" as well as "Charterhouse," an English corruption of "chartreuse." Bruno only lived in the Chartreuse for six years, but he left such an impression that legal documents of 1084 bear only a notation, *"L'an que l'Hermite est venu"* ("The year the hermit arrived").

Carthusian legend persists that in these very early days of the order, the Blessed Virgin appeared and told the monks to recite her Office, known as the "Little Office," for the grace of stability at the Grande Chartreuse. Bruno was greatly devoted to the Blessed Virgin, and the Carthusians regard her as the first contemplative. Because she was the first to be very close to Christ, the statutes of the order emphasize the Carthusians' closeness to the Blessed Virgin, "whom we are accustomed to call the Mother in particular of all Carthusians." The Divine Office, or Opus Dei, the public prayers of the Catholic Church, comprise the eight hours, or segments of prayer, that are said at appointed times throughout the day. Matins, Lauds, and Vespers are the three major hours, and Prime, Terce, Sext, None, and Compline are called the "little hours" and are commonly recited by Carthusian monks in cell, where their real lives take place. The hours of the Office of the Blessed Virgin Mary (BVM) are always said in cell. The monks bow, stand, and sit, putting their cowls up or down, carrying out the same ritual that they would in church. They pray that the Blessed Virgin will engender Christ in their hearts.

Impressed by the sanctity and sanity of the Carthusians, and by the Charterhouse that came to be called the Grande Chartreuse, other men started Charterhouses. During the twelfth century, the Carthusians established thirty-eight Charterhouses. St. Bruno hadn't intended to found an order and left no guidelines. He hadn't even left a book or sermon, certainly not a rule for monks; in fact, only two of his letters survive, written around 1099. Yet a special form of hermit life had evolved with him, and he had handed on his experience to succeeding generations of monks, not by the written word but by continuous example. Practice preceded statutes. The monks would try things out to see what worked; then, when they got together, they would consider making what worked part of the statutes. The first Carthusians simply delved into the common usages and customs of the eleventh-century monastic world that were handed down from the first hermits and monks. In 1127, the monks of the new Charterhouses asked Guigo, the fifth Prior of the Grande Chartreuse, to write down the customs of Bruno's original group. In this document, Guigo says that many Carthusian customs come from the Rule of St. Benedict, St. Jerome (340?–420), John Cassian (360–430), and the Desert Fathers (monks of the early Church who went into the desert to live a solitary life), as well as from Cluny and the other great abbeys of the period.

From the beginning, the Carthusian monks zealously guarded these customs. They have always been strongly independent, resisting any change to their traditions. They were almost totally unaffected by the Council of Trent (1545–1563), which changed many aspects of the Church. They have continued to wear a rough hair shirt day and night. The doors of the cells that Paddy and the others were about to occupy follow the custom of the ancient Egyptian monasteries of the Thebaid; they are marked by letters with a distinct religious quotation under the letter. The monks never, under any circumstances, eat any meat or poultry, nor do they enjoy smoking or chewing tobacco. Except for Sundays or major feasts, they also keep the great monastic fast, a remnant of a fifth-century Catholic tradition, that runs from September 14, the feast of the Exaltation of the Holy Cross, to Easter. During the Great Fast, the monks only eat one meal a day, and when Advent and Lent begin, they exclude any dairy products from their one meal. They have their own Carthusian sign of the cross: to honor the Trinity, they make the sign of the cross with their first two fingers and thumb held together, their gesture describing a uniquely large cross, with their hands brushing the outside of each shoulder. When they meet each other, there is no eye contact. Instead, each monk bows slightly, and raises his hands to the corresponding sides of his cowl.

Thirteen years after Guigo compiled the Carthusian customs, the Priors of the thirty or so Charterhouses assembled at the Grande Chartreuse. Thus, the Carthusian order began. They decided that the ultimate authority of the order would reside in a General Chapter attended by a representative from each Charterhouse. Each Prior who attended this first General Chapter brought a letter from his bishop, renouncing the bishop's ecclesiastical jurisdiction in favor of the General Chapter. In 1248, the order incorporated the nuns of a nearby convent. The nuns (always very few in number) had recreation every day and, like the lay brothers, had separate rooms; the nuns did not have cells because women were regarded as being psychologically unsuited for the rigors of solitude and silence. At the time of this account, 1960, there were five Charterhouses of nuns.

In 1271, the General Chapter combined Guigo's document with new ordinances and called this document the Statuta Antiqua. Nearly a hundred years later, in 1368, the General Chapter added other documents, calling the new compilation the Statuta Nova. The tone of Charterhouse life at this time can be seen in a detail of the Statuta Nova: A statute required each Charterhouse to have a prison for recalcitrant monks and those trying to escape. Visitors to the museum of the Charterhouse of Ittingen, Switzerland, can still see its prison. In 1509, the General Chapter added further documents in a third compilation. The Council of Trent reduced these documents to one body, called the Nova Collectio (1582). Over the years, the General Chapters introduced some minor modifications, and the Statuta Ordinis Cartusiensis (1926) brought the statutes into accord with the recently revised Code of Canon Law. But not until the Vatican insisted on changes in 1965 did the Carthusian order make any substantial modifications to what had first been codified in 1127.

The monks were feisty and even, at times, combative. When St. Bruno died on October 6, 1101, the monks battled so hard over his successor that Pope Pascal II had to intervene. Critics in the fourteenth century said that the order had no rule at all. Indeed, the Carthusians had no specific spirituality. Yet, to insure that Bruno's customs were observed, the order instituted the practice of Visitation. Every other year, two monk visitors from other Charterhouses spent several days at a particular Charterhouse and talked to every monk. The visitor assured each monk that whatever he said was confidential. Even the novices were encouraged to give their opinions on the spiritual conditions, on the other monks, and on the general running of the house. This practice, which constantly monitored each Charterhouse, helped ensure that the order could continue to boast, *"Cartusia nunquam reformata quia nunquam deformata"*—"never reformed, because never deformed."

The order reports directly to the Pope, with the biennial General Chapter running the order. The Prior of the Grande Chartreuse, called the Reverend Father, is president of the General Chapter, and when the Chapter is not in session, he holds its power. Elected only by the resident monks who made their first profession at the Grande Chartreuse, the Reverend Father controls appointments and can move solemnly professed monks to other Charterhouses according to the needs of various monasteries or to prevent factions. At each General Chapter, all the superiors of the order, including the Reverend Father, present their resignations, asking for relief from their administrative positions so that they can return to the purely contemplative life. The monks refer to this custom as asking for *misericordia,* or "mercy." The General Chapter then reinstates or removes them at will and also appoints the Prior of each Charterhouse. The Priors make their promises to the General Chapter: "I, Brother N., promise obedience to the common chapter for myself and for my house." The Prior of each Charterhouse is *primus inter pares*, first among equals. Although not an abbot, he is the ultimate authority in his Charterhouse. Unlike the Benedictines or Trappists, the Prior's clothes do not differ from those of the other monks; nothing announces his position, not even a pectoral cross.

Just before the Protestant Reformation (beginning in the early 1500s), there were 195 Charterhouses, even though the Black Death had killed 900 Carthusians in 1349. The order would never be more flourishing. Each Charterhouse has its own patron saint but is known by its location. The very simple and austere Chartreuse de Portes, begun in 1115, was the second French Charterhouse; with its simple twelve cells, it maintains the ancient tradition. Many Charterhouses were as simple as Portes, but by the time of the Reformation, others were magnificently ornate, such as the Charterhouse of Miraflores near Burgos, Spain, and the Charterhouses of Pavia and Padula in Italy. Between 1600 and 1667, the Carthusians founded twenty-two monasteries. Around 1700, Dom Innocent Le Masson records that "we number about 2500 choir monks and 1300 lay brothers and donates." Donates are brothers who are not professed members of the community. After this growth period, the Carthusians did not build any Charterhouses until the nineteenth century. Throughout the centuries, they have created 282 Charterhouses.

⊕

Each Charterhouse is vast. It must be. Its vastness protects what the Carthusian monks call "the life," the day in, day out, unchanging, monastic regimen. Layers of concentric circles wrap the monk in solitude, enclose him, protect him from any awareness of secular life. The first circle is the land surrounding the Charterhouse. To protect their solitude, Carthusians acquire very large amounts of land, sometimes thousands of acres. The exceptionally high walls around the monastic complex provide the next protective circle. Although the monks are not unfriendly, they do not offer hospitality; outsiders, in fact, have an extraordinarily difficult time getting into the Charterhouse at all. Within the exterior walls, the high walls of the monk's cell provide another layer of privacy, and finally, his ultimate privacy is the inner room in the cell, the *cubiculum*, where no one can enter without the monk's permission. He is entirely cut off from the world. No newspapers enter a cell, no magazines, no secular books, no telephones, no TV, no radio, not even any musical instruments. At the center of these protective circles, the monk's own diligence and prayer protect his interior life.

The order is so protective of its privacy that it is even averse to canonizing its members; in the eighteenth century, Pope Benedict XIV commented, "The Carthusians prefer to make saints rather than to reveal to the world the saintliness of the lives of the Order." The English Catholic Church insisted on the canonization of the patron saint of Parkminster, the order's first public saint, Hugh, Bishop of Lincoln. A much more recent example of the Carthusians' desire to avoid publicity occurred during World War II. A young brother, Edmund Tippen, had left Parkminster to fight in the war. Brother Edmund said, "I am the youngest, and it is my duty to fight for my country." He returned to Parkminster the very day he was discharged, covered with military honors. By nightfall, he had changed his uniform for a habit and was at his place for Night Office. When the newspapers called the Charterhouse for the story, the Procurator told them, "We are strongly opposed to any sort of publicity." Brother Edmund was universally loved in the order, being rough, humble, and nonjudgmental.

Each Charterhouse follows basically the same blueprint. In the beginning, the monks imitated the dwellings of the early Desert

Fathers. Three years after Bruno's death, in 1104, Guibert, Abbot of Nogent-Sous-Coucy, described the first Charterhouse:

> The church stands upon a ridge . . . thirteen monks dwell there, who have a sufficiently convenient cloister, in accordance with the cenobitic custom, but do not live together *claustraliter* like other monks. Each has his own cell around the cloister, and in these, they work, sleep and eat.

Gradually, the Charterhouse expanded, and the monks added other buildings for necessary functions. Basic to the life, of course, are the individual houses, or hermitages, of each monk—usually twelve to thirteen in a Charterhouse. The monks refer to them as "cells," as do many monastic orders.

Carthusian cells are usually four-room, two-story dwellings. Each two-story cell contains about 1,500 square feet. In 1960, some Charterhouses still had neither electricity nor central heating. The cell encloses the monk, and inside it he has everything he needs. The upper floor has two rooms. The monk's most private space, his *cubiculum,* has a bed in the form of a cupboard with a straw mattress (until the end of the eighteenth century, wooden shutters instead of curtains kept out the cold), a stove, a worktable, and a small oratory with a prie-dieu (a built-in kneeler and book stand) facing the wall with a crucifix hanging over it. Each *cubiculum* also has some bookshelves, a bell above the bed, and a small built-in dining table with a drawer.

Adjacent to the *cubiculum,* a small room that the monks call their "Ave Maria" room opens to a staircase. At the bottom of the stairs, an ambulatory leads to an ample garden of perhaps 1,200 square feet in size. The ambulatory has generous windows, and when snow covers the ground, the monks use it during their recreation time. The far end of the ambulatory leads to three separate conjoining areas: a small bathroom, a workroom, and a large storage room for wood and coal. When the monk leaves his cell three times a day to go to church, he exits into the enclosed cloister that guides him to the church. Next to the door of the cell, a hatch, or pass-through, allows a brother to place food inside the cell; the brother never sees the monk, nor the monk the brother. A large garden, or garth, enclosed by the U-shaped cloister, separates the cells, creating visual and aural space. Within these solitary cells, the monks work out their days.

The monks designed the church not to celebrate Mass, as in an ordinary Catholic Church, but rather to sing the Divine Office. A rood screen (a screen surmounted by a cross that divided the floor of the church into two parts) separated the monks from the lay brothers. The Carthusian liturgy, as was the practice in eleventh-century Lyons, exposed only the most solemn moments of the liturgy to the brothers and laypeople. The monks built the churches to suit the chant, and this design remains unchanged today. Instead of pews, individual choir stalls face each other on each side of the rood screen. The monks refer to the side where the Prior sits as the Prior's side, the other side as the Antiquior's side. Each side has two permanent cantors who lead the chant: the job of the First Cantor is to keep the monks on pitch and singing at a slow pace; the Second Cantor supports him so that he can hear another voice on pitch, similar to singing next to a piano. The monks read the lessons of the Office from a lectern in the center of the church between the choir stalls, six feet back from the sanctuary light; a huge pull-down lamp suspended from the attic hovers over the lectern. Imitating the very early monks, the monks pray standing instead of kneeling. From the earliest days of the order, all Carthusian churches had misericords, ten-inch ledges attached to the lower side of the hinged seats in the choir stalls to provide support while the monks are standing. They rest their buttocks against the ledge—and avoid back problems.

The small size of Carthusian communities, and their insistence on privacy, encourages a simple chant that inspires the monks to pray and to soberly look into their innermost selves. The roots of the chant are Gregorian, a form of plainchant derived from the Jewish and early Christian chant to which Pope St. Gregory the Great (540–604) contributed. Carthusian chant is unaccompanied, slow, and low pitched. In 1130, the Carthusians simplified the seventh-century Gregorian chant for their own use. The Divine Office, usually referred to as the "Office," spans the entire day, turning the monks' minds to God. Like Jews, Muslims, and even Hindus, the monks chant carefully spaced vocal prayers throughout the day. The Office stipulates eight distinct times for prayer; these times are called the hours of the Office. Morning prayer and night prayer were the first hours, derived from Jewish practice. Later, additional hours were added.

The other community buildings cluster around the church. The second most important building is the library; Carthusians cherish books. A quarter century after Bruno's death, Peter the Venerable notes that the monks' manual labor consists "chiefly of transcribing books." The early Carthusian monks, in fact, made their libraries by borrowing and copying books. Three years after Bruno's death, Guibert, the Benedictine Abbot of Nogent-Sous-Coucy, observes: "Although they submit to every kind of privation, they accumulate a very rich library." Books are the monk's most intimate companions; they nurture and sustain him throughout his life. In 1127, Guigo I instructed his monks: "Books forsooth, we wish to be kept very carefully as the everlasting food of our souls, and most industriously to be made, so that since we cannot do so by the mouth, we may preach the word of God with our hands." The manuscript collection of each Charterhouse was its major treasure. In 1371, immediately after the monks had completed the restoration of the Grande Chartreuse after one of its innumerable fires, another fire broke out. When the Prior saw the severity of the flames, he shouted above the tumult, "My fathers, my fathers, *ad libros, ad libros;* let the rest burn, but save the books."

Johannes Gutenberg invented the printing press in 1436, and as early as 1477, the Carthusians were printing; at least fifteen monasteries possessed printing equipment. The Carthusians not only printed books, they wrote them. Writing in 1881, a Carthusian author suggests that there were at least 800 Carthusian authors. In about 1150, Guigo II, the ninth Prior of the Grande Chartreuse, who was named the "Angelic" for his ascetic works, wrote one of the Carthusians' most famous contemplative works, *Scala Claustralium, The Ladder for Monks.* The most productive author, Denys de Ryckel (1402–1471), known as Denys the Carthusian or the "Ecstatic Doctor," was perhaps the most prolific writer of the Middle Ages. Parkminster's edition of his works includes forty leather-bound volumes, plus two index volumes; each quarto weighs 4.4 pounds. During the Reformation, he was the touchstone of orthodoxy, being reissued some twenty times. His most famous tract is *De Contemplatione.* According to him, contemplation is "a prompt, exact and loving knowledge of God." When the French government closed the Charterhouses, the Carthusians saved many precious, and not so precious, books by sending them to Parkminster. Books by Denys the Carthusian not only filled the library but the shelves in the novices' cells and even the huge bookcase, about three feet wide with seven shelves, by the novices' conference room.

Other buildings include a Chapter House where the monks meet to make decisions, for sermons, and for other business. Carthusians always read sermons from a written text to avoid any histrionics and to eliminate pride as far as possible. The content is supposed to impress itself on the listeners' minds, not on their sensibilities. On Sundays and feast days, the monks eat together in silence in what is usually a very plain and austere Refectory. Everyone washes their hands on their way from church in a built-in washbasin. While the monks eat, the Lector Refectorii, the reader in the Refectory, chants from the Bible, the statutes, or even from the Fathers of the Church. In the early days of the order, the Reliquary Chapel was very important; the relics could be parts of the body or clothing, some articles of personal use, or the like of departed saints or other holy persons. All Charterhouses have a Guest House where families of the monks stay for their yearly two-night visit. The monks also have greenhouses where they grow vegetables and flowers for the altars.

To protect the monks from the distractions of their physical needs, lay brothers do all of the manual labor. In the beginning of the order, the monks were educated men who could read and speak Latin; the brothers were usually illiterate. Not until the fourteenth century were the lay brothers even brought inside the main cloister. Until Vatican II, the monks and brothers were completely separated, working and living in different parts of the Charterhouse. Even in church, the rood screen separated them. While the choir monks sang the hours of the Divine Office, the brothers in their choir stalls prayed their rosaries in front of their own altar. At Parkminster, as in all Charterhouses, the brothers had two altars—one with a huge painting of St. Bruno above it, the other with an equally large painting of John the Baptist. The brothers did the jobs of cooking, laundry, shaving, cutting hair, nursing, delivering meals, heating hot water for the monks' fortnightly baths, gardening, bookbinding, running the printing press, tailoring, making cider, tending the beehives, and any other necessary work. They lived in rooms above their workshops called their "obediences." Now they live in cells if they wish. To isolate the choir monks from the sounds and smells of the obediences, Carthusians always build them as far as possible from the monks' cells.

⊕

The monks' major work is Night Office, the most intense time of Carthusian life. Night Office gives meaning to the order. Anyone wanting to be a Carthusian would savor the quiet time, the special responsibility of being awake when everyone else was asleep. The tradition, started in the fifteenth century, of getting up in the middle of the night, of being on duty, on call, keeping watch, harmonized with the life. The monks keep vigil like the shepherds in Bethlehem. Night Office is usually said between 11:00 PM and 2:00 AM. The Carthusians prize this time as their signature contribution to other men. All the monks agree on the primacy of Night Office—the biggest and most difficult task of the day and the toughest penance. Some monks never get used to interrupted sleep—or the resulting short days.

At the first stroke of the church bell for Night Office (or Mass or Vespers), the monks are by their cell doors. They open them at the same time and walk toward the church at the same pace. The major part of Night Office is Matins, the longest and most ancient of the Offices. A solemn Matins of twelve lessons is divided into three nocturns, from the Latin for "night". Each nocturn has six psalms, replaced by three canticles for the third nocturn, with their antiphons (sung liturgical responses), and four lessons or readings. The shorter Office of Lauds follows. Night Office is different every day, but it is always special.

After Night Office is finished, about 2:30 AM, after more prayers in cell, the monks return to sleep until about 6:00 AM, when they are awakened for the conventual Mass. None of the five young men pulling the bell rope of the Gatehouse would have recognized the Carthusian Mass. When Pope Pius V, later St. Pius V, reformed the Roman rite in 1568, he gave religious orders the choice of keeping their own rite if they could show that they had used it for at least 200 years. Clearly, the Carthusians qualified. Guigo, the fifth Prior of the Grande Chartreuse, had compiled the missal and the prayers for Mass between 1121 and 1128. In contrast to the Roman rite, the Carthusian rite is substantially that of the eleventh-century Lyons and Grenoble rituals, which are of Eastern origin.

All Carthusian monks become priests, and after the community Mass in church, every solemnly professed monk who has already been ordained says his own Mass in his private chapel, which contains an altar and a large cupboard for his chalice and vestments. The novices serve these Masses, at which both priest and novice receive communion. According to the wisdom of the order, by saying a private Mass, the monk unites his solitary life with the sacrifice of Christ. Before the Mass, the monk and novice together pray the little hour of Terce, the fourth official prayer of the Divine Office. The monks have already prayed Matins and Lauds at Night Office; they pray Prime, the first little hour and the official morning prayer of the Catholic Church, in their cells as soon as the Excitator, the bell ringer, wakes them. During the next thirteen hours, with the exception of Vespers, which they pray in church, they pray the other little hours of the Divine Office in their cells: Sext, None, and Compline. In contrast to the Roman liturgy, which has a feast day nearly every day, the monks have perhaps fifty feast days a year. They usually celebrate the liturgy of the Church year.

Changes of various sorts occurred after Vatican II, but from Bruno's time to the first half of the 1960s, every day was essentially the same in each Charterhouse. Some days were more pleasant than others. All the monks liked Saturdays because twice a month they could take a hot bath, shave, and get clean clothes. Some novices hated and some loved the days when they had classes. All the young monks braced for Fridays, when they fasted on bread and water. Some monks liked Sunday because of the *collatio*, a second meal, that was served even in Lent, and because on Sunday there were community gatherings. The conventual Mass was longer, the monks prayed all the hours together in church except Prime and Compline, they all listened to a sermon in the Chapter House, and they ate together. The monks had a short recreation, but the novices, who were continually being tested and trained, also had a conference and their Chapter of Faults. Since the third century, monastic groups held regular meetings at which the monks confessed their faults.

Carthusians have always been strongly independent, clinging fiercely to their unique identity and resisting any change to their traditions. Until the modifications of Vatican II, the Carthusians successfully resisted every attempt, even papal attempts, to substantially modify their austere and primitive rule. Carthusians report that in the early fourteenth century, the Carthusians sent a deputation of twenty-seven monks to the Pope in Avignon to protest against the command to eat meat when ill: The youngest monk was eighty-eight years of age, the oldest ninety-five. This convinced the Pope that the Carthusian rule did not shorten life. Later in the century, another Pope, Urban V, thinking to please the Carthusians, introduced modifications to ease the severity of their rule, which threw the order into a panic. The General Chapter immediately sent an ambassador to the Pope to beg him not to force them to accept the more relaxed rules. The ambassador opened his papal audience with: "These new Rules, so far from being of use to us, will lead to no less than the destruction of our Order." His words astonished Urban V, who immediately told the attending cardinals that the Carthusians "do not wish for the modifications I thought fit to offer them; let them follow their pious inclinations and courageously persevere in their primitive observances." The monks did, however, agree to obey the Pope's command to wear hats in bad weather.

The Carthusians' unique identity resides, to a considerable extent, in the Grande Chartreuse. The psychic power of the first Charterhouse seems nearly unique, rather like the power of Jerusalem for Jews and Arabs. Rather than just being a collection of religious buildings, the Grande Chartreuse itself seems an ancient state. As early as January 30, 1132, an avalanche buried the entire Charterhouse, killing seven of the monks. In 1561, during the wars of religion, the Grande Chartreuse was plundered and burned to the ground, not for the first time. The monks reconstructed it. After it was again in perfect repair, in 1676, the Chartreuse burned for the eighth time. Perhaps the most significant Prior of the Grande Chartreuse, Dom Innocent Le Masson, rebuilt the Charterhouse, at tremendous expense, in stone. The Grande Chartreuse "Annals" record that the rebuilding was nearing conclusion in 1686. Then in 1792, the French Revolution forced the monks to flee; over the course of the revolutionary years, many things were carted away and even destroyed, such as the crosses in the cemetery and some paintings. When the monks reentered in 1816, they set about rebuilding. In 1903, during the period of anti-clerical legislation, the French government confiscated the Grande Chartreuse, but this time the monks were prepared.

The monks unanimously decided to resist as far as they could—that is, until the soldiers violently removed them. They locked the gates of the Charterhouse and carried on their normal activities, twice refusing to even speak with the examining magistrate and his policemen. The French government needed a battalion of infantry, fifty mounted police, two squadrons of heavily armed cavalrymen, a detachment of bomb experts, a squad of military engineers, and reinforcements of mounted police to remove twenty-three Carthusians from their Charterhouse. After breaking through the assembly of thousands of local protesters, the authorities got to the main gate, which the monks still refused to open. Once they had broken through all the outer and inner gates, the authorities found the monks praying in church. They still refused to leave. The police captain brought warrants of arrest and removed the monks amid jeers from the inhabitants of the surrounding villages. By this time, the authorities were having second thoughts. For fear of making them martyrs, after questioning the monks, the police told them that they were free. All the monks immediately went back into the Charterhouse. The Prior said, "I need no authorization to reenter my own house." They did not leave until surrounded by soldiers with fixed bayonets. They were finally expelled on April 19, 1903. They resettled in the Italian Charterhouse in Farneta, but they had already built a double Charterhouse in England to house the monks and store the treasures they had sent ahead. The order carried on in exile without missing a heartbeat, not returning to the Grande Chartreuse until 1940, during the unsettled conditions of World War II.

THE CARTHUSIANS IN ENGLAND

England, not historically an easy country for Catholics, now has a Charterhouse on the scale of the Grande Chartreuse (its cloister is longer but it has slightly less enclosed acreage). In 1178, in partial reparation for the death of Thomas à Becket, Henry II himself built the first English Charterhouse. After the first two Priors failed to stabilize the new foundation, Henry personally selected Hugh of Lincoln, then Procurator of the Grande Chartreuse. A native Frenchman, Hugh lived most of his adult life in England. Hugh's mother died when he was eight years old, and his father placed him in a small French monastery to be educated along with other sons of the nobility. At age fifteen,

Hugh made his profession as an Augustinian Canon and was ordained a deacon at age nineteen. Hugh probably thought that he was settled for life, but when he visited the nearby Grande Chartreuse, he immediately asked to join. The Prior of the Canons tried to dissuade him, but Hugh joined the Carthusian order when he was twenty-three. Hugh liked being a solitary monk, but twenty-one years later, when he was forty-four years old, the Reverend Father assigned Hugh the job of establishing Witham, the first Charterhouse in England.

Henry later insisted that Hugh be created the bishop of the Lincoln diocese, the largest diocese (a district under the jurisdiction of a bishop) in England. Hugh of Lincoln and Henry II had a close but complex relationship, particularly because Hugh took a firm stand against secular aggression, earning the title the "Hammer of Kings." By the time of Henry VIII (1491–1547), the Carthusian order had eleven Charterhouses in the British Isles, and very distinguished peers attended Sunday Mass at the London Charterhouse. Sir Thomas More, later St. Thomas More, lived in its Guest House for three years, and Sebastian Newdigate, a prominent member of Henry VIII's court, even joined the order. But when Henry demanded that Englishmen validate his claim to be the head of the Church of England, the London Carthusians refused to do so.

Between 1535 and 1540, Henry VIII executed eighteen monks from the London Charterhouse; of these, seven were hanged, drawn, and quartered, an excruciatingly painful death. Tightly lashed to hurdles dragged by a team of horses, the monks first suffered the torture of the three-mile trip from the Tower of London to Tyburn. The executioner at Tyburn skillfully hanged them, one at a time, so that they were still alive when cut down; his task was to keep them conscious as long as possible. A surviving monk of the Charterhouse recorded the disemboweling of the London Prior: after cutting off his genitals, the executioner "ripped open his belly with an upward cut, tore his entrails apart and flung all to be burnt on a large bonfire erected there." After tearing out the monks' innards, the executioner cut off their heads and quartered their bodies, boiling the body parts in cauldrons of tar. The preserved body parts were hung in public places around London, including the gate of the London Charterhouse. Henry allowed the surviving monks to live in the Charterhouse until 1537. By early 1540, however, he had successfully confiscated all the Charterhouses, and many of the surviving monks gradually and stealthily left for the Continent.

What did Paddy, Hans, Bernie, Chuck, and Dave know of all this as they pulled the bell rope of Parkminster's Gatehouse? Chuck was totally ignorant. Hans conceived only of "a hermit's life with a few elements of community life." Paddy had some idea. Bernie had read books about the Carthusians. Dave, who had just left a seminary, had used its library to good advantage and had a pretty good idea of what was coming.

CHAPTER 3

Parkminster (1883–1965)

When the small door inside the large double door opened and the brother gatekeeper's paraffin lantern lit his friendly smile, Chuck Henley felt as if the ominous black was merely the deep-toned background of a Rembrandt canvas, throwing into sharp relief the richness of the highlighted face. This image stayed with Chuck as a symbol of the richness of monastic life in spite of its stark appearance. This was home. When Paddy, Hans, Bernie, Chuck, and Dave went through the Gatehouse door, they entered a unique world. None of them had ever seen anything at all like it. Even Dave Lynch was stunned by Parkminster's sheer size.

The walls of St. Hugh's Charterhouse, Parkminster, Horsham, West Sussex, England, usually referred to as "Parkminster," enclose ten acres of gardens and approximately seventy buildings. The sheer size, the scale, of Parkminster grabs the soul. Walking through the cloisters gives an unbearably exhilarating, breathless feeling of being in another world, on another planet, in a different reality. The Charterhouse exudes a sense of limitless space and chill. Everything, including its ceremonies, is simple, stark, and austere. Hans's soul felt expanded by the sheer space of the Charterhouse.

When the English Catholics invited the Carthusians back to England in 1863, they came with a flourish, perhaps with a vengeance. Indeed, at Parkminster, the coats of arms of the confiscated Charterhouses hang in the Prior's antechamber. Buying land for a Charterhouse was not easy in a country hostile to Catholics. And even so, there was an initial mishap. In the early 1870s, the Reverend Father had sent the first Prior of St. Hugh's to England with a large sum of money to purchase property and to build a Charterhouse. Instead, the Prior took the money and went to South America. The Reverend Father tracked down the renegade Prior, who repented and returned to the Grande Chartreuse, where he lived a life of penance. On the second attempt, after searching for the best site, the Carthusians chose an estate about forty miles outside London in West Sussex. One of the monks, Dom Jean-Louis de Nicholaÿ, a Russian baron and former general in the Russian army, wearing a fur-lined cloak, negotiated the sale and bought the property at considerably above the normal price. Only when Dom Jean-Louis signed the deed, designating his home as the Grande Chartreuse, did the former owner, a zealous Protestant, realize that he had sold his home to an order of Catholic monks. The monks changed the name of the farm from Parknowle to Parkminster and began building in 1876. They laid the foundation stone the following year.

Carthusians were always capitalists, having substantial revenues from land, but in this case they used the proceeds from the sale of green and yellow Chartreuse liqueur to fund their largest foundation. They worked quickly, employing 600–700 workmen of various nationalities. The workmen, among other things, produced 30,000 bricks a week using three kilns, rapidly moving toward the estimated 6 million needed for the entire project. The monks used stone from Bath and nearby Horsham for the arches and dressing, but they imported costly Belgian flagstones for the cloister walks and French oak for the intricately carved woodwork. After seven years of construction, in 1883, the Charterhouse at Parkminster was completed, and Carthusian business again began in England. By the turn of the twentieth century, the exiled French Carthusians, expelled in 1901–1903, took up residence. Books, relics, and printing presses followed, filling Parkminster's library, Reliquary Chapel, and printing house. Nearly 100 monks from various Charterhouses bedded down at Parkminster. The house was as full as the builders had intended.

At Parkminster, a 4,400-square-foot church anchors the Charterhouse. The five young men at the Gatehouse would attend choir in the Visitors Loft and see none of the interior until they became postulants—from the Latin *postulare*, "to request, to ask admittance to the order." Sixteen chapels form a U against the north church wall, with each chapel looking out at the carefully cultivated common garden.

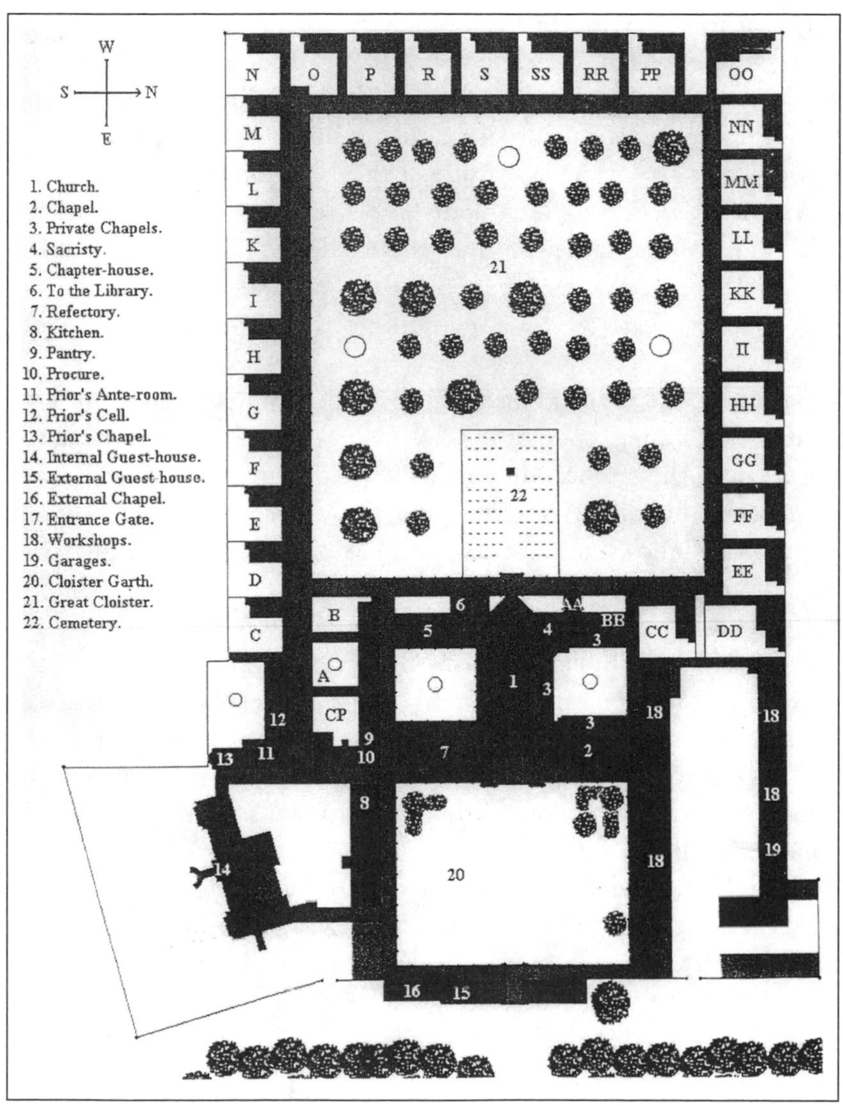

Drawing of Parkminster

Sixteen of the solemnly professed priests have their own chapel with a saint's name etched in glass on the transom above the door. In total, scattered all over, there are an additional fifteen chapels at Parkminster. Adjacent to the church, a small cemetery—with no gravestones, only anonymous wooden crosses to mark each grave—opens to a five-acre garth, or enclosed garden. On the outside edge of the U-shaped cloister, the monks live in thirty-six cells; each monk has his own. The novices' cells are on the north side of the Charterhouse, distinguished by the double letters on their doors; the solemnly professed are on the south side, with single letters. The exterior design of Parkminster is late medieval French. White stone sets off the gray stone of the buildings, and a half circle of carved stone outlines the top of the upstairs cell windows.

Seen from the air, Parkminster forms a squared figure eight, with the church at the intersection of the two circles, the monks occupying the larger circle, the brothers the smaller. At the center of the figure eight, community buildings cluster around the church. Enclosed cloisters, with solid windows on the outside wall, nearly a mile in length, connect the monks (and brothers) to the community buildings. Next to the church, on its southwest side, the monks meet for business in the Chapter House. Although a life-size humble plaster statue of St. Joseph stands above the door, the Chapter House is especially ornate. Like the church, this room is long and narrow, with high ceilings. From the cloister outside the Chapter House, an ornate spiral stone staircase leads to the vast library of rare books and manuscripts, about 30,000 volumes in all.

Behind the Chapter House, on the east end of the church, the monks eat together on Sundays and feast days in the huge and beautiful Refectory. No one ever speaks inside the Refectory. The floor gleams with polished red, black, and beige square tiles, and carved wooden wainscoting distinguishes the walls. The brothers put white cloths on the tables that sit on raised wooden platforms. The Prior sits alone at a table opposite the door; an immense wooden cross with a corpus twice as large as life hangs on the wall behind his table. The white walls have no ornamentation, but high above the tables, an intricately carved pulpit dominates the wall to the Prior's right. The Lector Refectorii, the reader in the Refectory, climbs the ornate stairs in the back to reach his place in the pulpit.

Above the Refectory, next to the library, the five young men ringing the Gatehouse bell will find one of the most ornate rooms in the Charterhouse. Forty-odd stairs lead to the Reliquary Chapel, containing flat glass-fronted cabinets that reach to the lofty ceiling. Not all the monks appreciate the relics. Dom Gregory, an older novice, found that being surrounded by bones, despite their being such holy ones, was somewhat depressing. Above the intricately carved altar, inside a shrine, stands a large statue of the Sacred Heart of Jesus. The entire body of St. Boniface, brought from Rome in 1895, is under the altar, glassed in on three sides.

On either side and above the altar and all around the room, the glass cases hold hundreds and hundreds of relics encased in gold and bronze. In the Charterhouse's list of a thousand-some relics, the monks consider only about 200 of them authentic. The relic of the cross on which Jesus died was marked "authentic," but some monks have wondered about the hair and piece of veil of the Blessed Virgin. Could the Charterhouse really have a piece of St. Joseph's cloak? Parkminster has some bones and clothes of St. Ignatius Loyola and some bones of St. John of the Cross. The chapel even has a part of the brain and skin of St. Rosaline, the first Carthusian nun to be canonized.

The large internal Guest House, the former estate house, is used for newcomers, for important male guests, usually priests and bishops, and for monks who are leaving the order. The building has not been kept up, and a visitor may be somewhat shocked by its dilapidated condition. A wide black brick path leads from the monks' quarters west of the church to the brothers' garth. On one side, the north side, are the brothers' sleeping rooms and the workshops: tailoring shop, beehives, bookbindery, cider press, laundry, repair shop, and garages. Earlier, the workshops also included a forge, a sawmill, and a printing press. On the south side, the kitchen dominates, with more sleeping rooms for the brothers.

Outside the walls of the Charterhouse, near the main gate, visiting family members and neighboring Catholics, sometimes as many as fifty, attend Sunday Mass in a small, sparse chapel, named after St. Rosaline. The thirty-minute Sunday Mass is the shortest in Sussex. Next to it, a fairly comfortable "extern" (the monks still use this archaic term) Guest House accommodates the monks' families on their yearly two-night visit. On the other side of the entrance gate, the monks use the

"North Parlor" for receiving guests and occasionally for sleeping quarters if the extern Guest House is occupied. When I visited Parkminster, family members were staying in the extern Guest House, and I found the North Parlor anything but inviting. The one small window has bars on it. My first impressions: cold, damp, dank; two antique sideboards, one with a crucifix above it, the other with a clock that chimes every half hour; lots of straight-back chairs. There is a flushing toilet, but no hot water, no towel rack, no wastebasket, no hangers. But when I arrived, a brother had already covered a large table with a flowered oilcloth and had set a place. A box of chocolates and two loaves of bread were on the table with a carafe of water.

The buildings at Parkminster have an old-house smell. Nothing is quite clean, dust is in the air, and the damp is pervasive and permanent, getting deeper into the walls every decade. The books, even those used every day, smell of mildew and mold. Priceless vellum manuscripts survive without heat or air-conditioning, much less climate control. In winter, the cloisters sweat and are clammy. The damp in the walls never leaves, even on the hottest summer day. And always there is the peculiar smell of damp, sweaty, wool habits. The buildings absorb the monks who come and go, leaving their imprints: another wooden spoon, a hand-carved walking stick, an extra-large habit, and especially wide walking boots.

At the time of this story, 1960–1965, about sixteen solemnly professed monks carried on the ancient Carthusian tradition. During those years, the Prior was Dom Bonaventure, an ex-Benedictine from the Chartreuse de la Valsainte, set in the mountains of Switzerland—the only surviving Charterhouse of the seven original Swiss Charterhouses. The Prior always has five officers. The Vicar is second in rank; Dom Bruno, a native Englishman, had been professed at Parkminster after wartime service in the Royal Navy. Dom Humphrey, the Antiquior (usually the most senior monk), had been a Carthusian for thirty-eight years, since November 1922. Before World War II, Dom Humphrey had been sent to the Italian Charterhouse of Farneta. The Vatican warned the Farneta monks that war was imminent and advised the French and English to leave Italy. The Prior and Dom Humphrey went to Selignac, where Dom Humphrey was Vicar. When the Germans took over the Selignac Charterhouse, they sent Dom Humphrey to an internment camp in Paris. Dom Humphrey's father, J. F. Pawsey, was famous as a radio inventor. The Procurator (the monk in charge of economic affairs), Dom Guy, had been a partner in the distinguished international law firm of Denton, Hall and Burgin. The fourth-ranking officer, the Sacristan, Dom Francis, has the important, and time-consuming, job of keeping track of the monks' time; his cell has a door going right into the vestry of the church near the bell rope. He rings the bell for all the hours of the Divine Office whether in church or in cell. Dom Francis was nondescript, almost invisible, his slight beautiful features contrasting with the rough creamy wool of his cowl. He was from Kerala, India, and had been a Carthusian for twenty-five years, since August 1935.

The Novice Master is the last officer. Yet in a quite real sense, he is one of the most powerful and influential monks—the keystone of the order, the one who educates and trains the new members. Parkminster's forty-four-year-old Novice Master, Dom Joseph, would be the official superior of Paddy, Hans, Bernie, Chuck, and Dave for the next five years. The monks all refer to him as "Father Master." In the early days of the order, the Prior himself directed each novice. After the Council of Trent mandated Novice Masters, the Prior appointed one man to form all the recruits, and to a considerable degree, the Novice Master decides who stays and who leaves. The collective decisions of the various Novice Masters more or less determine the membership of the order. Dom Joseph himself had joined the order after ten years of being a Catholic priest in Melbourne, Australia, and did not make final profession until March 25, 1957. A little more than three years later, he got the job of Novice Master.

During the 1960s, other solemnly professed members of the Charterhouse included many resilient and successful men. The novices' main teacher, Dom Anselm, son of an Antwerp jeweler, was an ex-Benedictine with two doctorates from Louvain. The father of Dom Marianus was the Duke of Saxe-Meinigen. When he entered religion, Dom Marianus gave up his right to the title to his cousin; his sister married the heir to the Habsburg throne. Dom Marianus's best friend told the monks that Dom Marianus had been considered for the position of Prince Consort for Queen Elizabeth II of England. Dom Emmanuel, a French cavalry officer with a degree in pure mathematics, made profession when he was forty-nine years old and served as Vicar before Dom Bruno. He was still very active in his nineties. Dom

Ludolph, an athlete, had been a member of New Zealand's National Rugby Team. His paternal ancestors were from Sussex; before going to New Zealand, his grandfather had been a horseman for the Duke of Norfolk, the senior Catholic layman in England. Dom Jerome, an Anglican convert, graduated from Oxford with a degree in classics; after graduation, he immediately joined an Anglican religious society and stayed for three years; on Easter 1946, he was received into the Catholic Church at Prinknash Abbey and entered Parkminster two years later. Dom Boniface came from the richest Catholic family in New Zealand. One of the first MPs of the Polish government after World War I, Dom Casimir was vice counsel in Danzig, which had been made a free city to allow the Poles to establish a navy. The Danzig corridor gave them access; when the Nazis took over, they reclaimed Danzig and imprisoned high officials. Dom Casimir heard Polish women being tortured; they were electrified to bring on labor pains and left to be racked to death. The Nazis released him during an exchange of prisoners. Another elderly monk, Dom Hugo-Maria had been Procurator at a German Charterhouse, then near Düsseldorf, and illegally helped people who suffered under the Nazis. He was forced into exile.

Carthusians refer to Parkminster as the "English" Charterhouse, but it was rather an international Charterhouse, occupied by very courageous, successful, and resourceful men. The five young men at the Gatehouse door were attempting to join a distinguished group, many of whom had endured great hardship long before they entered Parkminster. The caliber of the Carthusians was, in a way, a warning: Only the strongest would survive Parkminster's rigors. Only one of the five hopeful novices in 1960 is still a member of the order.

CHAPTER 4

Inside the Charterhouse (1960–1961)

In the 1950s, three New Zealanders and four Australians arrived at Parkminster, making a total of twelve novices. At that time, the community was astounded. There had not been such a large novitiate since the expulsion of the order from France in 1903. In the early 1960s, twenty novices arrived. The community interpreted their presence as a sign of miraculous growth. Thomas Merton's *The Seven Storey Mountain*, first published in 1948, influenced many of the young men entering the Charterhouse. Merton's controversial but impressive book sold 600,000 copies in the original edition in its first twelve months; the *New York Times* refused to put it on their best-seller list because it was a "religious book." *Seven Storey Mountain*, in all editions, has since sold many millions. Merton has been translated into twenty-seven languages. Two of the translations were first published in 2003.

Paddy, Hans, Bernie, Chuck, and Dave entered Parkminster toward the end of what later became known as the era of the "golden horde of novices." The gregarious Paddy brought an analytical and well-trained mind, as did Hans. Bernie carried with him the very recent memory of the glorious girl he had met on the *Mauretania*. Chuck arrived with the wholehearted conviction that he had found his place on earth. Dave possessed an innate reticence, intellect, and familiarity with solitude. They had to integrate these qualities to life in cell, the most overwhelming event of their arrival was encountering the cell. They did it in various ways. Some were immediately comfortable; some found the cell terrifying. In one way or another, they all had to come to terms with the cell.

Paddy O'Connell arrived at the Charterhouse on July 13, 1960, which by sheer coincidence was the same day that Dom Joseph had been newly assigned Novice Master. No sooner did he walk into the Novice Master's quarters than he had to deal with Paddy. Under the circumstances, Dom Joseph was quite cordial. He immediately installed Paddy in Cell II and showed him the practical things monks do, as well as showing him the layout of the cell. So from the first day, Paddy more or less followed the normal life of the monks. Paddy's first impression was that Dom Joseph was friendly and more intelligent than his Trappist equivalent. Dom Joseph closed the cell door when he left, and there Paddy was: alone. He thought, "Just me and, hopefully, God." Dom Joseph had given him a passe-partout, a four-inch metal-pronged key with a wooden handle (which the brothers made from scraps of tin and wood) to latch and unlatch the iron lock in the paneled door of his cell. For the next month, Paddy would live in cell and follow the monastic routine but would not go on the walks or participate in the Office.

Hans Klein arrived the very next day. He was very thin, rather ethereal, with huge eyes, and he looked a bit like a character in an El Greco painting. Paddy only saw him in the Visitors Loft, where those testing their vocations attended Mass and the Office, and at Dom Joseph's private Mass in the Chapter House where the newcomers received communion. Paddy and Hans never talked, but Paddy knew, of course, that Hans was also there for a month-long retreat.

Hans had visited the Charterhouse earlier that year to talk to the Prior, so he had some sense of the physical layout. After the first visit, Hans had written to his parents in Germany, "All the 'hardships' which are disturbing you (no meat, food only once a day, break of sleep, solitude) really are not hard for a young man full of fervour." When he returned for his retreat on July 14, Dom Joseph immediately showed him to Cell KK. Hans stood on the threshold and tried to imagine it as home, maybe for the rest of his life. At the upstairs door, he could smell the musty books and see the patchy whitewashing on the walls; the *cubiculum* had no life or spirit. Was this deliberate? The German Hans was very precise, so he paced off the cell dimensions so he could report its dimensions to his parents, about fifty-six feet by forty-six feet, he thought, including the enclosed garden. The upstairs ceiling had exposed wooden beams and undressed wood paneling. He looked for an escape and saw one large window from which he could see only a run-to-seed garden, with no other cell in sight. The blue chintz curtains hiding the straw pallet in the wooden box drew his attention, as did the bell above the bed.

Hans examined the built-in semicircular table by the window, the oratory with prie-dieu and fold-down chair, the attached quadrangular washbasin with a drain, the large block of wood for striking the side of the wooden bed so he could signal that he was awake when the Excitator made his morning wake-up rounds. Then he saw the discipline hanging on the outside wall between the bed and the oratory. He wondered uneasily about that white rope with knotted cords. He was happy to see a bookcase across from the washbasin crammed with old books: a Bible, the statutes of the order, a lot of nineteenth-century lives of the saints, and numerous Latin volumes by a medieval Carthusian called Denys. He went back into the anteroom, opened the door, and went down two or three steps to a landing that led to the ambulatory, which ran about forty feet, perpendicular to the cloister, and had a window. He admired the terra-cotta floor tile, but the garden outside was miserable. He was glad to see a walking stick: Hans loved mountain climbing and hiking more than anything. Even in the midst of escaping from East Germany in 1953, he had closely followed the media coverage of Edmund Hillary's ascent of Mount Everest.

In two medium-size rooms next to the ambulatory, he found one with wood and coal left over from the previous winter, and the other, a workroom, equipped with a pedal-driven lathe, a carpenter's bench, ax, and saw. Off the workroom was a doorless room so small he could barely squeeze into it. A toilet on the side wall had no tank. Next to the toilet was a spigot with a five-gallon leather bucket. Above the spigot, high up on the wall, he saw a very small window that opened and lent some light to the room. But what if he had to use the bathroom after dark?

The place felt like the eleventh century, as if he had passed through a portal and gone back in time. He had been required to leave his wristwatch with the brothers, and suddenly Hans felt a kind of vertigo, as if the passage of time had ceased all around him. He no longer had any sense of time. He grabbed the monastic schedule Dom Joseph had left him. Then he realized that he would have to depend on the bells to keep on schedule. When did the bell last ring? In fact, there seemed to be two different bells. Hans was sure that neither bell had rung in hours. And even if he did hear the bell ring, what did all those chimes mean?

Hans gradually began to understand the basic routines and rituals and to find his way around the Charterhouse. He was beginning to get a sense of the schedule. The church clock chimed at both three minutes to each quarter hour and again at the quarter hour. After the church clock stopped chiming, the Sacristan rang the church bell if he needed to alert the monks to a monastic duty. Hans adjusted quickly to the regime, but what disturbed him most were the bats in his cell. Bats swirled around him in his anteroom and flitted about while he prayed before Night Office, forcing him to shut the windows at dusk.

What surprised and delighted him most was the opulent meal signaled by the ringing of the bell above the bed at 11:30 AM. The meal took almost an hour to finish. This was a great improvement over the White Fathers' menu. The brothers' cider tasted like alcohol. When Hans wrote to his mother, he assured her, "The food is excellent. I never got four eggs a day with the White Fathers, or preserved raspberries, and a chocolate bar." A brother would bring the meal to the cell by trolley. Hans vaguely realized that the brothers grew, cooked, and delivered the food, but he never saw them. The brother placed the meal inside a wooden box with a handle and slatted sides, about the size of a fat carry-on flight bag, and then put the box inside the hatch. The invisible brother then pulled the bell rope outside the cell. Hans heard the bell and went down the steps to his ambulatory. Holding his box by the handle, Hans would carry it through his ambulatory, sometimes enjoying the sun pouring in through the large window, and up the steps to his *cubiculum*. After setting the box on the table in front of the window, he prayed over the food, then covered his clothes with a napkin the size of a small tablecloth. Then he would examine the contents of the box: a large pot of tea; three interlocking metal *gamelles*, which kept the food hot for quite a while, even half an hour; and resting above the tea and *gamelles*, an entire loaf of delicious, homemade black bread. On the upper shelf of the wooden box, he usually found a small salad and some honey in an old plastic margarine container. A large roughly carved wooden spoon and fork, a steel knife, and a mug were in the table drawer. Carthusian monks do not allow the luxury of plates, so they eat directly from the *gamelles*.

During his first meal, Paddy opened the *gamelles* one by one and wondered what he should eat first. He started with two herrings and mashed potatoes. Next he ate the side dish of green beans and the salad. Then lots of bread dripping with honey from the brothers' hives. Rhubarb for dessert. He ate slowly, letting his mind float, enjoying his food immensely. What mattered was that there was enough food to stoke his body. Thinking of the Great Fast only two months away, he mused, "When you only have one meal a day, you enjoy it even if it is herring and not mullet." Yet Paddy found eating alone very different from the Trappist community meals, and somewhat disturbing.

Friday was the day of the weekly fast, or *abstinentia.* The newcomers found it difficult to get used to the Friday fast; some never adjusted to it. The monks had all the bread they wanted but no other food and only plain water to drink. Except for the Fridays during the octaves (the day of the feast and the seven days following) of Christmas, Easter, and Pentecost, the monks fasted every Friday of the year, imitating Christ's forty-day fast in the desert, disciplining their bodies so that their souls would desire God. During the Great Fast, the monks had only bread and water from Thursday noon to Saturday noon—forty-eight hours of fasting. Paddy, more used to his mother's Friday meal of codfish cakes and boiled potatoes, appraised his first meal of dry bread and water, considering whether he should save some bread for a second meal after Vespers. He decided he should.

Newcomers spent time in the Chapter House, attending and serving the Novice Master's private Mass. On their first days, all of them were overwhelmed by both the ornateness and the gore of the Chapter House. Dark murals flanked either side of the altar. The grisly, life-size, and lifelike murals depicted the seven Carthusian monks who were hung, drawn, and quartered by Henry VIII. Over and on either side of the entrance door at the opposite end of the room, another mural continued the story. Antony Sublet, a French painter from Lyons, took three years to paint the martyrdom murals, completing the work in October 1891, at a cost to the order of 30,000 francs.

To the consternation of the monks who did not want to alienate the English Protestants, Sublet depicted the martyrdom in painstakingly graphic detail, even showing the executioners cutting the monks open and eviscerating them. One novice left the order because he couldn't tolerate seeing the ax about to fall every Sunday. The red and black tones were relieved only by the white of the monks' habits and the lightsome angels flying down from Heaven. The novices found it encouraging that three angels came down from Heaven to pluck up the souls of the tortured Carthusians. But they wondered why the Novice Master, Dom Joseph, said his private Mass in the Chapter House. Did he meditate on these murals? The murals between the series of arched windows were cheerier, of angels and Carthusian saints, including St. Rosaline, also painted by Sublet.

Part of the Novice Master's job is to question newcomers on why they had come to Parkminster. Paddy had thought a lot about this and had prepared his explanation for thinking about leaving the Trappists:

> The Trappist life is essentially a community life. There is in me a desire for more solitude and direct contact with God. And my questioning mind is hard to handle for my Trappist Novice Master who is of a more simple disposition. I am perhaps too intellectual.

He added, somewhat ironically, that "to be a Trappist you also have to have a vocation to be a farmer. Actually, pulling turnips can be pleasant. It leaves your mind free to pray." But Paddy admitted, "I don't like farming. My position is that weeds, frequently mowed, make a nice lawn." He compared the Carthusian life to that of the Trappists. He hadn't worn a hair shirt yet, but the thought of it didn't trouble him. The broken sleep was new, and what sounded like a cowbell over his head had come as a definite shock to his nervous system. But except for broken sleep, the Carthusian life was easier for him physically: better food, baths and clean clothes every two weeks, and best of all, hot water.

The monks took their baths in a room underneath the Prior's cell, and on bath day, the brothers spent the entire day stoking the stove to provide enough hot water for the baths. Each monk had a half hour for his bath. It was a regular, rare, sensuous occasion when the monks took off their hair shirts. A certain discomfort disappeared for the entire bath. A rough soap made by the brothers was in a dish by the bathtub, and the novices used it rigorously until their flesh tingled and looked a spotty red. They especially appreciated shaving with hot water; cold water really didn't do a good job. Dom Joseph provided razor blades once a month; by the end of the month, shaving was a penance. The novices tried to arrange things so that their habit and underwear would be back from the laundry on Friday so they could put on clean clothes after their baths. It felt very good to be clean, even with a hair shirt under their habits. Before or after their baths, the monks would go to the *rasura*, or shaving room, for a haircut.

By the end of his trial month, Paddy had decided to transfer to the Charterhouse, although he certainly wished Parkminster were in Ireland. As he formulated it to himself: "It can't be worse than what I now have and it does seem to go more directly to the goal, union with God." So Paddy went back to the Trappists to return his habit and left with their blessing. He visited his family in Dublin for a few days. After drinking too much, he took the plane to London; his entire family saw him off. He fell asleep on the train from Victoria Station and missed the Horsham station, ending up in Brighton, twenty miles away. It had been a hard day. Paddy returned on the feast of the Assumption on August 15, 1960. Dom Joseph put him back in Cell II, and he was almost immediately received as a postulant. In the ceremony, Dom Joseph slowly washed Paddy's feet while reciting Psalm 50, the "Miserere": "Wash me to the bottom of my guilt, from my sins cleanse me." With that, Paddy began his journey into Carthusian life. Dom Joseph then put the Carthusian white stockings with stirrups and flannel slippers on Paddy's feet and then coarse leather boots. Paddy continued to wear his secular clothes to choir (a symbol of the world that he had not completely left), but over them, he wore a wide black cloak reaching to the floor, without sleeves and hood, and a biretta, a black quadrangular hat then worn by parish priests.

For Hans, after six weeks of farewells to his family in Germany, returning to the Charterhouse was quite different. When he was on retreat, he knew he would have time to say good-bye to the "world." Now there was no exit, entering was final, and he had burned all the bridges to his former life. He had determined to stay at Parkminster no matter what. But when the door of his cell slammed shut, the "world" suddenly appeared very attractive.

Every month, the White Fathers had allowed the young men to go into London for sight-seeing, in secular clothes and always in groups of three. Hans had especially enjoyed the trips to Foyle's, at the time the world's largest bookstore. He was amused by Madame Tussaud's but looked forward more to visiting the Tate Gallery and then eating at the Lyons's Tea Shops that were on every corner. The black waiters cleaning the tables astonished him; he had never before seen a black person. He thought London quite old-fashioned compared to Germany: shops with tiny windows, schoolchildren in uniforms, men with bowler hats, and the old-fashioned taxicabs.

Hans had started taking notes during his religious retreats with the Jesuits and had kept up the practice. On September 7, 1960, two days after his arrival at Parkminster, he wrote:

> Only now I feel: No idealism can keep us here, God's help only. How quickly I lost my self-confidence! I now want to cry for help all the time. Is it home sickness? More than that! Only now I feel the farewell; I feel how it must have been for mother. Every time I think of my parents it chokes me. And the damp weather . . . And the cold . . . And the lack of appetite, the nausea . . . All this increases my discouragement. Had I known this three months ago, I probably would have turned aside . . . To me who always gave wise counsels to others it now is so incredibly difficult if not insurmountable.

Hans, for all his resourcefulness, admitted to himself that he simply did not know how to cope. Yet the sheer beauty of the Carthusian life began to seduce him. Within a short time, he cherished every day in the Charterhouse, but he particularly loved the pre-dawn time; he liked the sense of the day beginning, the openness of possibility. How were the monks this morning? How might he learn to know them better? Hans was very intuitive, and he felt connected to the monks; he sensed their well-being, or the lack of it when things were amiss. He looked forward to time spent in church and classes. Hans believed with all his heart that his monk brothers were always with him before God's face. He also kept up a conversation with his journal.

As the weeks went by, he and Paddy studied Latin and learned the statutes of the order. They also learned how to cope with the changing seasons. The daylight hours had changed; during the long monastic fast that began on September 14, their diet was more limited, and the cold and damp got worse and worse as winter approached. The glistening stone of the Charterhouse made the cold English winter even colder. It became impossible to work in the garden. Even keeping clean was a problem: Apart from the fortnightly baths, they depended on water warmed in the sun in a watering can for showering. But that didn't work in winter.

When Bernie Shea arrived in early October, a week later than expected because of his detour to Manchester, Paddy and Hans could smell the cigarette smoke on his clothes. Bernie arrived just in time for the feast of St. Bruno, on October 6. Bernie was slightly out of practice being a monk, but his Trappist Novice Master had given him books about the Carthusians. Dom Joseph put Bernie in Cell HH, and after several weeks, the Prior decided that Bernie could stay. He gave him the postulant's black mantle and biretta. Bernie's expectation of the Carthusian life did not match his initial experience of it. The life felt heavy on his shoulders—he admitted to Dom Joseph that he felt "oppressed." He missed human contact: in choir, for example, there were no human glances. The monks behaved like soldiers on parade. No one attempted to create an emotional or personal connection. Solitude seemed to envelop him like a silent blanket of white fog.

While struggling with all this confusion and disappointment, Bernie was cold. The late autumn was chilly and damp all the time. Bernie didn't have monk clothes yet, and he continued to wear pajamas for bed—as if he were in a centrally heated house. He was trying to behave appropriately, and wearing a sweater to bed did not seem right. When his mother sent long underwear and a note saying, "A monk that's warm prays better," Dom Joseph wouldn't let him keep it, considering long underwear indulgent. An older English novice, Dom Gregory, tried to cheer him up by telling him that the English always go to bed with everything being damp. In mid-October, Bernie decided to start a fire in his cell, which hadn't been lived in for decades. He'd never been a good boy scout—in fact, he had been asked to leave two groups for disruptive behavior—so his attempts to start a fire ended in a cell full of smoke. He opened all the windows. One of the solemns, Dom Ludolph, came to see if he was all right and remarked that fires weren't encouraged until November 1. When that day arrived, Bernie again tried to light the fire—with the same results. Finally, Dom Joseph asked Bernie's neighbor in the next cell to help, and he immediately discovered that the chimney pipe had never been cleaned and was totally clogged with soot. Bernie wasn't sure if he could make it through another day. He was totally overwrought.

By mid-November, Bernie was struggling to improve his Latin, had become bored by the statutes, and remained unconvinced that the ancient paths to God were really necessary: He felt a great inner conviction that he should leave the Carthusians. So he decided to leave, either to find his own mountain or to join the Camaldolese in California. He told Dom Joseph of his decision. Aware that newcomers tended to focus on solving the problems that they have inevitably brought with them, Dom Joseph tried in every way to dissuade him and failed. Bernie made an appointment to see the Prior, but before he left his cell, he knelt in his small Ave Maria room and asked the Blessed Virgin to stop him if he was wrong, before it was too late. The distance between his cell and the Prior's was long enough to do the trick. Nothing happened, no logical syllogism appeared, but by the time Bernie Shea arrived at Dom Bonaventure's cell, he simply knew, was certain, that he should remain at Parkminster. He told the Prior that he had been mistaken. Looking over his round horn-rims, Dom Bonaventure was greatly surprised, but he told Bernie that he had had no intention of trying to argue with him.

Once winter set in, the three young men found the Friday fast much harder. Bernie, especially, found it a shock to his system, and a humbling one. He was somewhat ashamed that while others in the world were starving, he found it difficult to go forty-eight hours on bread and water. Like most Americans, he was used to central heating, and without any fish or vegetables to stoke his body, a damp, cold day in Sussex stretched out forever. It was hard to keep from shaking with cold. Even when he received a *gilet*, a thick vest the monks wore under their habits in cold weather, it didn't help much. No matter what he did, he remained cold.

Chuck Henley arrived very late on the evening of December 2 as violent storms pounded England. The flooding in some places was the most devastating in more than a century. A brother opened the small door in the large double doors and contacted Dom Joseph, who soon arrived. He led Chuck to his assigned cell, designated "PP," about as far from the front gate as possible. Chuck was very glad to be under cover. Dom Joseph built up the fire in the coal stove to last until morning, and while Chuck, skinny as a stick, ate some food a brother had brought, Dom Joseph instructed him on surviving the night: how to light a paraffin lamp, how to bucket flush the ground-level toilet, how to find the washbasin, and how to acknowledge the Excitator's bell.

After his first sleep of four hours, a brother led Chuck to the Visitors Loft at the western end of the church for Night Office, his only source of light the paraffin lantern, or lanthorn, as the monks called it, that the brother had given him. The rood screen prevented Chuck from seeing the monks in their choir stalls or the brothers beneath him. The only other light came from lamps above the choir stalls, so the dimensions and features of the vast church disappeared into flickering shadows. The vaulted aisles of the church magnified every sound. Chuck could hear the sound of the brothers and monks taking their places in the darkness far below, with the occasional soft thud of the misericords. The church grew quiet, and in the dark, the Prior knocked three times on his choir stall with his passe-partout to let the cantor of the week, responsible for intoning the chant, know that the office should begin. The chant rose into the church, tapping into a thousand-year-old tradition of prayer. It was like nothing Chuck had ever experienced.

For the doctor's son from Pennsylvania, each new detail of this strange place was as gothic and alluring as anything he had read in the classic English novels. Other than the thin book that his Jesuit chaplain had given him, Chuck had read nothing about monasticism or Parkminster. His *tabula* was *rasa* and ready. During the period preceding his arrival and his early months at Parkminster, he experienced neither fear nor hope. His compulsive striving had dissolved in his moment of decision, in the ageless calm of cell and cloisters, garth and Refectory, on the walking paths of Sussex, in the chant, in the monastic literature introducing him to a divine friend, perhaps imaginary, perhaps not.

Chuck adapted to the Charterhouse so well that he was almost invisible. He had what he had always wanted—rules that told him exactly what to do. He did not have to make decisions; he didn't have to assert himself. He melted into the "golden horde" as if he had always been part of the tribe. He felt safe and happy. Although the Charterhouse felt like home to Chuck, everything about it surprised him. He liked it all. He reflected that monastic life was not odd, not unnatural, it was "just one mode, one wonderful mode, of normal human activity." Even during the very early days, he never yearned for the outside world. Becoming a monk solved his deepest dilemma: He had had no idea what to do with his life. Monastic life was not a formidable challenge but a simple resolution to a much larger and more complex problem. The idea of a life of prayer, completely new and novel to Chuck, was better than anything he had hoped for. That decision completely removed the tension he had felt since he started high school.

Chuck kept everything in his cell clean and tidy. Every month he cleaned the small window in his bathroom. He always made his bed and swept the floor of the *cubiculum* when he returned to his cell after Mass. The unfinished floor got dirty quickly, but he swept it vigorously with a primitive broom. Every few months, he scrubbed the floors of the *cubiculum* and the Ave Maria room with a hand scrub brush, soda crystals, and cold water; he used old sacking to soak up the water from the wooden floor. He decided to get serious about his garden and do something useful. He discovered that the ground was so compacted and rocky that little would grow there. On warm winter days, he worked at breaking it up, collecting buckets of rocks. He planned a real garden and looked forward to spring, when he could start planting. He also looked forward to being clothed as a novice.

Of the five young men, Paddy was the first to be clothed. Throughout the five-year process, following the practice of monastic seniority, he would always be the first. His clothing ceremony took place on the feast of St. Bruno, a few days after Bernie's arrival. The Prior and Dom Joseph named him Leo. As the first of the novices to be clothed, Dom Leo generously wanted to help the others learn how to cope. He was always ready to offer advice, although his good intentions were sometimes misinterpreted. Dom Leo recognized Bernie's initial distress. As the Cistercian Saint Bernard had often said, "Monks aren't teachers," but Dom Leo thought that he could share his experience to help Bernie get through his first weeks in the Charterhouse. He told him how he had coped with his first days with the Trappists:

> I kept going by a spiritual practice inspired from a 1938 film, *Angels with Dirty Faces,* starring James Cagney as a condemned murderer waiting to be executed in twenty-four hours' time. I tried to live each day as if it were my last. In the morning, on awakening, I received the gift of life. Each night, I gave it back into God's hands. All during the day, I would repeat to myself, "Tonight I die." Everything is a question of proportion. We can support many things for a limited time. And I gradually became

familiar with death and began to perceive its true Christian sense of a threshold to life. I discovered that I had reinvented the wheel when I read of this practice in the writings of the Desert Fathers.

Bernie liked Dom Leo, and they were both ex-Trappists, but Dom Leo's spiritual practice didn't work for him. Unlike Chuck, Bernie was in no hurry to be clothed.

After Christmas, the weather got colder and damper. New Year's Day, the feast of the Circumcision, a big feast day for the Carthusians, was a slight break; all the monks got a small bottle of green Chartreuse with their supper. Through the winter, in spite of the cold, Chuck remained very happy at Parkminster. He loved to inhale the now familiar and comforting smell of church, of guttering candles, of damp stone, and of unwashed monk. He found Night Office especially magical. The austere white-and-gold high altar in the large church shimmered against the French dark oak wainscoting, and the sanctuary lamp glowed dimly in the cavernous church, revealing the bronze glint of the four massive, ornate, eight-foot-tall candlesticks in front of the altar. The white walls of the church were bare except for a large painting hanging over the main altar, depicting the apotheosis of St. Hugh of Lincoln, the first canonized Carthusian and the patron saint of Parkminster; at its base, two monks held a picture of Parkminster itself. A 100-foot velvet-encased bell rope dropped from the bell tower to the center of the narrow church.

Chuck particularly looked forward to ringing the church bell before Mass. The Sacristan, Dom Francis, his dark brown face nearly invisible in the early morning gloom, took a couple of long pulls on the bell rope. The weight of the bell almost swept the slight Sacristan off his feet. Each monk rang the bell until the next arriving monk took the rope from him. The last monk had the arduous and tricky task of stopping the enormous bell from swinging. Bracing his body to lock the bell, as the rope went up, the monk would restrain it, to slow down the momentum; he would then wait until the next up stroke to restrain it again. He then had to tie the rope to the hook on the side of the choir stalls nearest the altar. Only the athletic Dom Ludolph could stop the bell from ringing with one arm, with one pull. Chuck found this a marvel. From Dom Joseph's perspective, Chuck was a poster child for the order, and he moved rapidly into the novitiate. Chuck was clothed on the last feast day before Lent began. The Prior and Dom Joseph chose to name him "Damian" after the third-century Arabian martyr; Damian and his twin brother, Cosmos, were both noted physicians, as was Chuck's father.

Bernie was not a poster child. Indeed, Dom Joseph had disturbed Bernie's adjustment to the life by giving him a Christmas card sent by the young woman from the *Mauretania.* Her words were delicate and carefully chosen, but Bernie still felt that he had made a choice that was right for him and therefore for her. Yet he felt increasing guilt for this romantic encounter and put himself on a very ascetic regime. He used few or no coals in his stove, cut back on food and sleep, and focused his energies on totally mortifying his flesh. Soon, he had no circulation in his hands and fingers. Dom Joseph sent him to St. Anthony's Hospital in Cheam, run by nuns who greatly admired the Carthusians. Dom Damian said good-bye to Bernie before he left for the hospital, convinced that he would not return. A specialist failed to find any cause for the lack of circulation, but body heat could be affected by diet. When the great fast ended at Easter, the monks could feel the difference in the heat of their bodies. To avoid returning Bernie to Parkminster during Lent, with its even greater austerities, the hospital postponed his release and sent him to another hospital to convalesce. He stayed in hospitals for nearly five weeks, ate properly, put on weight, and thought again about the wisdom of joining the Carthusians.

CHAPTER 5

The Last Novice (1960–1961)

MARCH 4, 1961

In Carthusian jargon, the youngest novice is always referred to as "the last novice." Dave Lynch arrived on March 4, 1961, in the middle of the second week of Lent while Bernie was in the hospital. About ten days before he left for Parkminster, Dave's parents hosted a reception and farewell party for him in the ballroom of one of the posher Chicago hotels, the Edgewater Beach Hotel. Family friends, relatives, priests, and classmates gave him $5,000. For what, Dave could never figure out. What did he need money for? Besides saying good-bye to Dave, the 150 guests were still talking about the inauguration of the first Catholic president, John F. Kennedy, for whom Dave had cast his first, rather indifferent vote. Father Rob Lynch, chancellor of the Chicago Archdiocese, looked at his nephew—fit, thin as a rail, five feet ten, and confident he could do anything. Dave was an only child, born when his mother was forty, and had been a trophy child from the beginning, always able to do anything he wanted to do, good at sports, best at studies, good at everything. In a class of 200 young men, David was first in class in both the minor and major seminaries. He was an obvious candidate to be sent to Rome for further theological study. The party celebrated all his achievements, from his golf scores to his solos at Holy Name Cathedral. When things were really difficult in the early days, he remembered the awe of the guests at the farewell party; their adulation swept over him and kept him on track.

Dave had seen pictures of the Charterhouse; he knew he would have his own house, and he knew about the meatless meals and even about the Friday fast. To get himself ready for hardship, he had been sleeping on the floor in his seminary bedroom. For the last two years, he hadn't read any newspapers or magazines. He had even adapted golf, a sport he loved, to a solitary meditative pursuit, playing alone at the end of the day on an empty course. Apart from a few movies—he particularly liked Alfred Hitchcock's *North by Northwest,* and he had seen *Ben-Hur*—Dave Lynch paid no attention to current events. In a sense, he was already living in a monastery.

When Dave finally arrived at Parkminster, he spent his first night in the internal Guest House. The next day, Dom Joseph showed him to his cell, RR, and then left. Dave was alone in his cell. Entombed. He realized he would spend the rest of his life in this cell, or one like it. No one could get in without a key. No one with a key would come.

Nothing but base motives kept Dave from catching the next bus to Horsham. Dave's first thought was, "How long do I have to stay to have a good story?" He decided that after five months he would have enough to go on the lecture circuit. His second thought was the people who had come to his farewell party: "How long do I have to stay to save face?" He decided to "gut it out for three months" and collect some really good stories. That resolution put Parkminster into real time and out of eternity. During the worst of the early days, Dave could relax and comfort himself with the thought that he was not going to be there forever.

But he felt better when Lent was over. He was reading more and had become used to the rhythm of the place. He felt more engaged, more able to fill his time with things he wanted to do. During his second month, he had decided to enter the novitiate, that is, if he was accepted. He rejoiced with everyone else when Holy Week announced the end of Lent and the beginning of the great feast of Easter. After Easter, the monks ate two meals a day that included dairy products, and the novices relished cream soups, custards for dessert, and most of all, cheese. Every monk knew that Christ's resurrection had to be celebrated, and after the long fast, the brothers provided a huge plate of sweets, mostly milk chocolates, for each monk. The novices had to be careful not to overeat after forty days of fasting from dairy products.

On Easter Day, April 2, 1961, Dave wrote his first letter from the

Charterhouse. Four times a year, on major Carthusian feast days, the novices were allowed to write to their parents. Dave knew that his parents would be anxious about him. He found it hard to describe how he was. He atypically stumbled for words. He started by making the cross that the monks always put at the beginning of their correspondence.

†

Easter, 1961

Dear Mom and Dad,

I don't feel as if I exactly know where I am. Everything is totally different. I feel as if I have plunged into the ocean and will have to grow gills. Trust me, Mom, I haven't yet. But a metamorphosis will have to take place if I am to make it in this place. The game is on.

Well, at least I'm still alive—after almost a month. Life here is certainly different. As you probably guessed, I have no contact at all with the outside—no radio, no newspapers, no television. I like having my head clear of all that stuff, but I feel a shade disorientated. When the door of my cell closed on me last March 5th, I was frankly scared. As I looked around, I saw all the resources for the rest of my life—only the cell and me. Will this cell support me? Can I learn how to live off this cell? One of the cells has "Our conversation is in Heaven" on the door in Latin. We sure don't have any conversation here. And all our rituals are in Latin. I'm glad the seminary got me used to speaking Latin.

Dad, if you stood facing the church at the end of the cloister, making the church 12 o'clock, my cell would be at 6 o'clock. I'm about 200 yards from the church, a long Par 3. The Novice Master has the northwest corner cell at 7:30; the novices' cells are clustered around his cell. The solemnly professed have cells on the other side, starting at 1 o'clock. There are no empty cells right now. There are about fifteen solemnly professed monks here who are also priests. Everyone, even the professed brothers, wear white habits—which get pretty dirty in two weeks. People call us the "white monks." I think the Franciscans are smart to wear brown.

There was another postulant from Brooklyn, but he got sick

and has been in a hospital for five weeks. He came back yesterday, but I don't think he will stay. He and I are still wearing regular clothes, but I hope to join the novices in June. Right now, twenty of us report to Dom Joseph. I will be glad to be clothed as a novice and get out of these civvies.

When Dick Schmidt and I decided to find out what the contemplative life was about, I never thought I would end up here. I knew when we visited the Trappists at Gethsemane over Easter break that I wouldn't end up there. I saw Thomas Merton as we toured the abbey. I was never a fan of his—I've always thought he should make up his mind whether he is a monk or a celebrity, in or out. I'm sorry that I didn't talk to you guys about my decision. But, once I realized that this was the life for me, there wasn't much to talk about. You must have been really shocked when I told you I was leaving for a Carthusian Charterhouse in England. You certainly weren't expecting that announcement when we got together on visiting Sunday in the seminary.

The brothers do all the cooking, and all the other manual labor. I see them working around the place, but, of course, I never talk to them. They apparently live a more communal life. I am not even sure where they live. The professed brothers all have beards—a sign of penitence or something.

Easter week here was different, interesting. On Good Friday, instead of bells ringing, the Sacristan walked around carrying an accordion-like instrument that the monks call a "rattle." He played it outside each cell to let us know when to go to church. Uncle Will would have loved to have one of those instruments.

Well, Happy Easter, and take care of yourselves. I will probably be able to write again on the feast of John the Baptist.

Dave

He read it over again, put it in the envelope that Dom Joseph had given him, and then put the unsealed envelope in Dom Joseph's hatch on his way to Vespers.

All five of the young men, over a six-month period, were now in the Charterhouse. They had begun their journey; three of the "golden horde" had already been clothed as novices. Paddy as Dom Leo on October 6, 1960, Hans as Dom Ignatius on December 8, 1960, and

Chuck as Dom Damian on February 2, 1961. They all went through the very same ritual.

For Hans, all the longing for the world he had left behind faded as the time of his reception into the novitiate approached—the feast of the Immaculate Conception of the Blessed Virgin. The postulant truly enters into monastic life on his clothing day, always a special feast day. Hans had no hesitations. Life in the Charterhouse had become customary, normal, even familiar. The life had worked on Hans, and he had absorbed the spirit of the place. Both he and Dom Joseph felt that he was ready to go forward. Dom Joseph advised him to ask for admission to the novitiate and explained the complex ceremony. Hans loved ancient ceremonials and knew that he would be comfortable with the formula. In the long, narrow, and high Chapter House, ten days before the feast of the Immaculate Conception, in front of all the monks sitting on benches on either side of the room, the Prior asked Hans several questions in his French-accented Latin: Had he made profession in another religious institute? Was he married? Did he have an incurable disease? Did he have any debts? Dom Joseph had warned Hans that if he concealed anything, he could be expelled, so Hans was scrupulously careful. The interrogation was carried out in Latin, in which Hans was fluent.

A few days later, Dom Joseph presented Hans's case to the solemns, setting forth both his good qualities and his defects. He recommended that Hans be admitted. Meeting in the Chapter House, the solemns used black and white beans that they slipped into a wooden box to vote the postulants in or out; the postulant needed 50 percent of the votes for admission and sometimes didn't get the votes. While he waited in the church for an anxious forty-five minutes, the solemns voted Hans into the novitiate. For the eight days before the feast of the Immaculate Conception, beginning on December 1, Hans went into retreat. Dom Joseph asked him to examine every aspect of his life in complete honesty to see if there was anything that would keep him from going forward. Hans found nothing. He certainly was not obsessing over women. Dom Joseph gave him daily personal conferences, and Hans took careful notes. Dom Joseph emphasized the difficulty of the life. In one of the conferences, Dom Joseph pointed out that it is only Jesus who could keep Hans in cell—and that the God-given strength to persevere in solitude is a much greater grace than the one he received to cross the threshold of the Charterhouse. He emphasized that there was "no escape!" Dom Joseph concluded, "In cell, which you are bound by rule not to leave, there is no getting away from oneself. One has to live through it." Hans had already learned that he could not escape from himself in cell and suspected that things would get worse. Yet, without any ambivalence, he decided to go forward.

When the feast day itself came, Hans was a little nervous, but when he lay prostrate on the wooden floor of the Chapter House, as novices had done since the time of Bruno, he had no doubts. When the Prior asked what he wanted, he said, *"Misericordia."* The Prior then told him to rise, and Hans repeated the ritual words: *"Supplico propter amorem Dei"* ("I ask for the love of God"), then continuing, "to be received for probation in the monastic habit, as the most humble servant of all, if this should be pleasing to you, Father, and to the community." Hans then faced another hurdle; the Prior read a sermon in Latin aimed at deterring him from seeking admission to the novitiate; the Prior detailed the hardships of the solitary life, stressing the strict enclosure and the necessity of "keeping to cell."

Hans, feeling totally overwhelmed by the solemnity and the import of what he was doing, and separated from his family's support, concentrated on the sun coming through the arched windows. When the Prior finished the sermon, Hans said, in Latin: "Relying solely on the goodness of God and the prayers of the monks, I will fulfill these obligations insofar as divine goodness allows." The Prior then emphasized not only that Hans would be free to leave any time during the next two years but also that the order could send him away if they thought he was not suitable. Hans assented to this, then knelt at the Prior's feet and placed his joined hands between the Prior's, feeling completely submissive to God. After that ritual, he received the kiss of peace from the Prior, then went to every monk, knelt down in front of him, and received a similar greeting; each monk then elevated him to his feet.

Hans was now a monk, but he still didn't look like one. He went to the *rasura,* where Brother Hugh gave him a monastic haircut. Upstairs, next to the Prior's Hall, the white-walled, smallish *rasura* was bare except for a large wooden crucifix. Brother Hugh, a fiery, bearded Scottish man in late middle age, shaved each monk's head with a sharp long razor. He left a band of hair, which he measured with a piece of string, starting about an inch above the ears, creating the monastic hairstyle called a tonsure. The monks thought of the tonsure as the *corona vitae,* the crown of life, which Jesus promised to those who love him. Later, the Prior would dismiss Brother Hugh as haircutter because he simply couldn't put up with the trouble of trimming the postulants' hair; he just shaved them bald. Those postulants who decided to leave Parkminster had to reenter the world with a haircut that was most uncommon at the time. Hans dreaded the long razor that left cuts that didn't heal in two weeks and would reopen with the next haircut, but he accepted the long, sharp razor as another part of the penance of the order.

Brother William, the tailor, brought all the monk paraphernalia Hans needed to Cell KK. The monks' clothes actually differed very little from the eleventh-century clothes worn by French mountain peasants. Hans received two habits (one for Sundays and feast days), two short, knee-length cowls without bands, stand-up flannel slippers that went into his shoes, stiff wool stockings with stirrups that tied off below the knee, two sets of long underwear, choir shoes, garden clogs, a *gilet,* and, of course, a hair shirt. A brother had made his hair shirt only the day before with fresh unsmoothed horsehair. The monks called the hair shirt a *cilicium.* In a short ceremony, the Vicar himself, Dom Bruno, gave Hans the knee-length cowl and the new hooded black cloak. Dom Bruno's manner was friendly, considerate, gregarious, almost chatty. In his typical, slightly strangled tone of voice, Dom Bruno told him to remember that "Cartusia nunquam reformata quia nunquam deformata." When Hans put his new clothes on, he found them incredibly heavy; the habit and cowl were made of very thick wool. Later in the day, Brother Bruno Maria, a novice brother from the Washington, D.C., area, came to his cell to measure his feet so he could make his choir shoes. Once he was clothed, Hans gave the Prior everything that he had brought with him: his clothes and books, as if on deposit. To stress that Hans would now own nothing, Dom Joseph had already given away the present Hans's parents had sent, a Latin dictionary. Hans had left all things to follow Christ. The order had one thing still to give him: his monastic name.

Before Vespers that day, the Prior gave Hans his new name. Dom Joseph led Hans to the church, where he prostrated and prayed on the inlaid wooden sanctuary steps. For this ceremony, the Prior wore a white wool church cowl with a white stole, a long decorated strip of cloth, loose over his chest. The Prior, and all the other monks who were leaning against their misericords, sang *"Veni, Sancte Spiritus"* ("Come, Holy Spirit"). After the Prior said two short Latin prayers, he led Hans back to his own cell, KK. With their cowls over their heads, the entire community followed, singing psalms. After the Prior came Dom Bruno carrying holy water, Dom Guy, the Procurator, and then the rest. The monks left the church, in the order of the date of their first profession, Dom Leo, Chuck, and Bernie at the end of the procession.

When the group arrived at the door of Hans's cell, the Prior sprinkled Hans, then the cell itself, with holy water, saying in Latin, "Peace to this house." Then taking Hans by the hand, the Prior led him into the cell and to his oratory. All the monks followed; the *cubiculum* could hardly hold them all. Hans knelt at his prie-dieu while the monks finished singing psalms. The Prior then said: "Keep the cell and the statutes in accordance with the observance and practice of our Order so that you can cling to God alone in silence and solitude, in constant prayer and ready penance." After that admonition, the Prior said, "Dom Ignatius, I hand you over to the care of Dom Joseph." Hans and all the other monks had waited for this moment—to learn his new name. The Prior and Dom Joseph had named him after the founder of the Jesuits, his earliest inspiration. It was the only name he would use now. The monks filed out, and unless Hans, now Dom Ignatius, were to become sick, no one would again enter his innermost sanctum. Even the Prior would need Dom Ignatius's permission to cross the threshold.

At last he was officially a "monk," both inside and out. Hans felt great satisfaction in that and in his new name. He inhaled the subtle odor of the wool habit with pleasure. Alone, with a half-inch crown of hair around his shaved head, Dom Ignatius hung his second, good habit on a wooden knob between his bed and oratory and sank into himself. From the moment he had put on the hair shirt, he could feel the stiffness of the new horsehair. It was as scratchy as he had expected. The woven shirt was attached by a strap over each shoulder and was kept in place by a rope threaded through the loops at the bottom. Dom Ignatius retied the rope at the bottom more tightly to maximize the unremitting discomfort. The itching kept him awake the first night, and then he decided not to be overly penitential and loosened it. The shirt still irritated his nipples. He didn't really understand the purpose of the hair shirt, but he liked the Carthusian traditions, and the hair shirt seemed to be part of them. Indeed, after a few weeks, it didn't bother him any more than a mosquito.

At the end of his first Night Office as a novice, at about 2:30 AM, Dom Ignatius returned to Cell KK and prayed Lauds (BVM); then he first took off his cowl, then the rosary beads wrapped around his cincture, a sturdy, three-inch wide, white leather belt with a buckle; then he took off his coarse, loosely fitting habit of unbleached wool, his *gilet*, and his choir shoes, lined with one-fourth inch of insulating cork, with rubber tire treads for soles. Hair shirts were supposed to be penitential, but they were warm, and he was glad that his order of monks never took them off. He kept on his long-sleeved wool undershirt and knee-length longjohns. Tonight, he even kept on his wool stockings and slippers. Then he put on a night habit over it all, a light cowl that the monks wore instead of a nightgown. By 2:45 AM, he was ready to extinguish his paraffin lamp and pull the coarse wool blanket over him. After a quick body check to make sure he was safely warm, he settled in for another quick sleep.

CHAPTER 6

The Novice Master (April 1961)

EASTER FRIDAY, APRIL 7, 1961

After putting the novices' Easter letters in the Prior's hatch, Dom Joseph returned to his cell. He was responsible for the twenty-some men from fourteen different countries—an unusually large and cosmopolitan group for a contemplative order. A small, shifting population of potential recruits came and went; many only stayed a day or two, few actually became novices. Statistically, only 10 percent of the novices, at best, would persevere. The fallout rate was high. Records kept since the sixteenth century, however, showed that about 95 percent of the solemnly professed monks persevered, with a dip in the nineteenth century to 90 percent. Right now, Dom Joseph had a bright and promising bunch. He wondered which ones would make it to final profession. Dom Joseph himself had only made final profession a little more than three years before, in 1957.

Dom Joseph had wanted to be Novice Master and felt prepared for the job; he resolved to do his best and run a tight ship. As an experienced Roman Catholic priest, a monsignor, no less, he had plenty of experience managing men. He had managed refugees after World War II and had been in charge of a Marriage Tribunal that adjudicated the validity of marriages. He thought he could manage his twenty-some men. Parkminster seemed to be a powerful community with enough lay brothers to maintain the estate—and all the cells were now occupied. The large novitiate promised continuity. Part of his job was to find what flaws he could in the novices and correct them. With this bright bunch, he had to guard against their intellectual appetites and introduce them to a monastic way of thinking.

Right now, the gritty Novice Master had to decide how to handle the new postulant Dave Lynch. Dave had a certain ease and assurance about him, ever in control. Dom Joseph thought about the letter he had just put in the Prior's hatch. He didn't see anything alarming about it. Dave ought to be great monk material: Catholic upbringing, intelligent, training in a major seminary, healthy as a horse. And even before he came to the Charterhouse, Dave could speak Latin. Lest he forget, Dom Joseph made a note on a scrap of paper to have Dave teach Latin to a new applicant from the States. Dom Joseph felt a kinship with Dave: They had both had Jesuit teachers, had prepared for the diocesan priesthood, and were interested in speculative theology. Most unusual for an American, Dom Joseph mused, Dave thrived on solitude, the biggest obstacle for most novices. Well, he thought, Dave was an only child, and his parents were old when he was born. Perhaps he was used to living alone.

But, how to turn him into a monk? Dom Joseph felt that Dave's main flaw was that he projected too few defects. He was too controlled, too sure of himself, too good a politician. Yet at the same time, he seemed uncomfortable with communal things, such as the Carthusian ceremonies and rituals. And there was his nationality. Americans had not done well among the Carthusians. They had trouble with the cold, for one thing, and they minded the absence of electricity and bathing. After a steady trickle of Europeans, the Americans had arrived all at once, and the other monks had started to think of them as a block of people rather than as individuals.

Dom Joseph worried about the effect such an onslaught of Americans would have on his novitiate, and the Americans were still coming. Many of the monks, especially the French, were skeptical of the Americans' spiritual maturity and their ability to live such an austere life. They said that "the Americans came to the monastery when the beaches shut down." Dom Joseph wondered if his thirteen years of settling matrimonial disputes would help him hold these men together. Americans didn't have an instinct for the ways things went in a Charterhouse. Another prejudice of the European monks was against the Irish. When Dom Stephen Mary Boylan wrote to Parkminster asking to join the order, the elderly Prior wrote back, saying, "It's no use. The Irish never make it." Not one to give up easily, Boylan started praying, and the Prior died. The new Prior accepted Boylan, the first Irishman in the order and currently the head of the Vermont foundation. Dom Joseph now found himself with three Irish Americans and two novices from Dublin.

Thinking about the American-Irish invasion, Dom Joseph decided to set some ground rules for the novitiate. He sat at his desk, pen in hand, and prepared an address for the following Sunday's conference. He roughed out his draft, entitling it, "The Tram We Are On."

> I will therefore ask of you that you think over the sources of your faults and difficulties, and that you reveal them to me and so allow me to discuss them with you in private in order that we come together for the adoption of some method of dealing with the fault right at its very root. We may not always be successful, but it would seem that in sheer principle it would be destined to greater success than mere open attack.

He paused, thinking about the German Dom Ignatius, who was fiercely protective of his privacy but also very rational. He sensed an unspoken resistance in Dom Ignatius, who seemed to resent his unannounced visits; he was cautious and reticent, not as open to him as Dom Joseph would like. Dom Joseph didn't realize, of course, although he might well have been expected to, that Dom Ignatius had learned to be cautious through his wartime experiences. Dom Joseph was not going to change him with a sermon, but he felt strongly that the novices had to confide in him if he was to turn them into Carthusian monks. He continued:

> As you readily see, this cooperation for which I ask is the very center of our mutual relationships. It is strictly rational, almost intellectual in character. What I ask of you is a very clear understanding of your mind, intentions, and ideas. So far as I am concerned this is all that matters to me. It is all important, as otherwise a mutual understanding is impossible, and it is the only thing of any importance, as anything else in our relationships, like or dislike, sympathy or antipathy, is entirely accidental.

After rereading his opening words, he stressed:

> I want to make this point very clear, as misunderstandings may easily arise if it is not grasped. I do not intend to work through

> the heart. I will treat you as men, both in public and in private, by talking to your minds, and I trust that you will respond as men, by giving me your mind. I want you to give your hearts to God and to no one else.

Dom Joseph's intellectual, non-emotional approach appealed to Dave Lynch; he wasn't about to give his heart to anyone. But Dom Joseph was a shade uneasy about Dom Leo. He and Dom Leo were so much alike that he feared he would have trouble with him. As he thought about this very bright group, he felt he needed to make explicit that in this novitiate, he was in charge. He concluded with a scarcely veiled threat:

> But if over a period of one or two years I should discover a particular novice unwilling to cooperate, then necessarily, I would feel in conscience bound to withdraw my side of the mutual understanding. Naturally such a novice would lose his security as a result, but he would lose it with his eyes open, of his own free will and by his own fault. My side is this. I will have no doubts about moving him out of the house.

Dom Joseph read it over and wondered if Dom Ignatius would see his last paragraph as a personal threat.

Each novice presented a different challenge to the combative Novice Master, and he had to figure out how to work with each of them. He still puzzled over Dave. Although admittedly a good candidate for the order, Dave was a very private person. He didn't open up at all. Dom Joseph had been a cardplayer in his earlier days, and he thought that Dave was probably a good poker player; he kept his cards close to his vest. Dave only went to Dom Joseph's cell if he was looking for something to read. Ever protective of his own solitude, Dave always tried to catch him after Vespers to limit the time he spent outside of cell. Dom Joseph thought that he had some justification for leaving Dave on his own. The statutes of the order instructed the Novice Master to let the newcomer experience the austerity of solitary life in cell:

> Each monk is placed in solitude from the very beginning of his new form of life and left to his own counsel. Now no longer a child but a man, let him not be tossed to and fro and carried about with every new wind, but rather let him try to find out what would please God and do it of his own free will, enjoying

with sober wisdom that liberty of God's children, concerning which he will have to render an account before God.

Yes, for Dave, Dom Joseph thought it right to take the stance, "if you need me, I'm here."

Dom Joseph had begun to think about a Carthusian name for Dave. Normally, the Novice Master conferred with the novice about the choice of his monastic name, but Dave had suggested the name of some obscure saint dedicated to poverty. Dom Joseph wasn't fond of obscure saints. Because Dave's clothing day would probably be June 24, the feast of St. John the Baptist, Dom Joseph thought that "John-Baptist" would be a good name, especially for someone so suited to solitude, but another monk already had that name. Dom Joseph thought about other solid, blue-collar saints. He considered the apostles; not many were left, but perhaps "Philip": A Dom Philip in the order had just died. He would pass that idea by the Prior, who would make the final decision. Dom Joseph was very comfortable with his relationship with the Prior; he had more influence on him than any of the other monks.

A few nights later, Dom Joseph's concern turned to his fellow solemnly professed monks. He knew that he had aroused the animosity of many of them. Dom Joseph's job as Novice Master meant that he seldom saw the other monks, but when he did meet them, they let him know that things had been different before his time. The statutes emphasized: "The progress or deterioration of the Order depends on the good or bad reception and formation of novices." The Novice Master's direction of the novices inevitably created conflict within the Charterhouse. Doms Joseph and Bruno, the former Novice Master, especially, were at loggerheads. Dom Bruno, a native Englishman, had been a Carthusian for ten years before being appointed Novice Master. Worse, Dom Bruno had been Dom Joseph's own Novice Master. Dom Bruno had not wanted to be responsible for watering down the Carthusian way of life and had followed the rules exactly; his novices, for example, only read traditional, approved monastic authors. Dom Joseph thought him immature and narrow and had always found his spirituality soft-centered and emotional. Dom Bruno had not helped his novices discover the stern, ascetic inwardness of the Desert Fathers, which was ironic to Dom Joseph since that very inwardness had drawn most of the novices to the order in the first place.

Dom Bruno was solidly built, working-class Yorkshire, Irish Catholic. When he graduated from high school, he had joined the Royal Navy before entering Parkminster. He had a distinctive walk and was instantly recognizable when he walked down the cloister. He tried to imitate the manners and breeding of the upper-class Englishmen in the Charterhouse, such as Doms Guy and Jerome. Dom Bruno had enthusiastically read some French textbook about Freud and had a tendency to interpret whatever you told him in Freudian terms. Dom Joseph had little patience with Freud. Since he'd taken over as Novice Master, Dom Joseph had kept Dom Bruno away from the novices, especially those who had previously had him as Novice Master. Dom Joseph blamed him for the clear failure of one English novice, who, Dom Joseph thought, would certainly have to leave soon. Dom Joseph seemed totally unable to reach this man—to move him in the direction of becoming a real monk—for he was still very much under the influence of Dom Bruno's teachings.

Dom Joseph felt that every contemporary novice needed to learn how to think, to have an intellectual grounding for prayer and meditation, rather than just religious fervor. The international voices he had heard in Rome, where he studied canon law, had motivated him to learn many languages. He spoke eight fluently; Dom Ignatius, the native German, considered Dom Joseph's German to be perfect—high praise indeed. Not surprisingly, he had some of the novices studying foreign languages and reading rather speculative theology. He particularly liked some German theologians, such as Dietrich von Hildebrand, Karl Rahner, and especially M. J. Scheeben, a nineteenth-century neo-scholastic scholar.

Dom Joseph also knew that he irritated not just the previous Novice Master but the other monks. All the solemns had a stake in the formation process. Would they persuade the Prior to remove Dom Joseph from his job? They were used to an entirely different novitiate and questioned everything he was doing. As a linguist, for example, Dom Joseph was very precise about correct Latin pronunciation. He preferred the Italian version, and he insisted that his novices pronounce Latin in the Italian way. Some of the older monks resented not just his own pronunciation but, worse, that all the novices were beginning to sound like him. Dom Joseph could feel the tension in choir when he intoned a psalm or read a lesson. He also felt resistance from the very intelligent, Jesuit-trained Dom Ignatius, who did not conform to his pronunciation at all. The other monks consistently made comments about the bad pronunciation of the novices. In an environment where the monks spoke so rarely and heard voices so infrequently, arguments about pronunciation acquired heroic, all-consuming proportions.

Three weeks later, on his way back from Vespers, Dom Joseph found a note from Dom Leo in his hatch. Dom Bruno's troublesome English novice was leaving the next day. Novices never knew when another novice might be leaving the order; Dom Joseph didn't want any of them to think about leaving or to be disturbed. But Dom Leo, who seemed to know everything, had found out and presumed to write to the departing novice. Dom Joseph decided not to give the note to the novice; he thought it "presumptuous" of Dom Leo to "prefer his own notion of charity to the rules." He needed to speak to him about that, but carefully, keeping his temper in check.

He pulled his thoughts together as he prepared the novices' Sunday conference, keeping in mind the new novices as well as his own hard experiences as a monk. He tried to encapsulate the dangers and pains of this spiritual adventure outside the known world:

> Many "try" solitude and come away in raptures. But they have never really experienced its total demand on human nature; whilst they were in cell, they knew that at the week-end they would be back home or at the sea-side. But solitude is far from romantic.

He thought of some of the applicants who had left, many during their first night in cell.

> Before entering, the postulant dreamed of closing his door upon himself and calling to Jesus the Beloved, but he did not dream that it would be a desperate cry for help. That is the only prayer he now knows. It is just "Jesus mercy, Jesus help" all day long. All his pretensions, all his confidence in self, all his assurance that he was strong enough for solitude, have gone long ago.

After rereading his draft, he decided to continue later. He wondered if Dave, who was so very sure of himself, would understand what he was talking about.

The next day at Mass, Dom Joseph encountered another sort of challenge. He noticed that Dom Damian was coughing, his skin pale and hands shaking. With some concern, Dom Joseph decided to visit his cell during the afternoon work period. With no capacity for subterfuge, Dom Damian was totally submissive to the life, unbelievably open and vulnerable. Dom Damian would become a monk, more slowly than Dave perhaps, but Dom Joseph felt sure that there was the stuff of a Carthusian in him. After ringing the bell of Cell PP, next to his own cell, Dom Joseph used his passe-partout to let himself into the ambulatory, leaving the door open about three inches, using the sliding iron bar fitted to the door just for this purpose. He found Dom Damian in the workshop on the ground floor, wearing the special white work apron made by the brothers. With beads of sweat on his forehead and bald head, and his one-half-inch crown of red hair wet with perspiration, Dom Damian was feverishly making a pair of egg cups on the pedal-driven lathe. Dom Joseph took one look at his flushed face and unsteady posture and said, "You should be in bed. I'll come round to see you tomorrow." He sent the Infirmarian to take his temperature and then told the brothers to take Dom Damian's food directly into his cell instead of putting it in his hatch. Dom Damian worried about the Infirmarian's visit. Once before, as a postulant, he had gotten constipated, and the Infirmarian, a short, shy, gentle brother, had administered a dynamite enema, using a length of black tubing and a portable toilet. Three days without movement was considered actionable. Dom Damian made sure he never reached three days again.

The next day, Dom Joseph found Dom Damian still very pale and listless, but his temperature was down. Dom Joseph wondered about taking him to a doctor. A Carthusian statute advised: "Let our sick monks, as benefits souls in search of solitude, receive the necessary treatment in their own cells." He asked Dom Damian how he felt. Dom Damian insisted he just had the flu. His father, after all, was a doctor, and he knew what the flu was. Dom Joseph reminded him of Chapter 27 of the statutes; Item 3 warns the sick monk:

> not to distress those in attendance on them by asking for superfluous or impossible things or perchance by grumbling; and, mindful of the religious state they have adapted, let them realize that, just as healthy monks differ from healthy layfolk, so too sick monks should differ from sick layfolk, lest—which Heaven for-

bid—on the occasion of illness, their souls grow narrow and this contact with the Lord prove vain.

Dom Damian, of course, wouldn't have thought of asking for anything, but after that bit of professional advice, Dom Joseph decided to chat a bit with him. Dom Joseph didn't usually indulge himself, but he started telling Dom Damian about the food at the Grande Chartreuse, particularly the French bread. Because monks weren't supposed to talk about food, Dom Damian didn't know how to respond, especially when Dom Joseph started complaining about Parkminster's cook, Brother Christopher. Dom Joseph didn't seem able to help himself.

Feeling guilty after this serious lapse, worse because he had given a bad example to a novice, Dom Joseph returned to his cell, reflecting on his own difficulties with the life. The novices would never know it, but he thought a lot about skiing. He was passionate about skiing, awed by mountains. When the wind whipped past him, he loved the new sensation, the new vision, the sense that he was slightly out of control and needed to use all his skill to survive. He liked danger. If he had the opportunity, he was afraid he would get into skiing clothes and take off. Knowing he was being seriously tempted, he went out into his garden to concentrate on a huge crucifix one of the novices, Dom Mark, had made for his garden.

The April day was unseasonably warm. He checked the two wisteria, his favorite vine, that he had planted in late autumn outside the novices' singing room. The mother of an English novice had sent the wisteria to Dom Joseph before she died, and he cherished the wisteria for that reason. She had been a charming, educated, and sophisticated woman. Dom Joseph found her very attractive, but he didn't have much understanding of human passion. Most Carthusians idealized women and marriage, and Dom Joseph idealized this novice's mother. She had sent her son jasmine that had flowered in the middle of winter—a splash of yellow in the general dank gloom of his cell garden. After recollecting himself, meditating on his job as Novice Master, and sorrowing for his grave fault, he went back to his fastidiously clean cell to do some spiritual reading before Vespers.

After Vespers, he checked on Bernie, who had just returned from his hospital stay, resolved to balance his life so that he could survive and persevere. Dom Joseph found him in his garden, turning over the soil and breaking up the clay. He was viciously attacking a strange plant that he called Indian bean. The weed was six feet tall, with roots that ran horizontally in every direction deep below the ground. The garden of Cell HH was overgrown with it. Dom Joseph could see that even in his weakened state, Bernie was a good match for the Indian bean. He also noticed other improvements in the cell. It occurred to Dom Joseph to move Bernie to other old and neglected cells so that he would use his strength and boundless physical energy to repair them. Bernie told him that the lathe in Cell HH was broken, so without a moment's thought, Dom Joseph gave him permission to take pieces from the lathes in other cells to put together one that worked. Bernie then asked Dom Joseph if he could ask the Procurator—the monk in charge of the monastic economy—for some putty so that he could repair his windows. The brothers did all the repair work, but nonetheless, Dom Joseph was surprised and delighted to give his permission. Perhaps he had underestimated Bernie. Or should Bernie perhaps become a brother? What about a name for him? Bernie seemed to have the great faith of a prophet, as well as a prophet's eccentricities. He felt a great pull toward solitude, and his faith came from his gut. The last minor prophet (fifth century B.C.) was Malachi; his name meant "messenger of Yahweh." He reminded people that God will do all he can to help his people. Maybe "Malachi" would work as a name for Bernie. The order needed a prophet, someone who would tell the monks about God through ordinary events.

Before returning to his cell for examination of conscience and prayer, Dom Joseph decided to check on Dom Columba, who was just about to make simple profession. Dom Columba was thin-faced with a prominent Roman nose, the same age as Dom Joseph. But Dom Columba had a lot more experience as a monk—thirteen years as a Trappist at Mount Melleray Abbey in Ireland. Dom Columba was also a medical doctor, which gave him additional authority—he had been a general practitioner during the war, working in England and Wales.

An experienced monk, Dom Columba didn't really need to learn about monk prayer, but Dom Joseph felt he needed to get used to the idea that now he was in a Carthusian novitiate. Dom Joseph was investigative and felt that he should know what his novices were doing with their time. He also felt that Dom Columba was not entirely open with him. After all, he had had Dom Bruno as his first Novice Master. He rang the bell of his cell, used his passe-partout, and entered, again leaving the door three inches ajar.

Dom Joseph found Dom Columba in his garden, cleaning out last season's dead leaves and planning his spring garden. Dom Columba was so tall that he seemed too big for the small garden. He seemed to stretch out forever, like a straight-backed crane. He was bending over the dead stalks, gathering them for compost. Dom Columba tried to talk to Dom Joseph about his favorite writer, the esoteric Spanish mystic St. John of the Cross, but Dom Joseph wasn't interested. Instead, he began to interrogate Dom Columba as to why he had left the Trappists to join Parkminster. Questions of this type were more usually asked of postulants, but Dom Columba was always happy to talk. He glowed with warmth, turned to Dom Joseph, and said, very simply, "I couldn't get enough solitude." After eleven years as a Trappist monk, he said to his Abbot, "There are many holy men here, holier than I can ever be, but I am a weak man, and I need strong medicine." His Abbot responded, "But can you tolerate the medicine?"

Dom Columba continued, "When I walked up the drive to Parkminster, I thought, I'll never see Ireland again, but I will be at home here." After a pause, Dom Columba added that he thought that a monk needed to have had other hard tests in life before coming to the Charterhouse. "A monk needs to say, 'I have experienced life, and I can adjust to this life.'" He feared that without that confidence, the life could crush a man. As a doctor, Dom Columba worried somewhat about the young novices. With some hesitation, Dom Columba then turned the question back on Dom Joseph, "Why did you come?" Dom Joseph was surprised at the question, but he said, "You're missing the point. Just realize you didn't make the choice. I don't think we can talk about it. The experience just doesn't translate. Frankly, I can't remember why I came." He curtailed his brusque tone by adding somewhat apologetically, "We only persevere if God supports us. He calls us, and He gives us the strength to keep up the fight. He enables us to live only for Him—*Soli Deo.*"

They ended up talking about the garden. Dom Columba's family had sent some gladioli, and he had been allowed to keep them. Last summer, their bright, rich colors provided a splash of welcome relief from the somber cell—he remembered their names, "Winston Churchill" and "Maria Goretti." Unfortunately, when Dom Francis, the Sacristan, had heard about the gladioli, he cut the lot for the altar. Dom Columba commented dryly to Dom Joseph, "It was good for detachment, I suppose." With that, the Novice Master went back to Cell OO, got out his maps, and, with delight, started planning Monday's walk.

CHAPTER 7

The Long Walk (May 8, 1961)

Except for Holy Week, every ferial Monday, that is, ordinary Mondays that are not feast days, the monks leave Parkminster for what they call a *spatiamentum*, a walking about. Only when the weather is really fierce do the monks postpone the walk until the next day, and then the next, until Friday. Historically, because the monks kept the strict Carthusian solitude, the walk had enormous importance. The *spatiamentum,* probably made a formal part of Carthusian life around the twelfth century, helped to keep the life balanced. When St. Bruno built the first Charterhouse in the French Alps, he invented a hermit life with some communal activities—to keep the hermits from going crazy. In his first extant letter, St. Bruno made clear the need for diversion, describing in detail the landscape at his second Charterhouse:

> I am living in a wilderness in Calabria. . . . How can I speak adequately about this solitude, its agreeable location, its healthful and temperate climate? It is in a wide, pleasant plain between the mountains, with verdant meadows and pastureland adorned with flowers. How can I describe the appearance of the gently rolling hills all around, and the secret of the shaded valleys where so many rivers flow, the brooks, and the springs? There are watered gardens and many fruit trees of various kinds.

St. Bruno then commented, "Scenes like these are often a relaxation and a diversion for fragile spirits wearied by a strict rule and attention to spiritual things." Because the novices were never allowed to speak to the solemns, they took a separate walk. The novices always assumed that the reason for this unbreakable rule was that they might scandalize the solemns. In fact, the reverse was true; the solemns had integrated their monastic life, to some extent, with their own personalities and had learned how to soften the harshness of the life. They had made compromises with the rule. If the idealistic novices had known of it, they would have been incredulous, as well as scandalized.

The Carthusian monk seeks solitude—the order's signature contribution to spiritual exploration. Yet the weekly walk was an opportunity to talk—a contrast to the rest of the week's journey into a private, internal world. Serious discussions on the walks were not encouraged. Even though the conversations the monks shared were short, never more than thirty minutes, they were consistent, week by week, year by year. Some of the solemns had been talking every week for forty years; a unique kind of restricted intimacy developed. They knew what other monks read, and they knew about each other's families and their health, but they didn't know about the other monks' interior lives, their journey into solitude. In 2003, when I met with two ex-monks who had been together in 1961 for only a month or so, they didn't recognize each other. After about fifteen minutes of conversation, one of them said, "The more we talk, the more I think we talked before."

Most of the novices looked forward to Monday's walk as a chance to stretch their legs, work up a sweat, and compare notes with the others. With self-congratulation, they breathed a sigh of relief; they had lasted another week. After six days of nearly total solitude punctuated only by bells, Monday's walk felt like an exuberant opportunity. Dom Ignatius loved to walk more than anything. He was so lithe, so light on his feet, that he looked beautiful when he walked—like a dancer defying gravity. Some weeks, he worked up such a sweat that he couldn't even feel his slippery hair shirt. On Tuesdays, he always woke up feeling terrific, his muscles rejuvenated.

Dom Joseph always varied the twelve-odd routes for the walks; he loved exploring the English countryside. When the group got lost or a decision was needed about which path to take, he spread out his huge official map of the intricate Sussex footpaths and squinted through his wire-rimmed glasses to decipher the fine lines. Dom Joseph and the novices would huddle around the map and debate the course; the novices liked the shared decision-making. Dave liked walking with the

Novice Master because he could not only change the course of the current walk but also lobby for other walks he wanted to take. He schemed on how he could borrow the maps and study them in his cell. He loved maps and thought one of the advantages of being Novice Master was planning the walks.

Most of the novices talked noisily. A few novices didn't like to talk, or they didn't like to talk to certain novices. As required by the customs of the order, Dom Joseph kept a rotation going, and he enjoyed doing this with precision. The novices walked in pairs; if there was an odd number, one of them rotated walking alone. Every half hour, they changed partners. Within two weeks, all the novices and postulants had had a conversation with each other. On the walk, of course, they spoke English. Or to be more precise, they spoke various kinds of English. Dom Ignatius spoke a Germanized English. He liked to tell the novices that he'd learned English when he was appointed "shopkeeper" for the White Fathers; he'd had long discussions at Woolworth's when trying to buy "pins," a word he didn't know. He'd asked for "needles without holes."

Some topics came up every week. The novices always talked about any new solemns they had seen in choir. Occasionally, monks transferred from other Charterhouses, adding a new face to the dynamics of Parkminster. Besides these permanent additions, a monk from the Grande Chartreuse visited Parkminster a few times a year to check on the order's finances in England—Dom Damian, always ready to mock, called him the order's official money launderer. Every other year, two Monk Visitors from other monasteries would be there for a week or so to do an audit on the spiritual and financial health of the house. Because their presence usually preceded changes in personnel, the Monk Visitors created discussion for weeks. Most of all, the novices were interested in any new recruits to the order, speculating on who would leave and when. In a day? Would they stay through the postulancy? If any solemns had been missing from choir, they too became much talked about. Were they sick? Had they left the order? No one officially mentioned a departure, no one posted an announcement on the huge notice board outside of church, but the novices would talk about it on their Monday walk. In Dom Joseph's words, "Nowhere does news travel faster."

News shouldn't, of course, have traveled at all; it was an intrusion into the solitary life. Some novices, Dom Ignatius, for one, would get permission to visit a monk in cell, to take flowers to him, for example, and under this pretext would share news. Dom Ignatius always liked to share and question things. When Jehovah's Witnesses left their pamphlets at his mother's shop in Berlin, Hans read them. At school, he would raise their anti-Catholic questions. His teachers came to see his parents to find out where Hans was getting such irreligious ideas. At other times, Dom Anselm, their Louvain professor, provided information in his classes. More or less secretly, Dom Anselm had been telling Dom Ignatius about the Second Vatican Council. Dom Ignatius was particularly eager to learn more about the sessions of the brilliant young German theologian Hans Küng.

News from the secular world did not travel at all. None of the novices knew that while they were journeying deep into inner space, other men had traveled to outer space. A month earlier, on April 12, 1961, the Soviet Yury Gagarin became the first man in space. A week earlier, on May 5, 1961, the American Alan Shepard flew a suborbital flight. But the monks were never aware of these and the subsequent flights and orbits. The Carthusian coat of arms that Bernie saw above the double doors of the Gatehouse symbolized the mindset of the order: an orb surmounted by a cross set in a constellation of seven stars, symbolizing St. Bruno and his six founding companions. Beneath the orb are these words: *"Stat Crux dum Volvitur Orbis"* ("The cross stands firm while the world moves on").

Once a year, in the spring, usually in the middle of May, all the monks took an eight-hour walk and had a picnic. The brothers put picnic food in the monks' hatches in the morning, and the monks packed their lunches and two bottles of cider in variously colored knapsacks made by the brothers. The long walk took the monks beyond their weekly routes. The Novice Master and the Vicar, who led the walk of the solemns, got together and checked their maps to be sure the two groups wouldn't cross paths.

Dave had heard about the tradition of the long walk from the older novices. Doms Leo and Ignatius had looked forward to it for months. The novices, and even the juniors—those who had made simple vows—were irrepressible, bubbling over with excitement at the prospect of being able to talk to everyone in one day, and to talk all day. They felt incredibly free and unfettered—their minds as well as their bodies loose and unencumbered. Perhaps prisoners feel like this when they are out on work detail, or writers when they have just put a major project in the mail and take off on a very long vacation.

After the private Masses, Dom Francis rang the bell calling the novices for walk prayers in the brothers' chapel. Unlike the monks' church, the bluish-colored brothers' chapel looked like every other Catholic Church, with pews, kneelers, and stations of the cross. A Queen of Heaven Madonna with the Christ child holding a globe stood guard over the altar; in front of the painting, a brother had put a bouquet of daffodils and budding apple blossoms. Fourteen novices and three postulants—Bernie, Dave, and a new postulant from Nigeria, Hyacinth Objidja—arrived at the brothers' chapel. A new recruit had just arrived as well.

According to a centuries-old tradition, the monks prepared themselves spiritually for the walk by praying and listening to a reading, perhaps to remind them that they should pay attention to God even outside the walls of the Charterhouse. The ritual started with Psalm 125, "Ad te levavi." Dom Ignatius loved the psalms and thought this a perfect start to the walk. He loved knowing that the same 150 psalms the monks sang had been sung daily in synagogues for thousands of years. The novices then said a lot of other prayers, after which Dom Joseph prayed alone:

> Let us pray. O Lord, we ask that you be attentive to our prayer and make sure that we are walking in the way of your salvation. That amongst all the varieties of ways in this life, you will always protect us with your help.
>
> We beseech you O Lord to help and oversee our actions that every prayer and action of ours always begin with you and end with you. Through Our Lord Jesus Christ who lives and reigns with you forever and ever.

By the time the prayers were finished, Doms Damian and Ignatius were about to burst, but they still had to sit through the reading—today, the seventeenth chapter of *The Imitation of Christ*, compiled by the fifteenth-century German priest Thomas à Kempis. Dom Damian desperately wanted to be a perfect monk, so he listened especially attentively as Dom Joseph read the chapter, "The Monastic Life":

> If you wish peace and concord with others, you must learn to break your will in many things. To live in monasteries or religious communities, to remain there without complaint, and to persevere faithfully till death is no small matter. Blessed indeed is he who there lives a good life and there ends his days in happiness.
>
> If you would persevere in seeking perfection, you must consider yourself a pilgrim, an exile on earth. If you would become a religious, you must be content to seem a fool for the sake of Christ. Habit and tonsure change a man but little; it is the change of life, the complete mortification of passions that endow a true religious.
>
> He who seeks anything but God alone and the salvation of his soul will only find trouble and grief, and he who does not try to become the least, the servant of all, cannot remain at peace for long.
>
> You have come to serve, not to rule. You must understand, too, that you have been called to suffer and to work, not to idle and gossip away your time. Here men are tried as gold in a furnace. Here no man can remain unless he desires with all his heart to humble himself before God.

Trying to keep those thoughts in mind, the group left the chapel for the 1961 long walk.

Holding their long walking sticks and wearing their knapsacks, the group left the brothers' chapel. They continued in silence along the brick pathway to the Gatehouse. Only once they were out of the Gatehouse could they speak. The huge Porter, Brother Raphael, saw the group coming and opened the massive double oak doors. Dom Damian and Dave were ahead of the pack, Dom Damian quietly muttering to Dave, "Whoopee, the inmates are out!" Brother Raphael overheard them and grinned as he locked the doors behind them.

This year, Dom Joseph had planned a fourteen-mile walk to the hills of the South Downs. Dom Joseph thought that the long walk should be an athletic event, a way to work off energy. He believed that if men didn't expend their energy, it would fester, and he assumed his novices were as fit and energetic as he was. He called out the first set of walking partners in rapid fire: "Dom Damian with Dom Columba, Dom Gregory with Hyacinth, Dave with Dom Mark. . . ." The novices milled together and then set off in a ragged line in the wake of Dom Joseph, who strode ahead.

If visitors had been in the upper floor of the extern Guest House and looked out the window, they would have seen a somewhat unusual sight. The group of twenty-some men looked odd, to say the least. The young men walked loosely in pairs with multicolored and raggedly made knapsacks on their backs. Their clothes technically were white, but in reality each habit was a different shade of gray. Some had been washed more times than others; some men are tidy, others aren't. Many habits were patched with very thick wool patches in various shades of white. To keep their clothes clean, the monks hitched up their habits and cowls with hooks attached midway up their habits. Some of the novices wore hats, some didn't. They hadn't had a haircut in ten days, and the tops of their heads were various colors and lengths. Some, like Dom Gregory, were going bald; Dom Damian had what looked like a reddish crew cut; Dom Leo's hair just looked bristly, as if he hadn't shaved for a few days. They wore heavy army boots or walking boots especially made by the brothers, with recycled truck tires for soles. The three postulants were variously dressed: Dave wearing golf pants and a jacket, Bernie in blue jeans and a heavy sweater, and Hyacinth in casual slacks and two sweaters. Some walked almost sedately, others were already waving their arms around and brandishing their variously carved walking sticks. The line they formed was hardly straight. The man at the front of the line was walking at a fierce pace, and the others struggled to keep up with him.

They set off at a good clip. Dom Ignatius felt like a high-powered car that was finally getting on the Autobahn. "This is a pretty athletic bunch," he thought. But Dom Columba talked so much and told so many stories that he and Dom Damian soon lagged far behind, especially since Dom Damian talked almost as much; he often talked about his father, but today he was excited about his Christmas cactus. Dom Joseph yelled, "OK, now Bernie with Dom Paul, Dom Columba with Dave. . . ." Most of Dom Columba's height seemed to be in his legs, and as he got warmed up, Dave had a hard time keeping up with him.

Dom Columba told Dave about the venerable monk Dom Hugo-Maria. During World War II, the Vicar always prayed for "victory" until Dom Hugo-Maria, a refugee from Germany, arrived; then the Vicar thoughtfully changed "victory" to "peace." The novices had never seen him; because he was old and ill, he never left his cell. The Infirmarian took care of him. Dom Columba had used his medical skills on him somewhat against the rule. Dom Columba told Dave that "he had been a Trappist before at some abbey in Poland or Slovakia or Hungary. When the Nazis dissolved the abbey, the monks went to the German abbey of Himmerod, near the river Moselle, and became Cistercians. Dom Hugo-Maria joined us instead." Dom Columba then continued, "Dom Hugo-Maria had brought some grape vines with him from Germany, then cultivated them in his garden and produced wine." Dom Columba qualified this with, "The wine was very sour" and added, almost *sub rosa,* "He also grew and ground his own snuff."

In ordinary human terms, monks have very limited experience. They have their lives before they arrived at the Charterhouse, their observations of the other monks, and what they read. Perhaps because of these limitations, from the days of the earliest monks, they appear to have been addicted to telling stories. The trait appears to be bred in monkish bones. John of Karpathos (seventh century) advised his monk disciples in Ethiopia: "Never form a friendship with someone who enjoys noisy and drunken feasts, or who likes telling dirty stories, even though he may have been a monk for many years."

Dom Ignatius liked to be the first with a new story. He had a prodigious memory and kept track of what happened in the monastery, recording events and observations on scraps of paper. He even borrowed Dom Joseph's sermons and copied them in German. Later, in 1963, while the novices were cleaning the Great Cloister, Dom Ignatius broke the news, and the great silence, to surreptitiously tell the novices that John F. Kennedy had been assassinated. Today he had a shocking story that he had saved to share with Dom Leo. Dom Joseph had told him that the plans for the new German Charterhouse Marienau (which only opened in 1964) showed that the monks were to have showers in the cells. Even though there would be no hot water, Dom Ignatius considered it a breakdown in Carthusian discipline to even allow showers.

The group had reached the outskirts of Partridge Green, a village of about 2,000 inhabitants. Dom Joseph planned the walk to avoid towns as much as possible, and the group usually walked along the easements at the edges of various properties. Many of the public footpaths were overgrown, and the novices had to tramp through brush and stinging nettles that pained and burned if you just touched them. The novices forged ahead, whacking a path with their staffs. Following the white cross-shaped signs marked "public footpath," or sometimes "bridle path," the novices tramped through fields just turning green and occasionally through a manicured estate with formal gardens crowded with heavily scented purple rhododendrons.

After an hour or so, Dave was walking with Dom Leo, who looked very Irish with a reddish one-half inch of hair around his shaved head. He always wore a hat on the walks, as he sunburned very easily. Behind his glasses, his eyes didn't miss much, and his wiry body easily coped with long walks. Dave suspected that Dom Leo had enjoyed more than one pint in the pub and knew how to buy a round. Dom Leo marveled at the kind of men who, in his words, became "God-struck." With a self-deprecating laugh, he kept saying to Dave, "I've got to get the rhythm, it's all a matter of rhythm." He was very self-assured and confident. In his soft, slurred Irish voice, he advised Dave, "Just let it flow around you." Dave thought Dom Leo the most capable of the bunch. He felt a kinship with him that he didn't feel with the other novices. They thought in the same way and kept out of the mainstream conversations, rarely venturing anything personal about themselves. After nearly three months in the Charterhouse, Dave found that Dom Leo was the only one he was connecting to as a person. As they walked, they talked about why the rest of the novices came to Parkminster. The two novices figured that the Carthusian vocation had to be something that hit the very core of a person. Dom Leo thought that the monks themselves probably didn't know why they came. The mystery was part of the attraction.

Unlike the other novices, Dom Leo always thought about the future. He set agendas and asked provocative questions that made the other novices think. He asked Bernie, for example, "What does Jesus Christ mean to you?" Bernie, also an ex-Trappist, was a man of simple faith and didn't know what to say. To him, Dom Leo seemed very advanced in the spiritual life. Bernie believed in Jesus Christ, but before Dom Leo asked the question, he had never thought about knowing Him; he couldn't say that he knew Him. Forty years later, Bernie is still turning over the question, "What does Jesus Christ mean to you?"

As they walked toward the Downs, Dave discussed the choir with Dom Gregory from Lancashire. Dom Gregory had a slight limp from having polio as a child, so he and Dave slowed down. He was tall, about six feet, with a round face and a big upper body. He looked a bit like Babe Ruth. He had started singing when he was eight years old and had received two three-year scholarships to the Royal Academy of Music. His teachers thought he would be the English equivalent of the famed German baritone Dietrich Fischer Dieskau. When he converted to Catholicism, he left the academy to devote himself totally to God. The famous alto soloist Kathleen Ferrier had been at the academy before Dom Gregory, and he delighted Dom Ignatius by teaching him her signature song, "Blow the Wind Southerly." In monastic terms, Dom Gregory was far ahead of Dave and the others. He had been in the Charterhouse since 1956, but the solemns couldn't make up their minds about admitting him to solemn vows and had required that he spend another year in the novitiate. Although Dom Gregory was always cordial, the others were somewhat guarded with him, and he with them.

Yet Dom Gregory was comfortable with Dave, and they chatted about how choir shattered their musical nerves. They particularly talked about the "Viri Galilei" antiphon for Ascension Thursday, only three days away. This short piece of plainsong resonated with both of them. Dave loved the ascending fourth that then rippled up, soaring into the last syllable of "Galilei." Dave told Dom Gregory that when he had arrived two months ago, he had been impressed by what he thought was a new kind of atonal music: The monks sang antiphonally and descended in semitones—which is not easy to do. But subsequent choir experience proved that they simply couldn't stay on pitch. Commiserating with each other, they weighed the doubtful benefits of having musical sensibilities. "Do they even try to stay on pitch?" Dave asked. Dom Gregory considered the possibility that they could drown them out. Dave didn't have a big voice, but he knew that Dom Gregory could drown out the entire choir by himself. Dom Gregory muttered something about "the choral-ignorance of Carthusian simplicity." Dave thought that Dom Gregory was more outspoken than most monks.

As Dave was walking with Dom Gregory, Dom Damian was walking briskly with Dom Mark, a preppie type from New Zealand. Dom

Mark sparkled when he talked. Dom Damian knew there was a lot going on inside Dom Mark's head. He came from an Italian family and was very handsome, rather like Tyrone Power; his hair was so dark that his whole head looked unshaven just days after a haircut. The two novices talked about the wooden objects, candlesticks, small tables, and chairs that they crafted on their lathes. Dom Damian sported a new walking stick he had just carved. The stick had a snake's head for a handle, and Dom Damian explained in great detail how he had carved it. He also bragged about the number of egg cups that he had made. Dom Mark then put his hand in his pocket and showed him a small, highly finished, inlaid box that he had made for his sister, to whom he was devoted, for her wedding. Dom Damian was amazed at how Dom Mark could have found such delicate tools and the wood for the inlay. In comparison, his snake head stick seemed quite rustic.

Then, Dom Mark asked him what he was reading. A good listener, he really wanted to know. Dom Damian told him about the books by a Benedictine monk, Abbot Columba Marmion, that Dom Joseph had given him to read. He read Marmion's *Christ the Life of the Soul* closely, but he found *Christ the Ideal of the Monk* more useful—solid and helpful, but dull. Dom Damian told him that he really liked St. Thérèse of Lisieux, whom he found encouraging. She had no visions, performed no mighty acts of the will, had no great earthly accomplishments, and died in the very depths of the Dark Night of the Soul. But, as Dom Damian pointed out, she was now a saint and a Doctor of the Church. For Dom Damian, St. Thérèse was the best the Catholic Church had to offer.

The novices frequently talked about what they were reading. As they learned to live in their minds, their closest companions were books. Some talked about the same author every time they walked together. Almost every week, Doms Ignatius and Gregory would discuss the writings of John Henry Newman. Dom Ignatius sent notes about Newman to Dom Gregory on the backs of old envelopes. Dom Ignatius liked Newman's letters and particularly his Anglican sermons, as well as *The Idea of a University*. Dom Gregory also cherished Newman's *Grammar of Assent*. But as much as they agreed on Newman, they frequently enjoyed disputing over whether Handel was a German or English composer.

Impatient with climbing over stiles between fields, and bursting with energy, the normally contained and taciturn Dom Paul started vaulting over the stiles, using his walking stick as a pole. His white cowl flapped out back and front as he flew over the stiles. The novices jeered, but it looked like fun, and soon most of them were trying it—pole-vaulting over the fences, competing for the highest jump. Dom Mark was very athletic and won, to Dom Damian's chagrin. Had any Sussex locals seen these vaulting monks, they would surely have believed Dom Damian's words from earlier in the day: The inmates really had escaped.

And so they continued, some picking up the threads of old conversations or debates, others keen to share or acquire new information, occasionally, in Dom Joseph's words, "darting into the woods for necessary business."

From Partridge Green, going south toward the Downs, the monks crossed the river Adur, a small twenty-five-foot wide stream that flowed toward the English Channel. A half mile further, the monks skirted the village of Henfield. Dom Joseph yelled out new walking partners, and Dom Ignatius was now walking with Dom Columba. Dom Ignatius instinctively liked Dom Columba and said to him, "You are older than I am, you have been a Trappist for thirteen years, you are a medical doctor, and I am just a young kid. I suppose we can't be friends." Dom Columba thought for a moment and gently said, "Friendship has nothing to do with these things." Dom Ignatius said, "Then I am your friend." After that, on each walk, they talked about their troubles and their thoughts and had very intimate conversations about prayer, about different ways of conducting interior prayer, and about the nature of contemplation. Dom Ignatius could only talk to Dom Columba in this way and only on the weekly walks outside Parkminster.

When Dom Columba made solemn profession in 1963, Dom Ignatius went to the Prior, whom he found a very kind spiritual director, and asked if Dom Columba could be his confessor. The Prior agreed, and Dom Ignatius went to Dom Columba's cell and said, "So as not to be abusing this privilege we will only talk on the fourth week of the month; on the others you will only hear my confession." Dom Columba thought that Dom Ignatius had proposed a good and wise plan. They were friends forever, a rare exception to the Carthusian saying, *"Secretum meum mihi"* ("My secret is my own," Isaiah 24:16).

About a mile beyond Henfield, the monks walked across fields toward the village of Small Dole. The town was so small that Dom Joseph decided to go right through it. On the main street, the greengrocer came out and said, "We haven't seen you for a long time. We've missed you." The terrain then changed from flat pastureland to gently rolling hills covered with a low, many branched spiny shrub as well as the usual brush and nettles. Hedges separated the fields, and grazing sheep dotted the landscape. The Nigerian Hyacinth Objidja, who had just been received as a postulant, tripped on a wire fence after being distracted by a very large tree sculpted against the developing downs. One of the shortest of the group, Hyacinth weighed about 140 pounds. The twenty-two-year-old postulant, from an upper-middle-class family in Nigeria, was very black; the brothers referred to him as "Snowdrop." Dom Joseph had asked Dave to show Hyacinth, just after his arrival, how to pray the Office in cell. Dave showed Hyacinth how to put the misericord up and down, how to bow, stand, and sit. Then, Dave looked up and saw, on the top of the prie-dieu, a human skull, below the cross hanging on the wall. He didn't know what to say. Later, after Hyacinth reported seeing angels, Dom Joseph asked him to leave. His disappearance prompted the other novices to consider how long they would be able to stay at Parkminster. Doms Columba and Ignatius never had any doubts, but Dave wondered if he would last long enough to make final vows in five years' time. Would he even last until his clothing ceremony next month?

About a mile beyond Small Dole, the group hit the foot of the Downs and began the 600-foot ascent to Truly Hill, a radio beacon. Dripping with sweat and with perspiring red faces, they walked up the steep sides toward the grassy knolls that looked like a whale's back. Ever practical, Dom Leo said, "I'm glad we're not doing this walk in the summer. These habits would have us in hospital with heat exhaustion." When they got to the flat top, after about three and a half hours of walking, they could see the English Channel. Tired, they collapsed on the ground, laying out flat on their cowls. After ten minutes' rest, they followed the ridge path called South Downs Way, which, after a mile and a half, led them to Devil's Dyke, a sight-seeing point. To the south, they saw the English Channel; to the north, they could see the Weald, the endlessly flat tract of land between the North and South Downs. The North Downs loomed on the horizon. Fields, small bits of woodland, and an occasional homestead divided the Weald into patchwork squares of green, gold, brown, and red. Perhaps only Dom Leo thought about the incongruity of an ancient and radical group of Catholic monks climbing through Stone Age burial grounds to get to a place called "Devil's Dyke."

The novices stopped for a moment to watch some yellow, blue, and red hang gliders soar on the thermals from the English Channel. Dom Leo and Dave noticed an earthwork circle covered with beech trees on top of the Downs and walked through the trees to investigate. Dom Leo told Dave that it was the Chanctonbury Ring, an Iron Age fortification, 783 feet above sea level, with ramparts dating from the sixth or fifth century B.C. From the top of the Downs, the novices could see the sea cutting in and out of the coastline. The sight made Dom Ignatius think of Psalm 134, which he really liked: "Whatsoever pleaseth the Lord He doth. In heaven and on earth, in the sea and all the deep." He wondered if the busy Dom Anselm, the ex-Benedictine from Louvain, would have time to teach him Hebrew so that he could read the psalms in their original language.

In this quiet wooded place, the novices formed a circle and prayed. Most of the novices felt this was a very special part of the day. At the third verse of the Angelus, *"Et verbum caro factum est"* (John 1:14), they knelt down and kissed the ground. They did not feel strange pausing there to pray the Angelus. At one time, people all over Europe stopped whatever they were doing to pray the Angelus. Then the monks all prayed the little hour of None (BVM) together. For this purpose, they carried a small breviary with a dark blue linen cover in their pockets; the first page read: *"Officium Beatae virginis Mariae, secundum usum et morem Sacri Ordinis Cartusiensis."* Praying and meditating together on the walk felt right to many of the novices, Doms Ignatius and Damian in particular.

They continued to walk for a while. Then, hungry after the four-hour trek, they stopped to eat their picnic after saying their usual before-meal prayers. The novices spread out their cheese, bread, apples, and a candy bar, and ate together, careful to mix food with the cider. Dom Damian told a story about an Englishman who had left shortly after Dom Damian arrived. He had drunk his cider before eating and had fallen over, intoxicated. He just flopped onto the ground like a beached white whale. Dom Damian mockingly wondered if that was what the statutes meant by the admonition to keep "spiritual sobriety." Did cider make some monks spiritually drunk?

On the return journey, Dom Joseph was yelling out the names of the walking partners like a drill sergeant. Some lay people visiting Devil's Dyke excitedly took pictures of the monks. On their way back, skirting villages and following winding minor roads, Dave fell into rotation with Dom Damian, who was rhapsodizing about the beauties of the countryside. To change the subject, and to jerk Dom Damian out of his sentimental mood, Dave asked him with some sarcasm, "Are you going to slap me on the back when I get the habit?" referring to the occasion when on the first walk after Dom Damian got his hair shirt, one of the older novices had slapped him on the back. Pressing his hand hard into his back, the novice then turned his hand in circles.

That jarred Dom Damian into bringing up the subject of hygiene: "I wish you would wash your underwear more often. You do smell. You really should try washing your underwear." Dave said he couldn't smell anything, and that he wasn't going to waste his time washing clothes. But Dom Damian wouldn't let it rest, mentioning the idea to Dom Columba, who backed him up completely. He rolled out in his most emphatic tones, "The whole church stinks, the odor is so bad in choir. It is awful." But no one joined Dom Damian in the cleanliness crusade, let alone followed his example. On the walks, he wore only his hair shirt and habit to keep his underwear cleaner and to keep cool. Wearing a hitched-up habit without underwear on the walks, however, meant that Dom Damian had to be very cautious about stinging nettles when climbing over stiles or underbrush.

Dave noticed, with concern, that for all Dom Damian's banter, the angular lines of his face seemed tense. He seemed uncertain, needing the reassurance of others. Often, he talked about Night Office. As he interrupted his sleep each night, Dom Damian charged out like a knight keeping watch while the rest of the country slept; he was on duty. He got so excited that he couldn't sleep when he finally got to bed for another three hours' sleep. Cumulatively, Dave feared, the strain from lost sleep would prove corrosive.

Bernie was now walking with Dom Columba. He, of course, inquired about Bernie's health, as Bernie had just come back from the hospital. Then he told him the story he always told new postulants by way of encouraging their vocation. As a young lad in Dublin, Dom Columba had haunted the secondhand bookstores along the banks of the river running through the town. The rolling sound of Dom Columba's voice had already mesmerized Bernie: "I used to browse there when young till I was told to clear off, but one day, I looked at a book called *The Contemplative Life, by a Carthusian.* You probably already know, we always publish anonymously. I don't know who wrote the work. I saw a picture of a monk kneeling, praying. I felt inwardly it had extraordinary meaning for me." He rolled out "extraordinary" so long that Bernie didn't know if he would continue. "I never forgot the picture, but I never saw it again." He stopped and turned to face Bernie, who also had to stop walking, as he continued the story. "When I came to Parkminster, Dom Bruno was the one to bring me into the Charterhouse on my first day." Dom Columba reflected in a wry aside, "I thought I was in Heaven, and then I realized that I would have to put up with him for five years. God has a sense of humor." Dom Columba continued, telling of how on his first day he had been taken into the brothers' part of the church. Then, suddenly grasping Bernie's arm for effect, he added, "I saw the very same picture, the original, over the right-hand altar. I stood, rooted to the ground. Dom Bruno didn't know what was wrong. I couldn't move or say anything. I'm sure it was supernatural. I knew without any doubt, that I had found my home."

By this time, those in the straggling procession had recrossed the river Adur, and they were about a mile and a half from Parkminster. Moments later they glimpsed the church spire. Apart from an unscheduled deviation to avoid a charging bull in Farmer Smyth's fields, which terrified Dom Damian and Hyacinth, they soon found themselves within the 200 acres that remained of the 622-acre property formerly belonging to the Carthusians. The 200-foot church spire bobbed above the countryside as they walked up and down the hills. Soon the outer wall and the upper story of the cells were visible, and as they approached the Gatehouse, their talk subsided. Dom Columba remembered the saying of St. Antony of the Desert, the father of all monks:

> Just as fish die if they stay too long out of water, so the monks who loiter outside their cells or pass their time with men of the world lose the intensity of inner peace. So, like a fish going towards the sea, we must hurry to reach our cell, for fear that if we delay outside we will lose our interior watchfulness.

By the time they could see the statue of the Blessed Virgin above the Charterhouse gate, they were quiet, already back in their cells.

As Dom Leo walked through the gate into the brothers' garth, the scent of the apple blossoms from the monks' garth, the five-acre orchard inside the Great Cloister, hit him. He inhaled the odor he had been sensing from his cell, a bit heady from exercise and unaccustomed stimulation, and felt how good it was to be there. The long walk was like dessert, but life in cell was where Dom Leo was learning to live, the meat and potatoes of the Charterhouse. His cell was his anchor, his stability, his real home. Returning from the long walk reaffirmed for him that this was where he wanted to be; it felt right.

Brushing the mud off his walking boots to keep them from cracking, Dom Ignatius also felt that he had had a very good day. On this special day, the brothers left a four-ounce bottle of 110-proof green Chartreuse in the monks' hatches with a summer supper of sardines on toast and a salad. Dom Ignatius enjoyed feeling the diminutive cork against his forefinger and the convex bottom of the glass bottle in the palm of his hand. As he quietly sat at his table looking out into the garden, he felt the good ache in his muscles and the tingle of his skin. It had indeed been a good day.

CHAPTER 8

Alone (March 1962)

⊕

Since their arrival, all five of the postulants had become novices. Dave from Chicago and Bernie from Brooklyn were clothed on June 24, 1961, the feast of John the Baptist, Dave as Dom Philip and Bernie as Dom Malachi. Whether a novice would stay in the Charterhouse depended on his ability to cope with unrelenting Carthusian solitude—being alone, behind closed doors, for most of every day. When the novices had a chance to talk, they loved to tell stories of those who hadn't persevered. Only at Sunday recreation could the novices talk to each other in a group. They milled around, almost like at a cocktail party. What Dom Ignatius enjoyed the most was the way everyone worked together to communicate, mixing languages and gestures, and helping each other out.

In bad weather, the novices would stay in Dom Joseph's cell; in good weather, they would go outside the Charterhouse. Sunday, March 4, 1962, was a good day, and after leaving Dom Joseph's cell, they went through the novices' cloister to the *tabula* (the area containing the communal notice board), took the path to the Gatehouse, and once outside the Gatehouse, they turned to the right. They then walked around the Charterhouse walls, past the extern Guest House and chapel, and along a winding, idyllic path through apple trees. Two minutes after leaving the Charterhouse gate, the novices could smell and hear the sheep just beyond the exterior walls of the solemns' cells. Then they were in a meadow on a warm March day. They pulled out some benches stashed in the nearby copse and started to talk.

On this March day, Dom Philip told his favorite story of a recruit who hadn't persevered—Father James Maguire. Dom Philip had served his Mass when Father Maguire had arrived from Scotland. After making numerous retreats over a period of many years, Father Maguire had finally decided to become a monk. The Novice Master showed him to his cell, and the monks saw him at Vespers, but they didn't see him at Night Office. Dom Philip loved getting to this part: "In fact, they never saw him again. He came and left in one day." Juicing up the story, Dom Philip's voice would rise in amazed incredulity: "He left in the middle of the night, before Matins. He left all his stuff and a note: 'Please send my things to Edinburgh.'"

Dom Damian, who also loved to tell stories, had one that Dom Philip didn't know—about an American named Tim O'Brien. Dom Damian began confidently, explaining that O'Brien had made a number of retreats at the Carthusian foundation in Vermont and inspired all that he met. Dom Stephen Mary Boylan assumed it was just a matter of time before he became the eighth star on the Carthusian coat of arms. Even his good-byes to friends were inspirational: He was going away, but he told them that he would be closer to them when he was gone. Everything monastic and Carthusian came easily to O'Brien. That is, until the cell door banged shut behind him. Once alone, he entered a zone of panic from which no amount of Librium could save him. The facts were blunt: in on Friday, out by noon on Sunday, two apples eaten. But the glimpse that the gatekeeper Brother Raphael got into his soul was unforgettable. The brother barely had time to open the door of the Charterhouse gate before O'Brien rushed through it. Brother Raphael never forgot that look. He gently joked with the brothers that he now used St. John of the Cross's *Dark Night of the Soul* for light reading.

Everyone knew that Dom Damian was stretching a lot; he had never even talked to Brother Raphael. So he lost his audience. Dom Columba, a master storyteller, immediately took over. He had been at Parkminster for four years and knew stories pre-dating the other novices. According to Dom Columba, on one clear night, about 11 PM, before Night Office began, an Italian postulant pounded on the Novice Master's door. Carrying a suitcase in either hand, he shouted, "Taxi, taxi." The Novice Master, then Dom Bruno, couldn't get a word out of him but "taxi," so he finally went to the Guest House and called a cab. Dom Columba threw his crane's head back, roared with laughter, and kept on telling stories. "Just two years ago," he said, "after three retreats, a newcomer from Poland jumped over the wall in the middle of the night, leaving a note, 'Hope has turned to fear.'" In his rhythmical Irish brogue, Dom Columba exclaimed, "But that's the thing of it!" Warmed up, Dom Columba then told the story of how a novice had kept a set of secular clothes and, once a week, climbed over the low side of the Charterhouse wall, about eight feet, and went to the local pub in Partridge Green. None of the novices believed that story. Yet neither did they believe Dom Columba capable of lying.

On Sunday recreations, Dom Leo usually just looked on, amused. But today's stories spurred him to participate, asking with a wry, savvy grin, "What, do you suppose, were the escaping men afraid of?" He then answered his own question: "fear of the next day . . . and the day after that, fear of the unknown, of annihilation, of death." He added a story of a Benedictine who had plagued his Abbot for twenty years to be allowed to join the Carthusians. After he spent a few hours in cell, he yelled, "Let me out of here." Unlike Dom Leo, he needed an Abbot and the company of other monks to survive. He couldn't tolerate being alone and responsible for his own spiritual life. As Dom Damian was saying, "just one more story," Dom Joseph rang the bell. Socializing was over for the week. They were all reminded of the ephemeral nature of their companionship.

⊕

The Novice Master's job was to weed out those he thought unable to persevere, and a really good Novice Master tried to find the best alternative for the novice. They were all being trained, but probably even more, tested. In his classic rule for monasteries, St. Benedict instructs the Novice Master "to try the soul to see if it really seeks God." Dom Joseph and the other solemns kept close watch on the novices. The practice of testing recruits went back to the Essenes. Their novices observed the ascetic rules of the group outside the community for a year; after this initial trial, the Essene novices shared in the rites but not the meals of the initiated.

The two-year Carthusian novitiate is the novices' first real experience of solitude. The interior tasks of the novitiate are relatively specific: separation from one's past life, adapting to the strict discipline, and developing one's prayer life. The novices, of course, also worked at understanding the religious vows they would make when professed. They were all able-bodied, idealistic, young men, and they quickly adjusted to the eleventh-century Carthusian way of life. More than a year after their arrivals, Doms Leo and Ignatius had become very comfortable with the routine and took the horarium in stride; the exterior religious observances had become instinctual.

Yet the novices gradually learned that the exterior observances weren't what the Charterhouse was about. The solitude, the routine, did the work. The novices all seemed to be in different places. They found it frustrating to talk about their life in cell because they had no shared interior experience. None felt they were in control. The regimen molded the monks as the ocean tides mold the shore. Solitude challenged the novice to inner prayer, to a closer relationship with God. Whatever the novice did with his time, he was supposed to be focusing on God, aspiring to see the face of God, to be in relationship with God while still on earth. His goal was to become the kind of monk that St. Augustine describes: "He is, he sees, he loves: the eternity of God is his life, the truth of God is his light, the goodness of God is his joy." This did not mean that he tried to experience an altered state of consciousness. Monastic life meant dull, pedestrian daily living. Dom Joseph said proudly and pointedly, "We practice the mysticism of faith." Being a monk meant learning to live out the consequences of faith.

By degrees, the novices learned to live in the solitude that brought out their own distinctive qualities. Each one had to find his own path into his interior life, his journey into God. Dom Leo from Dublin recognized the challenge of solitude most quickly. After a year and a half with the Trappists, he felt he had become somewhat comfortable with death—the basis of the ascetic life. Even during his monthlong retreat, he had realized that the real combat at Parkminster was in the mind: thoughts, emotions, self-doubts, and projections of the imagination—invisible, untouchable, silent. "Who was I, or who did I think I was? God was the only certitude I had and I clung to him." Solitude became a box filled with resonance. On bad days, Dom Leo was his own worst companion. He felt powerless and vulnerable; the dark force, a feeling that none of the life made sense, took over. He couldn't shake his awareness of his emotions, his thoughts, his desires, as he had before when he had worked with other monks; he became increasingly introspective. Dom Leo felt stunned and adrift. He observed the loss of his history, his intellect, and, with them, he saw his individuality receding. Would God take over? Would the void be filled? He had left the Trappists, who would have brought him to humility—thence to God. He hoped that "by going directly to God, I will be given another sort of humility, perhaps deeper, certainly not of my doing, perhaps not even conscious of itself."

Before he left Dublin for the Trappists, Paddy O'Connell had read voraciously—all the great authors, especially the Russians, and practically everything of importance in English, including his fellow Dubliners, George Bernard Shaw, James Joyce, and Samuel Beckett. *Waiting for Godot,* published in 1952, had made him think about the absurdity of secular life. Now he read other kinds of books. For Dom Leo, the new library of books helped him cope with the aloneness of the cell. Books became his companions. He was very ambitious and gregarious. Studies became an outlet for his ambition and intellect, but to live with his native gregariousness, he had to go ever deeper into himself and focus on another relationship, his interior life with God. Life in cell was difficult. Dom Leo studied Jean Déchanet's *Christian Yoga* in an effort to contain his frustration.

He had always needed to be physically active; rugby, hurling, and other sports translated into the walks and gardening. He didn't particularly like gardening—the twenty-foot wall ensured that it was utterly private—but it gave him a physical outlet. By Ash Wednesday, the worst of the winter days were over. Besides, the damp outside was no worse than the damp cell. As the days became longer and warmer, and plants began to sprout from the ground, Dom Leo planned to start digging and perhaps even move some plants. The phlox, sweet william, delphiniums, and lupines were now brown and stiff, as were the espaliered pear trees plastered to the cell wall. But the box elders bordering the four rectangular flowerbeds showed hints of green. Above the wall, all he could see was the heavy wrought-iron cross with finials and four curling ornaments anchored to the church spire. On rainy days, he worked at the lathe in his workshop. Working the pedal-driven lathe required muscle and provided more exercise than one would have thought, and he became quite proficient. On bad days, Dom Leo thought about the long years ahead with nothing specific to do, no work; only *hic et nunc,* here and now.

On the very worst days, he abandoned himself to God, trusting that He would see him through the day. Years later, he would say, "I think that I felt called to a more 'mystical' way, than a more ascetical, virtuous, way. The Trappists always told me I was too human. Precisely because of my weakness, it had to be God's work, not mine." Dom Leo kept in mind Dom Joseph's sermon that marked his becoming a novice.

> Carthusian life is commonly spoken of as solitude. If the thought stops there, if the concept holds no more than this, Carthusian life is an insult not only to man but also to his Creator. We should love to be with others. God made it so, and any inclination in the opposite direction is a perversion of human nature. We seek solitude, therefore not from a disposition of not wanting to be with others. We seek it for the very opposite reason.
>
> Solitude over a period of time banishes from the mind and heart all that separates it from God, all that tends to occupy the human mind and heart and usurps the place that God will make his own. . . . God wants it all, and human nature will not give it up. God wants it all because he wants to have complete union with the soul. . . . The Carthusian has adopted the most direct way, the most drastic of methods of getting to his goal, cost what it may. His strategy is to bypass the lot—to cut them dead at one fell swoop—to cast them aside—to make a clean sweep once and for all.

Sweeping aside Dublin and all it offered meant nothing unless Dom Leo could keep his mind open to God alone. That was his challenge.

Of the five novices, perhaps Dom Malachi found adapting to life in cell the most difficult. Dom Malachi wasn't an intellectual; he was a man of faith and deep feeling. Once, on a walk, Dom Damian had said to him that when he thought of his "center," it was between the eyes, behind the forehead. Dom Malachi's center was always below with all his emotions. He was aware of his emotions, the objects in his cell, of his own male physicality; and he tried to be attentive to them in a contemplative way. Dom Malachi's center mixed his guts and instinct. Before he had joined the Trappists, he had found that his life in Brooklyn was difficult, but there were ways to make it bearable. The more balanced life of the Trappists was tolerable, even pleasant. The Carthusian novitiate, however, took away the structural supports, the externals of religion, and left only solitude. The hermit's life asked him to support himself. As St. Bernard remarked somewhere, he needed to "leave God to find God." Dom Malachi wanted to let go of the exterior supports, but he found every day very difficult. He needed not only to believe in God's love for him, but he needed to believe, in some mysterious way, that he loved God.

Unlike Dom Philip and the others, he didn't particularly like to study. Then he came across *The Soliloquies of St. Augustine.* He would read just a few sentences and mull them over for a long time. St. Augustine was interested in God, in God the Father, the Father of Truth, God alone. He had no sense of other people, no sense of helping other people. His *Soliloquies* are highly intellectual, Platonic, abstract, even mathematical, such as, "a line cannot be longitudinally divided into two." Dom Malachi liked math; after all, he had planned to be an engineer. Most monks would not have been able to even read the *Soliloquies,* much less understand them. But they spoke to Dom Malachi. St. Augustine gave him the resource he needed to cope with hermit life. Like Dom Malachi, St. Augustine wanted to be "about his Father's business." St. Augustine believed that everything depended on God's grace. Dom Malachi read:

> Nothing else have I than the will: nothing else do I know than that fleeting and falling things are to be spurned, fixed and everlasting things to be sought. This I do, Father, because this alone I know, but from what quarter to approach Thee I do not know. Do Thou instruct me, show me, give me my provision for the way.

In the confusion and cold of his hermit life, he trusted that God would lead him to Himself. This belief gave him the strength to cope during the tests of the novitiate. He found that solitude helped him develop his perception of himself and the world around him; he hoped it would help him develop his relationship to God. He tried to communicate with the mysterious reality that the monks called God. He found that being alone with God made him depressed, overflowing, merry, happy, more often just peaceful, and sometimes terribly bored.

Dom Malachi's restless New York mind needed news. Without news of current affairs, Dom Malachi discovered a vast amount of information within himself. He began to think a lot about America. From the Charterhouse, he felt that he was seeing America as if from outer space. He thought that every American should get away from America to see it more clearly. Although outside the world, Dom Malachi did not want to feel wholly disconnected. He thought about the monastic tradition that the life and prayers of a monk had a particularly beneficial effect on the people who live near the monastery and turned his attention to the people of a nearby town as a source of motivation and purpose. This monastic prop, even if merely psychological, helped him find meaning in his pain and isolation.

In contrast, Dom Philip had come to like the Carthusians' stark simplicity. He liked their single-mindedness—the radicalness of the life—the rhythm and harmony. After his first months, Dom Philip was reveling in the solitude, in the freedom from other people's expectations. As an only child, he already knew how to live without any emotional dependency on other people. Most of the novices nearly went crazy without conversation, but Dom Philip was glad not to talk to anyone, to be away from all the mess of monks and human stuff. Dom Philip was able to sense the mood of a group, even if it was never articulated. This was a mixed blessing: On occasion, he felt every discord, discontent, and conflict in the group, and he found this very painful. He knew one thing for sure, and nothing would ever shake his belief that God loved him. God loved Dom Philip. He went toward God as if he were pulled by an irresistible magnet. Looking straight ahead at God, he could be totally oblivious of everyone and everything else. Except when they were singing off pitch, he was barely aware of the other monks.

But by September 1961, after Dom Philip had adjusted to the externals of the life, his mind had gotten very noisy. Dom Philip suddenly realized that the monk lives *in* solitude—he doesn't just do solitude for a few days of retreat. Devout Catholics go on weekend retreats when they don't talk to anyone for a few days, when they don't have the release of a movie, a joke, a favorite television show, but then they return to their ordinary life. A Carthusian monk is on retreat all the time—he isn't taking time off from his normal life. His normal life is solitude, living alone without any supports from the outside world. His emotions are under pressure, the solitude weighs on him, not momentarily or for a semester or the duration of a tour of duty but for life. The more the life works on the monk, the more total his detachment. It took almost a year for Dom Philip's mind to reach what St. Bruno called *quies*, in Bruno's words, "leisure that is occupied and activity that is tranquil." At all times, the monk was supposed to listen to his heart and allow God to enter through all its doors and passages—to find God in solitude and silence. Essential to Bruno's concept of the contemplative life, active and dynamic quiet was also essential to monastic survival. Until the monk got to *quies*, he flailed around a lot.

A Sunday reading in the Refectory had made Dom Philip especially reflective. He had had the job of Lector Refectorii. While the monks ate their meal of thick tomato soup, cooked turnips and parsnips, fish and eggs covered with a cream sauce, and an apple for dessert, Dom Philip read from the Bible in the same manner as he would chant psalms in church. In the course of the year, the monks heard the entire Bible read aloud, either in the Chapter House or Refectory, or in church. On this day, Dom Philip chanted, in Latin, from the First Book of Kings.

> But the word of the Lord came to him, and he said to him, "What are you doing here, Elijah?"
>
> "I have been very jealous for the Lord, the God of hosts," he said, "for the Israelites have forsaken the covenant with thee, thrown down thine altars, and slain thy prophets with the sword; and I, even I only, am left, and they are seeking to take away my life."
>
> "Go forth," he said, "and stand upon the mount before the Lord."
>
> Now behold, the Lord was passing by, and a great and mighty wind was rending the mountain and shattering the rocks before the Lord; but the Lord was not in the wind. After the wind came an earthquake, but the Lord was not in the earthquake. After the earthquake a fire; but the Lord was not in the fire, and after the fire the sound of a gentle whisper. Now as soon as Elijah perceived it, he wrapped his face in his mantle and went out and stood at the entrance of the cave. Then there came a voice to him and said, "What are you doing here, Elijah?"

Dom Philip thought about this reading for a long time. The author of the Book of Kings might as well have written, "What are you doing here, Dom Philip?" He tried hard to hear the gentle whisper and to be quiet enough so that God's voice would come to him. At Parkminster, Dom Philip could pull his cowl over his head and almost hear the whispers of God. He treasured being in one of the few places on earth quiet enough to hear God's gentle whisper.

Dom Philip felt that solitude was like plunging into a cold lake. Once you got used to it, you didn't want to get out. To quote John Henry Newman, *"Numquam minus solus quam solus"* ("Never less alone than when alone"). Yet in this intoxicating solitude, he had trouble keeping his mind on God, particularly during morning meditation. He tried to keep his mind blank, like someone who was staring at a white wall, so that God would speak to him. But his mind kept working, he couldn't keep it quiet. His thoughts were all over the place. Dom Philip loved to keep track of things, and instead of meditating, he counted his days in the order. He had now been in the Charterhouse for a full year. He felt very good about that. Then his attention wandered to the fire: Was it doing all right? Was it making peculiar noises? Would the fire be safely lit when he got back to his cell after church? Was that a sparrow that had flown by his window? Where would they go on next Monday's walk? He wondered if he were fully prepared for today's classes. He groaned at his inability to be open to God. He prayed Psalm 12 of "Feria Quinta ad Primam" again: "How long, O Lord, wilt Thou quite forget me? How long yet wilt Thou hide Thy face from me?" He felt that some force was pulling him away from his interior vision of God. The struggle felt like hand-to-hand combat—pulling his attention to and from God.

Dom Philip looked at the tranquil old monks in choir, and their presence gave him hope. They looked more eager as they got older, like athletes in a triathlon as they neared the finish line—jubilant almost. When the Lector Refectorii read Exodus at the Sunday meal, Dom Philip paid particular attention to 34:29–31: "Moses himself did not know that his skin was in a glow after conversing with God; but Aaron and the Israelites all saw that the skin of Moses' face was in a glow." Dom Philip tried to see the faces of the older monks, and he thought they definitely had a glow.

ASH WEDNESDAY, MARCH 7, 1962

Most people are aware of late winter days when Catholics have smudged ashes on their foreheads. Ash Wednesday begins the penitential season of Lent. The cross of ashes reminds Catholics that from ashes they came and to ashes they will return—death is coming. During Lent, Church vestments are purple—the penitential color of mourning for sin. Catholics go to Mass more often and make special sacrifices. These practices symbolically mourn the death of Christ and prepare for his resurrection. But for Carthusians, nearly every day is a Lenten Day.

The novices found that the Carthusian order did not encourage special penances during Lent, though a few other minor penances had been added to help clear the monks' minds of trivialities: Instead of sitting during part of the Office, for example, the monks would lean on their misericords throughout. Each monk prayed the seven penitential psalms (6, 31, 37, 50, 101, 129, and 142) that express sorrow and awareness of sin besides his regular prayers, and after Vespers all the monks together prayed the "Miserere," Psalm 50—the great prayer of sinners, the great prayer of trust: "A sacrifice to God is a broken spirit; a contrite and humbled heart, O God, Thou wilt not despise." Ash Wednesday itself, of course, called for special observances. The statutes transferred the Friday bread and water fast to Ash Wednesday, and the monks did not leave their cells, even for classes, except to go to church. Dom Francis burned the palms from the previous Palm Sunday, and on Ash Wednesday, each monk knelt before the hebdomadary priest, who created a cross of ashes across the monks' entire shaved head, about six inches in each direction. The Lenten dinner began an hour and fifteen minutes later than usual and initiated the Lenten abstinence from dairy foods. Some of the monks believed that dairy foods kept them warmer during Night Office, so for them this penance was significant.

The order also transferred the Friday discipline to Ash Wednesday. In imitation of Christ's scourging, the monks scourged themselves on their thighs with the discipline, a white knotted rope that hung on the wall by the oratory. Dom Joseph recommended that the novices take the discipline after Night Office to warm themselves. Although the discipline was nothing compared to fasting for forty-eight hours, some of the younger novices dreaded it. The weekly ritual filled one young

English novice with total dread and repugnance. He really disliked the scourging. He would give himself timid swishes, and then try to screw up all his courage to try and give himself a decent swipe. He completed the whole exercise with indecent haste. He wondered if this was something he should confess at the weekly Chapter of Faults.

The daily rhythm reinforced itself the day after Ash Wednesday. The basic ritual did not change on this ordinary Thursday. Dom Ignatius was the Excitator this week. As it had all week, the shrill buzzing of the windup alarm wrenched him out of a sound sleep. He lunged out of bed—as if it were on fire, to quote St. Benedict. He hurriedly dressed, and stuck the stem of a woody flower that he had collected last fall into the embers of the stove and transferred the flame to the lanthorn. With the lanthorn lit, he threw his hood over his head and put on his novice's black cloak. He pulled on the bell rope outside each monk's cell until the monk inside banged the block of wood against his bed board so that the Excitator would know that he was awake. Once all the monks were roused, Dom Ignatius went back to his own cell to pray and meditate.

When Dom Francis rang the church bell, thirty-some white-robed monks with smudged black crosses on their heads came scurrying out of their cells holding paraffin lanterns to navigate the dark cloister. A pale sphere of light surrounded each monk; they were spaced out regularly by the distance of one cell door from another. Grateful for the shelter of the wide, enclosed cloister, as custom dictated, they walked as closely as they could to the inside cloister wall, to make meditation easier. Dom Ignatius's shoes quickly and lightly hit the smooth black Belgian marble paving stones. He anxiously counted the Bath-stone arches that seemed to go on forever as he walked along the cloister. An indefinable smell, perhaps the smell of damp stone, enveloped him. The Charterhouse flowed around him.

As he passed other cell doors, he sensed the monks coming out of their cells. He hurried. He did not want to be the last monk in church and have to tie off the bell rope. When he entered the church, he made the sign of the cross in the Carthusian manner and then bowed deeply toward the high altar, which shimmered against the French dark oak wainscoting. In the darkness, Dom Ignatius found his place at the novices' end of the choir stalls and stood with his cowl up facing the altar. During the Mass, with his head down and cowl up, he absorbed what he could sense of God in this holy, hidden, secret place. The sun started to rise, and the walls gradually became luminescent. By the time the sun started coming through the stained-glass windows, the conventual Mass was over. Dom Ignatius and the other novices went outside the church in the semi-dark to the private chapels.

This week, Dom Ignatius looked forward to serving Mass for Dom Emmanuel. The novices thought that Dom Emmanuel did financial work for the Grande Chartreuse during his manual labor break. They had even heard that he had a typewriter in his cell. Dom Ignatius followed him to his chapel, observing his distinctive walk. He thought to himself that Dom Emmanuel always walked as though he had just jumped off his horse and was hastening to deliver some important, strategic message to the commander. Dom Emmanuel had been a French cavalry officer for nearly twenty-five years before joining the order, but, as Dom Ignatius watched him, he saw an old, small, and bent monk. Even so, at age seventy-five, Dom Emmanuel was still vigorous and wiry.

Bringing his mind to attention, Dom Ignatius prayed the little office of Terce, the fourth official prayer of the Divine Office, with Dom Emmanuel before the private Mass. At the end of the Mass, both monks received communion. Then Dom Emmanuel bowed low and prayed Latin words in a heavy French accent:

> Most holy Trinity, may my act of worship be pleasing to you. Accept this sacrifice of praise which I, your unworthy servant, have offered to you. May it draw down your mercy upon myself, and upon all those for whom I have offered it, even to the gift of eternal life.

After Dom Ignatius placed the purple Lenten vestments on hangers and put them away in the specially designed cupboard, Doms Emmanuel and Ignatius meditated; Dom Emmanuel prostrated with his right elbow on the altar step, Dom Ignatius lay a bit behind him on the floor. Dom Ignatius didn't know the origin of this monastic tradition of the almost fetal prostration, but he accepted it as he did all the other customs of the order. He meditated until Dom Emmanuel got up. Then he could get up, too. Even without looking at him, Dom Ignatius sensed Dom Emmanuel's extraordinarily friendly radiance. Dom Ignatius loved being in the company of these men of different ages, nationalities, and backgrounds. He went back to his cell to pray the little office of Terce (BVM). After that, he relaxed for a few minutes before starting his studies.

By 9:30 AM, all the novices, with faint black crosses on their heads, were at their desks ready to study. Dom Philip couldn't wait to get to his books. As a first-year novice, he had already read a lot, much of it in Latin: his academic books, for example, the Bible, St. Augustine, and St. Jerome. He worked at improving his Greek so that he could read the Church Fathers in the original. He stumbled through St. Clement of Alexandria (circa 215 A.D.), who wrote:

> God has given the universe a musical arrangement. He has placed the dissonant elements under the discipline of harmony that the whole world may be a symphony in his ears. . . . He has orchestrated this pure concert of the universe.

Dom Philip thought that he would have liked St. Clement. He relished St. Thomas Aquinas, who commented: "The First Philosophy is the knowledge of truth, not any truth but truth which is the source of all truth." Today, searching for this truth, he read St. Augustine. He made a note. Monks didn't use new paper, so Dom Philip made the note, in the smallest handwriting he could, on the inside of an envelope sent by his father:

> The study of philosophy does not mean to learn what others have thought but to learn what is the truth of the thing. A chance perusal of any of Aug's writings, even a page from his most abstract work "On the Trinity" will convey the unmistakable impression—this was thought and written by a man of flesh and blood.

Both Aquinas and Augustine were, it seemed, making the same point. When Dom Philip realized this, he was as excited as an astrophysicist postulating a new theory of the universe.

Classes for the priesthood began during the second year in the novitiate. The novices attended classes from noon to 1:25 on Tuesdays and Thursdays, the usual time for theological study.

Dom Anselm taught most of the courses. In his mid-fifties, Dom

Anselm was short, stocky, and roundish of body. Though jowly and stern looking, he had a sweet smile. He always seemed busy and in a hurry and was very down-to-earth. Dom Anselm had previously lectured at the Belgian University of Louvain on the history of theology. Founded on December 9, 1425, the university added the faculty of theology in 1431, which later vigorously resisted Protestantism. The university could receive students from all over the world, and if the student received a doctorate, he could teach anywhere in the world. Its distinguished reputation caused Sir Thomas More to enroll. During the seventeenth and eighteenth centuries, Louvain was one of the strongest intellectual centers of the West. In 1797, the French Republican troops suppressed the university, but in less than fifty years, in 1843, the Pope restored the university in its old buildings, independent of the state. The University of Louvain is the only Belgian university with a theological faculty.

Dom Anselm taught in Latin, but he frequently inserted a *"n'est-ce pas."* He taught philosophy, moral theology, dogmatic theology, the New and Old Testaments, canon law, and Christology, as well as other classes. Besides teaching the novices, he continued his own research into medieval theology. Dom Anselm wrote historical articles for learned journals. He needed to use microfilm and was the only monk to have electricity in his cell. Once, Dom Anselm had left the room to his *cubiculum* open, and Dom Malachi caught sight of shelves and shelves of books, with books on the floor and all over the place. He had thought that he smelled photo developing fluid but concluded that he must be wrong. Dom Anselm's microfilm reader and his contact with outside scholars were a source of tension—certainly for Doms Bruno, Jerome, and perhaps Ludolph. Dom Anselm had the life the other monks desired, but which their own interpretation of Carthusian monasticism, and their own upbringing and talents, prevented. Dom Anselm was well aware of the feelings surrounding him, and he kept his balance by projecting a rather gruff bearing at community gatherings. Dom Anselm appeared to look on the community life and internal politics with a certain disdain, which, of course, irritated the solemns even more. Their irritation made Dom Anselm take even greater pleasure in teaching the young, unprejudiced novices.

When the first novice entered Dom Anselm's cell, using his passepartout as usual, he left the door ajar. Putting their cowls down, the novices would greet Dom Anselm, saying either *"Benedicite"* or *"Laudetur Jesus Christus."* Dom Anselm would answer, *"Dominus"* or *"In aeternum."* Although they might be taking the same class, they came from different educational backgrounds: Dom Ignatius, for example, had had three years of philosophy and one year of theology, Dom Philip had studied philosophy for three years and had begun theology, but Dom Damian hadn't even finished college. There were two or three in a class, or occasionally just one novice. The Tuesday De S. Scriptura V. T. class that Dom Philip took in 1964, two years later, included Doms Leo, Damian, and himself. The three of them worked diligently studying the Old Testament with Father Anselm. When the novices took oral exams, the Prior and Dom Joseph would also be present. Dom Damian was particularly nervous at these exams, which were held in Prior's Hall, outside the Prior's cell. The twelve escutcheons of the first English Charterhouses destroyed by Henry VIII were at the top of the wall, and Dom Damian's gaze always drifted upward to the meticulously crafted, intricate, wooden ceiling. Because he had not finished college, much less been to a seminary, Dom Damian never did as well as Doms Leo or Philip on the tests. Dom Damian fretted about them. Dom Philip tried to help by getting the right books to him. As the monks habitually did, he wrote a note to Dom Leo on a tiny recycled scrap of old paper, and he suggested that they rotate the book systematically. Dom Leo was happy to help, and they tried this, but Dom Damian kept forgetting to pass the book to the next person, so that ended the book rotation exercise.

On Thursdays, Dom Philip took "De Praeceptis," a course on moral theology, with Dom Ignatius. Moral theology is a branch of theology that deals with what is right and wrong, or what the Catholic Church would define as sin, either venial or mortal. A mortal sin sends one straight to Hell unless the sin is confessed with proper contrition. They used Noldin's huge Latin textbook, but because they were studying for the priesthood, they also used a separate volume allowed only in high-level courses, *De Castitate* (Of Chastity), printed in 1958. This volume would later have huge repercussions for Dom Ignatius.

On the walks, Dom Gregory would say, pointing to the power lines above, "That's the only place around here where there is more tension

than in the Charterhouse." The monks irritated each other a lot. Dom Philip thought that the monks were more aware of other people's oddities because they didn't talk. Dom Bonaventure loved to tell the story about the monk who entered his cell in such a state of anger and agitation that he couldn't even speak. Eventually, he calmed down enough to say that Dom X really hated him. When Dom Bonaventure asked him why, he said, "Didn't you see the way he handed me the bell rope last week?"

The Novice Master had to weed out those novices who were overly sensitive, who didn't have sufficient tolerance to live with the eccentricities of the others. The monks had only themselves, humanly speaking, for companionship, and the novices had to learn how to live peacefully in a community of hermits. Some monks just couldn't do it. Dom Philip had weighed the difficulty of solitude before he came to the Charterhouse. He had not weighed the problem of the other monks. He was taken aback at the tension between men who didn't even talk to each other. The solitary regimen actually encouraged tensions. Although the monks left their cells three times a day, they only talked to each other during an hourlong Sunday recreation and on the walks, which meant perhaps an hour's conversation with each monk every month. But indirect conversations every week or so did not resolve tensions. This sort of tension, what some might call pettiness, is a temptation in an environment with little external stimulus; some monks succumb to it, others are not affected. Hidden under the cloak of charity, the monks might, perhaps, mention their irritation obliquely on the weekly walks, but they could only talk directly to their confessor. Unless the monks were able to sublimate their irritation by meditation, or by yoga as Dom Leo did, these tensions continued unabated, driving some of them into illness and out of the Charterhouse, slowly but surely. Since no new information came inside the cloister to change the monks' ideas, the Charterhouse offered fertile ground for unmediated opposition, for prejudice, for factions. Doms Gregory and Leo, for example, had a lifelong animosity over the nature of choir; Dom Leo didn't care how it sounded, and Dom Gregory did.

The purpose of the ancient tradition of the Chapter of Faults was to encourage mutual understanding and humility, and to guard religious discipline. The verbal formulas from the eighth and ninth centuries had not changed.

De defectibus in Divino Officio (concerning faults in Divine Office)

Maxime in officio/iis (especially in the Office/s of)

Sacerdotis hebdomadarii (Priest of the week)
Diaconi hebdomadarii (Deacon of the week)
Cantoris hebdomadarii (Cantor of the week)
Lectoris Refectorii (Reader in the Refectory)

De Statutis and Ceremoniis male observatis (concerning statutes and ceremonies poorly observed)

De erroribus and confusionibus in choro factis (concerning errors and commotions made in choir)

De tarditate veniendi ad Ecclesiam (concerning coming late to church)

(etiam ab infirmario requisitus) (even requiring the time of the Infirmarian)

De fractione silentii, cum ___ *in* ___ (concerning breaking silence, with ___ in ___)

De absentia a divinis (concerning absence from Divine Office)

De egressu cellae inordinato temporibus prohibitis (concerning inordinate departure from the cell at prohibited times)

De ceteris defectibus meis (concerning all my other defects).

The Carthusian order encouraged the monks to confess faults committed against the other monks, against the statutes, and especially against breaking silence, which required a public penance.

For their Chapter of Faults, the novices went to Dom Joseph's cell, which was at the northwest corner, Cell OO, larger than the rest, and climbed up the stairs to the conference room, right above the music room. They took the first door to the right and sat at the benches that faced the window. If Dom Joseph hadn't let his prized wisteria get out of control, the novices could have seen the church. Dom Joseph sat at his table, facing west, with the large window behind him.

The Chapter of Faults didn't bother Dom Philip at all; he considered it a formality. Dom Columba was grateful for the chance to apologize to his fellow monks for what he considered his many failings. Dom Damian was always nervous and uncomfortable about the Chapter of Faults, but he was more nervous today because he had had an argument with Dom Joseph over whether passing wind while praying the Office in cell was a fault. Dom Joseph tried to reason with him, asking, "Wouldn't it be irreverent if a priest passed wind during the consecration of the Mass?" Dom Damian loudly said, "No." He felt that he had been quite courageous to stand up for his beliefs. It wasn't his fault that a diet heavy with root vegetables and beans made passing wind a real and present danger.

Dom Joseph instructed the novices to keep it short. Each novice in turn flipped his cowl in front of him and then prostrated on the floor in front of the bench, with his legs drawn up, lying on his right side with his two hands together and his body curled. He held his list of faults in his hands and read them. The novices were very impressed that Dom Philip didn't write out his faults; he just talked from notes, which Dom Malachi thought looked hieroglyphic. Dom Malachi was so nervous that he had to write it all out. Dom Ignatius believed that the rules required him to write it out. Dom Damian wrote pages.

Everyone knew what Dom Philip would say: "I confess that I overslept and failed to wake the monks before Night Office." He had confessed that about ten times already. Even putting the alarm clock in a tin pail hadn't helped wake him. He was glad that he hadn't talked to anyone, but he felt that he should add something, so he said, "*À propos* religious decorum, I confess to sitting in an indecent posture." The phrase *à propos* impressed Dom Malachi. Dom Damian had a tendency to overdo, and he confessed in great and convoluted detail "discussing a matter I had no duty or right to discuss although I thought I did at the time because I failed to think, becoming at times fascinated by my singing; once about to bless myself on rising from confessing a fault I caught myself and pretended some other indescribable gesture for the benefit of an approaching novice; attaching importance to the simplest externals, such as shutting choir gates; priding myself and boasting to others of my lack of external modesty; saying things I thought Fr. Master would like to hear." Dom Damian felt Dom Joseph's eye on him, so he concluded.

Dom Ignatius confessed, "When I got some powder against fleas, instead of being grateful, I complained about its smell." He also confessed to wasting the Charterhouse's poor quality matches by using too many to light his stove. He then confessed that "for several months I did not bother to omit the pronunciation of the 'H' in the choir readings, preferring to follow my own ideas in the matter." He also confessed to praying the Office in cell while sitting and failing to take manual exercise. Dom Malachi again confessed to breaking the glass in his paraffin lamp when he lit the lamp after Night Office, to passing wind in church, to skipping his manual exercise, to late rising through sloth, and to talking to Dom Ignatius after Vespers outside his cell last Friday. Following the Carthusian custom about breaking silence, Dom Malachi took his cowl off, and Dom Joseph tapped his shoulder with a bundle of birch rods; this action instructed Dom Malachi to use his discipline when he returned to his cell—for the space of the twenty-one verses of Psalm 50, "Miserere," about two to three minutes. Dom Leo confessed to being outside of cell without cause, to using nicknames, to appearing casual before seculars, and to not praying the Angelus. Dom Columba accused himself of preferring himself to another monk while eating in the Refectory. And so on.

Dom Malachi had puzzled all week over whether or not to confess that he had hidden some religious pictures. Because Dom Malachi liked cleaning things up, Dom Joseph had assigned him the task of cleaning out an old cell. Dom Malachi was scandalized by what he found; nineteenth-century pictures of a curly haired, blond Jesus and pious saints. He found these disgraceful, certainly not helpful for a hermit monk. In order to protect future inhabitants of the cell from this sentimentality, he had taken all the old pictures and hidden them under the stairs in the coal bin. He wondered whether he really needed to confess this deed. He decided to keep it to himself. In God's providence, they would come to light sooner or later. And maybe it wasn't a fault.

Later in the week, while Doms Ignatius and Philip were at the Thursday class, Dom Malachi was in cell. He had learned to keep his stove well stoked and his cell warm. Dom Malachi was lonely in cell, but when he came together with the other novices, he only felt more loneliness, even more aware of how much he needed other people. After being together for over a year, the novices weren't feeling closer. They didn't slap each other on the back and say, "How's it going?" The monastic observances created distance rather than collegiality: the rigid formality of calling each other "Dom," for example, or "Venerable Father" if they wrote to each other. He took off his *gilet* and sat at his semicircular table looking out the window.

Dom Malachi was a practical man, and during his manual labor breaks he enjoyed fixing things. His cell was always in excellent condition, and he liked to invent ways to improve the efficiency of the cell. His current project was to invent and manufacture metal pieces to protect the always charred paper shades of the paraffin lamps. When the clock bell chimed 5:15 PM, all the monks examined their consciences. Then for nearly an hour and a half, until the little hour of Compline, the prayer before going to bed, the monks had nothing specific on their schedule. Dom Malachi stood on the window sill of his cell to see the sun set behind the surrounding walls.

When the bell rang for Compline, the novices genuflected in their anterooms, saying an Ave Maria in front of the fourteen-inch white statue of the Blessed Virgin, and prepared their minds for evening prayer. Throwing out all the distracting thoughts clamoring in their minds, they recollected and calmed themselves. Then they lit their reading lamps, knelt down at their prie-dieus, and prayed Compline, the final official prayer of the day. They began with a Pater and Ave in silence, then said the Confiteor, a prayer acknowledging sins, and prayed Psalms 4, 90, and 133. They thought about the sixth verse of Psalm 90: *"Non timebis a timore nocturno . . . ab incursu et dæmonio meridiano"* ("Thou shall not fear the terrors of night . . . nor the attack of the noonday demon"). Most felt reassured, as always, by the hymn *"Christe qui lux es et dies"* ("O Christ, you who are the light and the day"), and its comforting verse, "Defend us in this night, let our eyes capture sleep. We who rest in you, give us a quiet night." Then a short reading from Jeremiah 14: "Thou, O Lord, art among us, and Thy holy Name is called upon by us: forsake us not, O Lord our God." At the end of Compline, they paid particular attention to the Oratio:

> Visit, we beseech Thee, O Lord, this dwelling and drive far from it all snares of the enemy; let Thy holy Angels dwell herein, who may keep us in peace, and let Thy blessing be always upon us.

The quiet absorbed everything.

Things were wrapped up for the day. Dom Malachi used the toilet on the ground floor, threw a bucket of water into it to flush it, and climbed the inside stairway to the upper floor living area. He had forgotten to put water on the stove to heat, so he poured cold water into his washbasin and cleaned his face and hands. He put some more coals on the fire, took off his cowl, cincture, habit, *gilet*, and shoes, put on his night habit, settled into the straw pallet as best he could, pulled the curtains shut to keep out the cold, tugged at the straw pillow, and pulled the blanket over him.

Published posthumously at the end of the nineteenth century, a poem about the Carthusians by the Catholic poet Ernest Dowson commented, perhaps a bit melodramatically:

A cloistered company, they are companionless,
None knoweth here the secret of his brother's heart:
They are but come together for more loneliness,
Whose bond is solitude and silence all their part.

He wasn't too far from the mark. He certainly understood Dom Malachi.

CHAPTER 9

Desire (Summer 1962)

In the solitude of the Charterhouse, a void opens so that the monk can listen to God. St. Bruno's original aspiration was to "see the face of God," and every Carthusian perseveres with the same ultimate hope. One monk, whom Dom Joseph had ejected from the Charterhouse, said, "I didn't see the promised land, but I did see the glow of the promised land." Yet there are very few records in which a Carthusian monk articulates his experience of God. In 1487, a Carthusian monk at Mount Grace in England left evidence that at least one monk succeeded in his quest. Richard Methley kept a personal diary for slightly over two months. In it he recounts an experience of God that so overpowered him he could scarcely speak. As he journeyed deeper into God, the pain of love became more intense, like an unending musical crescendo, culminating in mystical ecstasy. When the journey ended, he was unable to speak a single word but "Ah":

> On the feast of St. Peter in Chains I was in the church at Mount Grace, and after celebrating Mass was engaged upon thanksgiving in prayer and meditation, when God visited me in power, and I yearned with love so as almost to give up the ghost. How this could be I will tell you, my brethren, as best I can by the grace of God. Love and longing for the Beloved raised me in spirit into heaven, so that save for this mortal life nothing (so far as I know) would have been lacking to me of the glory of God Who sitteth on the throne. Then did I forget all pain and fear and deliberate thought of anything, and even of the Creator. And as men who

> fear the peril of fire do not cry, "Fire hath come upon my house; come ye and help me" since in their strait and agony they can scarce speak a single word, but cry "Fire, Fire, Fire!" Or, if their fear be greater they cry "Ah! Ah! Ah!" wishing to impart their peril in this single cry so I, in my poor way. For first, I oft commended my soul to God, saying, "Into thy hands," either in words or (as I think rather) in spirit. But as the pain of love grew more powerful I could scarce have thought at all, forming within my spirit these words: "Love! Love! Love!" And at last, ceasing from this, I deemed that I would wholly yield up my soul, singing rather than crying, in spirit through joy. "Ah! Ah! Ah."

This desire for God is what compels men to enter the Charterhouse. Monks, like mountaineers, feel a compelling attraction for the extremes of human experience. They want to push the limits in their search for God. *O Bonitas!*

One of the perils for the monks is that having emptied their world of social routines and conventions, they are very vulnerable if they falter. If the monks are not attentive to God, other desires will surface. Their former lives, their former selves, lurk in the background—always waiting to break through their new monastic identity. When the novices received letters from home four times each year, they were transported back—flooded with memories and desires. During the process of becoming a monk, these letters were both eagerly awaited and dreaded. They were dangerous—psychologically, they brought them back to their previous identity. Dom Leo, for example, might have felt again the pleasure of being the president of the debating society or going dancing with a girlfriend, or Dom Philip of shooting under par on a golf course. Dom Malachi might again recall the young woman on the *Mauretania.* Sometimes, the letters stirred up desires for trivialities: a young novice from New York, for example, yearned for pork chops. Dom Joseph himself craved the French bread he had had at the Grande Chartreuse, and his secret passion for skiing never disappeared. Later, when the Reverend Father reassigned Dom Joseph to Italy as Vicar of the Carthusian nuns at the Certosa di San Francesco near Turin, his niece visited and gave him a gift of skis. He finally succumbed to his great passion. His delight in skiing put him in touch with his audacity, his love of freedom, with his own nature. Dom

Ignatius never mastered his curiosity for what was going on in the church outside the Charterhouse, a desire shared by many new arrivals unaccustomed to total seclusion. Occasionally, a newcomer continued to be interested in the secular world. On November 20, 1962, one or two days after China invaded India, just when political and military matters had suddenly become really gripping, an Englishman entered Parkminster. Much of the press, and the Englishman, thought World War III was about to begin. A huge six- by eight-foot notice board outside the church posts information. The notice board is divided into panels to organize the information, such as permanent rules, a list of monks' names and their cell letters, and the choir assignments for the week. The Prior also pins, in Latin, selected events from the secular world. A week or so after he arrived, the newcomer saw a tiny notice posted. He read Latin poorly and thought that the notice said that, indeed, World War III *had* started. For months, he had to curb his curiosity until a new postulant, the only source of secular news, came. Then, he had to wait for a Monday walk to find out what was going on. He discovered that the Chinese had only advanced up to what was called the MacMahon Line, which was a disputed border left by the British in colonial times. World War III had not begun.

Some monks found it harder to suppress their nonspiritual desires than others. Sometimes the desire was trivial, but suddenly, at a certain psychological moment, it seemed essential. A cheerful Italian novice from Buffalo, New York, an ex-Trappist, had difficulty suppressing his desire for spontaneous gratification. He electrified everyone during a confession of faults by confessing that in the middle of the night, after Night Office, he had left his cell. This in itself was monstrous, because no monk ever left his cell except to go to church. The novice didn't stop there. Dom Leo wryly thought to himself, "This gets worse and worse." He proceeded to confess that he had gone into the garth, forbidden territory, and gathered up some half-rotten apples that the brothers had left on the ground. Dom Leo hoped that he would stop there. The novices wondered what could possibly be worse. Monks never ate between meals. Then he confessed that he put the Cox's Pippin apples in his mug and baked them on the top of his stove . . . and then, in the middle of the night, ate them, using his big wooden spoon. A frisson of shock ran through the group. No one knew what to think. Dom Damian was glad he was required to guard his eyes because he wouldn't have known where to look. Everyone wondered if Dom Joseph would ask the novice to leave. In fact, he was gone within weeks.

As the Desert Fathers said, when the spiritual life isn't going well, the monk is much more prone to the temptations of the flesh. Always alert for obstacles to their concentrated attention to God, one of the monks' greatest concerns has always been the threat of women. The ferocious banishment of women is part of an ancient tradition. This theological and ascetic attitude goes back to Aristotle, St. Augustine, St. Thomas Aquinas, and earlier monks such as St. Jerome. The Carthusians imported it along with other monastic traditions. Guigo, the fifth Prior of the order, wrote: "Neither the wise man, nor the prophet, nor the judge, nor the host, nor the sons of God, nor the very first man formed by the hands of God, could elude the blandishments and deceits of women." Within days of the arrival of Bruno at the Chartreuse, Hugh of Grenoble issued a letter to all the people in his diocese, forbidding, among other things, "women to enter the territory of the Carthusians who seek to do God's pleasure by fleeing from the world and its tumult." The regnant queen in the country of the Charterhouse, if she wants to, can get beyond the extern Guest House. Yet Queen Victoria of England needed a letter from the Pope to get into the Grande Chartreuse on the occasion of her Golden Jubilee. St. Hugh of Lincoln is preeminent among monks, not because he was canonized or was the Bishop of Lincoln but because he warmly embraced a woman he knew, and was obviously fond of, at an Episcopal reception. The monks take this embrace as a sign of his extraordinarily advanced holiness. An ordinary monk would fear risking his soul if he embraced a woman.

To the monks, the epitome of "woman" was the Blessed Virgin. Dom Malachi, as well as others, missed the femininity of life, intuition, and mysticism. Over the long history of the order, a certain legalism set moral judgments and denied feminine qualities. At times, the monks, probably unconsciously, sublimated their sexuality, transferring it to the Blessed Virgin. Dom Joseph mentioned to Dom Malachi that when he was a diocesan priest, women who repeatedly confessed their adultery to him often continued the affair. He simply couldn't understand. He once went to Dom Malachi's cell in considerable confusion and asked him what he thought about a novice who had dreams with sexual allusions about the Blessed Virgin. Dom Joseph didn't know what to do or think. Dom Malachi, who considered himself a man of the world, was not shocked, but Dom Joseph clearly was. Dom Damian felt that the Song of Songs contained the most beautiful words ever written.

> My beloved put his hand through the key hole, and my bowels were moved at his touch. I arose up to open to my beloved: my hands dropped with myrrh, and my fingers were full of the choicest myrrh. I opened the bolt of the door to my beloved: but he had turned aside, and was gone. My soul melted when he spoke: I sought him, and found him not: I called, and he did not answer me. (Song of Songs 5:4–6)

On the other hand, Dom Philip hated the Song of Songs, seeing it as an intrusion of sex into his monastic life. Dom Malachi also avoided reading the Song of Songs. Though others did not know what the Bride of the Song of Songs meant, Dom Damian felt lucky that she spoke to him. He was not sure what the words meant, but they spoke to his deepest self, a self he perhaps could not admit to his consciousness. When he served Mass in the Reliquary Chapel, he worried about the statue of the Blessed Virgin, presented as a beautiful young woman with high cheekbones holding the child out in front of her. He had to be careful not to look at her. He worried that he might be, in Dom Joseph's words, "seething with concupiscence."

By the time a Carthusian novice reaches his fourth or fifth year, he has usually sorted out his need for women, or for simple companionship. That is not to say, however, that he might not respond to a woman if he unexpectedly encountered one. Dom Damian remembered how he felt when he rounded a curve in the path on one of the Monday walks, and a young woman on horseback nearly ran into him. She merely said, "Good day, Sir," but Dom Damian felt great for a week. At the Chapter of Faults, he confessed to having "distractions," but he didn't go into details. At least one novice had obsessional thoughts of a sexual nature. These thoughts diminished when the novice was reading or studying but came back full force when his mind was not consciously occupied with work.

The Carthusian attitude toward women can best be illustrated anecdotally. When Dom Malachi was struck with appendicitis, he "turned orange and was feeling a real wrench in my gut. I collapsed on the floor, all two hundred pounds of me." Father Prior stopped Night Office and called for an ambulance. Dom Malachi, stretched out on the floor of the cold church, heard the sirens blaring as they came down the road into the Charterhouse. Brother Raphael opened the gates to the brothers' garth. Just as Dom Malachi had calmed down, reassured that help was on the way, he heard the ambulance leaving. Father Prior had seen that a nurse, a woman, was in the ambulance! The ambulance had to back out and leave the woman outside the Charterhouse before it could return for Dom Malachi. After he thought about it for a minute, he reflected cheerfully, "At least they did come back."

Dom David had just turned twenty-one. His Jewish mother had refused to let him leave Melbourne for Parkminster before his twenty-first birthday. He was very susceptible to the distractions of women. On one walk he had to put his cowl up over his head, *ex toto,* to avoid the temptations of one small town. He could barely see in front of him. Dom Leo was amused; he had seen plenty of girls, enough to know that he preferred redheads. Having lived in the secular world as an adult, Dom Leo was comfortable with women, and he understood that women were different from men—but not idealized creatures. Dom David's distress at seeing girls inspired Dom Leo to talk about the women he had left behind, especially Thérèse, whom he had almost married. Dom Joseph asked Dom David to leave in July of 1964— girls were still very much on his mind. In early February 1965, in a letter to Dom Joseph, he admitted he was still homesick for the Charterhouse, but a year later, he wrote that he was "extremely happy about the way things are going, in study and in general." He finished the letter with "a kind thought for our suffering brothers, inside and out." Many novices who were asked to leave were advised to "get married." Dom David perhaps took the advice too seriously. He married on June 1, 1968, in a baroque Nuptial Mass with flute, violin, and organ. He immediately remarried when his first marriage was finally annulled in 1985. He has five children, is again divorced, had been in a relationship with a Russian architect, and is now formally engaged to a businesswoman from the Philippines. In early 1993, he returned to Judaism.

Few monks who stayed to make solemn profession had serious problems with heterosexual desire. The monks very rarely saw women, and the books they read certainly didn't feature them. Probably all of the men in this novitiate, including the Novice Master, were virgins, with little or no sexual experience. None of the monks talked about sex among themselves or with the Novice Master. Unless there was a problem, sex did not exist.

Or rather, if sex existed, there was a problem in the Charterhouse. The Catholic Church was terrified of homosexuality; both male and female religious were warned of "particular friendships." The monks themselves lived in horror of the possibility of homosexuality. Although never spoken of, fear of homosexuality was always there; the solemns were always on the alert for it. Even more frightening to the monks was what the Catholic Church called the sin of "self-abuse." Origen, a brilliant third-century precursor of monasticism, was said to have castrated himself to avoid "self-abuse." An early Irish Penitential (circa seventh century) reads, "He who desires to sin during sleep, or is unintentionally polluted, fifteen psalms, he who sins and is not polluted, twenty-four." The Penitential assigns the greater penance to the man who desires to sin, not the one who is unintentionally polluted. The novices were convinced that there was no sexual expression at Parkminster, yet when they first came, there were more than twenty novices, and all except Dom Columba were young men. Subconscious sexual fantasy had to be common, even among young monks. The novices found it difficult to seek advice about this issue in a closed society. When Dom Malachi confessed to Dom Emmanuel that he had felt an "uncontrollably strong urge" when he woke during the night, his confessor was shocked and demanded a general confession of the sins of his entire life. After this one sexual episode, Dom Malachi had peace and inner harmony for the years that followed. Other novices had the same experience with seeking advice on "self-abuse," with, in some cases, even more extreme results. Dom Joseph gave one novice some twine for assistance. The novice bound his hands together, then constructed a twine sling to loop over his neck, thus safely immobilizing his hands. Then he made sure he never slept on his back. But the novice got terrible headaches. Quite quickly, he was asked to leave and advised to "get married." Following Dom Joseph's advice, he entered into a disastrous marriage two months after leaving Parkminster. The novice from Buffalo also had a hard time with sex. He had been in the Charterhouse a year and a half longer than Dom Damian and had explained to him his intricate methods for not suffering so much, how at all costs to avoid the sin of self-abuse.

When answering Dom Joseph's question as to why he wanted to

become a Carthusian, Dom Philip said, "The horror of homosexuality interfered with my relationships with my classmates, but I wanted to connect with people. I was sitting in the Philosophy House's chapel, waiting for a conference to begin. I had always wondered if anyone could understand me. I looked at the crucifix and realized that God understood me completely." He felt he had been letting God down, that he hadn't been paying attention to Him. God as a person came through. He told Dom Joseph, "I saw being a Carthusian a tremendous opportunity to search for this person. How do you meet God?"

This very intensity for God left the novices more vulnerable to human imbalance. More than anything, for example, Dom Philip wanted to be alone in his cell. The time after Vespers was his favorite time of day. He would sit on the fold-down chair in his oratory and savor the sense of completeness. The sun would soon be going down; he felt like a farmer with the day's chores completed, enjoying the rhythm of the seasons and the quiet of the early evening. The end of the day felt buoyant; he could lean back into the evening—the noise was gone, choir for the day was over. Before the day ended, he walked around his garden, watching the mice. Nothing else moved in his world. When he heard the church clock chime 6:57 PM, he went back inside his cell. Dom Philip wanted this life to continue. He wasn't worrying about women. But neither was he thinking about his humanity, his psychological balance, his fellow novices, or his community.

CHAPTER 10

Profession (June 16–24, 1963)

By June 1963, two years after Dom Philip had been clothed as a novice, the solemns were ready to vote on whether to allow Doms Malachi and Philip to join Doms Leo, Ignatius, and Damian in making simple profession for three years.

After making simple profession, the novice can no longer leave without a dispensation. To do so would be similar to deserting from the army. Only under grave circumstances can the simply professed ask for a dispensation. He promises to observe obedience, stability within the Charterhouse, and conversion of morals (to adapt his life to that within the Charterhouse). During this time, he continues to live in the novitiate under the supervision of the Novice Master, but he is technically referred to as a "junior," and he has more responsibility. He is, and feels, much more a part of the order. He begins to sense the more subtle difficulties of the life. If this permits an ever deeper understanding of Carthusian life, all will be well. If not, the person may hit a wall and will probably be asked to leave.

Simple profession gives the junior monk the opportunity to test whether he will be able to endure and cope within the community and also allows the community to further evaluate him. If he successfully completes the three years, he can petition to make solemn profession, which will bind him to the community for life. The Vatican alone can release a monk from solemn vows.

On June 16, Doms Malachi and Philip began their eight-day retreat before simple profession. They would neither take part in Monday's walk nor do any studying. The June night was quiet and cool. Dom Philip wasn't. He knelt at his prie-dieu. Soon, the church bell would call him to Night Office. He concentrated on the psalms, especially Psalm 24, "Who can ascend the mountain of the Lord? And who can stand in his holy place?" Could he really stand in God's holy place? Could he ascend the mountain in the wilderness?

He had his windows open, and the bats were flitting around his head. He didn't mind them. His mind swirled with the import of June 24, the feast of St. John the Baptist, his profession day. Dom Joseph had presented Doms Malachi and Philip to the community a few weeks earlier, and the solemns had voted to allow them to proceed. Dom Philip had felt relieved about that because the solemns often weeded novices out at first profession. He had figured that the odds were about 50–50. A week from today, he would be taking vows committing him to stay at Parkminster for the next three years. That was altogether different from being a novice and wondering from day to day if he could survive. Making simple profession meant that he intended to stay at Parkminster for life, probably surrounded by these same off-pitch monks. Carthusian life looked entirely different from the perspective he had had two years ago. He knew the painful rituals, and he was beginning to sense the bitter politics beneath the exterior calm of monastic life.

Dom Philip believed that just surviving the life for two and a half years meant that he had a vocation, that he should continue. He felt that he shouldn't even think of throwing away the extraordinary gift of his vocation; he thought about Esau, who sold his birthright for a mess of porridge and couldn't get it back (Genesis 25:29–34). Dom Philip liked his life in cell; he also liked the walks and recreation. Aside from choir, the life seemed to provide everything he wanted. Only when the dark force, a sense that his life was being wasted, made him feel that he couldn't last another day, when the going was very difficult, did he doubt himself. He never could be sure whether the dark force was a trial from God, a test to strengthen his faith, or a sign that he should quit. Having been present at the simple profession of Doms Leo, Ignatius, and Damian, he knew exactly what to expect at the simple profession ceremony. Dom Philip hated ceremony and wished he could just sign the paper and be done with it. But, he reflected, if he planned to take a vow of obedience, he couldn't very well object to a religious ceremony. When Dom Philip was in the minor seminary, he was often master of ceremonies and had to be in charge of the liturgy. He just hated all the fuss.

After Night Office, lying awake, he thought about the formula of the vows.

> I, Brother Philip, promise, for three years, stability, obedience, and conversion of my life, before God, his saints, and the relics belonging to this hermitage, which was built in honor of God, the Blessed Mary ever Virgin, and Blessed John the Baptist, in the presence of Dom Bonaventure, Prior.

He was glad that he had John the Baptist as a patron. Dom Philip liked his starkness; solitude was the Baptist's whole being, his identity. His birth had been miraculous, and his parents had been saints. John the Baptist knew from the beginning that God had called him for an extraordinary role, the harbinger of the Lord. He knew he had to make the way straight for the Lord; fleeing the world, he went to the solitude of the desert to prepare himself. Imitating him, the monks went into the desert of their cells. Taking comfort in that thought, Dom Philip dozed off, too sleepy to worry.

Dom Malachi, also making profession on the feast of St. John the Baptist, was nervous in a different way. He had begun to doubt the life itself. Just a few months after his arrival, Dom Malachi realized that he had not grown very much as a human being in the Charterhouse. How does one grow as a human in a Charterhouse? When the moment came to make simple vows, his anxiety became so intense that Dom Joseph called in a psychologist. Dom Malachi was perfectly sane, and the psychologist could not shake his determination to make simple profession. Dom Malachi believed that he was where God wanted him to be. He would concentrate on the here and now, the *hic et nunc.*

For the week before their profession, Doms Malachi and Philip would read and reflect on only one book. Dom Philip really liked the Jesuit Jean-Pierre De Caussade, and Dom Joseph gave him *Self-Abandonment to Divine Providence* for his retreat book. Dom Philip delved into the book. A Frenchman, De Caussade had been born in 1675, but Dom Philip felt that he could have been writing for a Chicago cab driver. He was so simple. Not eighty-nine classes or gradations of prayer, prayers of this, prayers of that. No scholastic taxonomy with *pars prima, pars secunda.* Dom Philip felt that men shouldn't try to break down something that was as simple as God. De Caussade hadn't even meant to write a book; a fellow Jesuit found his notes in 1861 and compiled the book from letters and sermons. Dom Philip wondered if anyone would ever compile his own notes.

On the first day of the retreat, Dom Philip got to page thirty-one of *Self-Abandonment to Divine Providence.* He read, "We are well instructed only by the words that God speaks to us personally. . . . What instructs us is what happens from moment to moment." Dom Philip thought, "This makes sense. I just have to respond to what happens." He thought, "We only have 'now' and 'death.' I don't need to make a plan." The second day he got to page forty-eight and read that faith "knows how to see and hear God in all that happens from moment to moment." After mulling that over, Dom Philip conceded, "If God wants the monks to be off pitch, then I just have to put up with them." Then he wondered, "Is De Caussade too passive?" He concluded that De Caussade could hardly be too passive for a monk. But he wondered how a Jesuit, a religious son of the aggressive Ignatius Loyola, could write such notes.

At the Sunday conference on June 23, Doms Malachi and Philip made their annual confession of faults. After the confession of faults, Dom Joseph read a sermon before all the novices but addressed to just the two of them. Its tone and language were impersonal. Carthusian sermons were not meant to be emotional. It was a theoretical discourse, with no congratulations for having persevered or recognition of their individual personalities. Dom Joseph laid out the bare facts of their future.

> Doms Malachi and Philip have nothing and nobody but God, and Him alone, in whom to find both the motive to go on living and the strength to do so. The meaning of cell has now become terribly clear to them. It is: get to God, or get out. As their choice is now made, Doms Malachi and Philip are simply forced to draw all their courage and strength at almost every moment from Him in whom they live and move. And with a loving lack of mercy God rains down his blows upon the soul that He might present it to Himself as a glorious bride without stain or wrinkle.

In sharp contrast to the severity of Dom Joseph's sermon, Dom Malachi inadvertently remembered a time when he thought about getting out instead of getting to God. The image was sharp and eerily clear. During a winter walk, he had seen a house, with lots of lights on and smoke coming out of the chimney. He imagined the warmth by the hearth. He had wanted to go into that house. A fleeting, normal reaction, surely, but the reaction disturbed Dom Malachi, and he was careful that it didn't happen again.

The afternoon was warm and safe, but Dom Philip's hands were cold and clammy and his stomach churning. Instead of going straight to church for Vespers, all the monks went to the Chapter House. Doms Philip and Malachi prostrated themselves on the polished wood floor and repeated the official ritual as their predecessors had done since the time of Bruno. They asked for *misericordia*, and Dom Bonaventure said, "Rise," and then they stood and asked to be received for Profession as the most humble servant of all:

> *Supplico propter amorem Dei me ad primam professionem recipi pro humillimo omnium servo, si tibi, venerabilis pater, ceterisque venerabilibus patribus placuerit.*
>
> (I beseech, for the love of God, to be received to first profession as the most humble servant of all, if it pleases you, venerable Father and the other venerable fathers.)

Then they stood up. Dom Philip stared straight ahead at Sublet's grisly dark murals while Dom Bonaventure read a short sermon in Latin. Fidgeting with his hands, Dom Bonaventure read the sermon that attempted to deter them from going forward:

> *Carissimi in Christo, iam per duos annos nostram vitam experiri potuisti, et nunc optas hic stabiliter permanere. Quo proposito? Iam ipse vidisti in Cartusia non dare opportunitates praedicandi, ministrandi, studendi sicut in pluribus aliis religionibus. Non datur exterius ministerium.*
>
> (Malachi and Philip, beloved in Christ, for two years now, you have chosen to live our life. And now you choose to remain here. For what end? You have already seen that there are not opportunities in the Charterhouse for preaching, for ministering, and for

studying, as there are in many other religious orders. There is no external ministry.)

He continued:

> Our own Reverend Father General has been exempted from being present at the ecumenical council held in Rome. We well know, moreover, how necessary is the ministry among souls . . . and how momentous are the wise decrees about to come forth from the council. Why do you with the little flock of our order choose to leave the external battle and fly to the mountain?
>
> One thing only can our life satisfy for your conscience. Give up all else that you may be a man of prayer. Leave the common people on the plain and with Moses climb the mountain to pray to God. . . .

After more prescriptions about prayer, Dom Bonaventure ended:

> And therefore, Malachi and Philip, beloved in Christ, since you have petitioned to stay in the Carthusian vocation, have high in your mind that to the degree that you will be a true Carthusian, to that degree, you will be a man of prayer. To this end, all of your being is directed.

The sermon stayed with both of them: "Give up all else that you may be a man of prayer. Leave the common people on the plain and with Moses climb the mountain to pray to God." Could they really do nothing but pray for the rest of their lives?

Then all the monks went to Vespers and proceeded with the rest of their day.

Dom Philip tossed on his straw mattress all that night. He knew that he had decided to make simple profession in the morning, but still, vows of stability, obedience, and conversion of morals were serious stuff. He couldn't own as much as a walking stick. He didn't mind giving up the right to own property, and he certainly wasn't concerned about women, but stability and obedience were hard. Stability meant that he would never leave the Charterhouse, never leave the enclosure; he couldn't even move to a different Charterhouse unless the Reverend Father reassigned him. Except for the walks, he hadn't been outside the walls for two and a half years. Although he didn't want to leave, after taking vows he no longer had the choice. Stability meant that he would be incorporated into the fellowship of hermit Carthusians. Could he settle down at Parkminster in mind and body? Dom Philip thought it would probably be helpful. The dark force would be less powerful here. In the Charterhouse, there were no distractions, none of the stimuli that made him chase after things that weren't God, that made him less likely to think about God. The dark force had fewer disguises to use in the Charterhouse; it was easier to see it coming.

When the bell above his bed rang at 6 AM, Dom Philip hurriedly dressed, putting on his best habit, and prayed hard until Dom Francis rang the church bell for Mass. Instead of going to the church, Dom Philip again went to the Chapter House. He saw that two candles had been lit on the large white altar. Dom Joseph had put new, longer cowls by Doms Malachi and Philip's places on the wooden benches. They took the new cowls with narrow bands in their hands and went to the sanctuary steps, made a profound bow, put down the cowl, and then stood in front of the steps. Dom Bonaventure lumbered over to them and said some prayers; he then blessed the cowls and with his hand extended, prayed: "In your great goodness, bless these habits which our fathers choose to wear as a sign of innocence and humility in renouncing the world." After that, with typically restless and agitated movements, Dom Bonaventure sprinkled the cowls with holy water. Doms Malachi and Philip then knelt in front of Dom Bonaventure on the first step of the sanctuary and loudly recited in unison, in Latin, of course, the first part of Psalm 15:

> Preserve me, O Lord, for in Thee I place my trust. I say to the Lord: Thou art my God, Thou art my only good.
>
> Upon the Saints who are in the land, on the nobleminded; in whom is all my delight,
>
> They have heaped manifold sorrows, and some they have put to death.
>
> I will not share in their bloody offerings, not even shall their names be on my lips.
>
> The Lord is the allotted portion of my cup, Thou it is Who gavest me my lot.
>
> The lots have fallen happily for me, therefore my portion is precious to me.

Dom Malachi made his profession first. Then, with the help of the very calm and gentle Sacristan and Dom Joseph, Dom Bonaventure removed Dom Philip's black novice cape and short knee-length cowl. At the same time that they were removing the cowl, Dom Bonaventure prayed, "May the Lord put off from you your old self with its past deeds." While Dom Bonaventure put the long cowl of the professed monk over Dom Philip's head, he prayed, "and may he clothe you with the new man, created in God's image, whose justice and holiness are born of truth." After this, Dom Philip read the formula of Profession. Dom Philip then handed the signed paper to Dom Bonaventure, who would later sign, date, and deposit it in the Charterhouse archives. Doms Malachi and Philip then finished reciting Psalm 15 in unison:

> I praise the Lord, Who giveth me counsel, even at night my heart exhorteth me thereto.
>
> Ever will I keep the Lord before mine eyes, for with Him at my right I shall not falter.
>
> Therefore my heart is glad and my tongue rejoiceth, my body too shall rest in hope;
>
> Because thou wilt not leave my soul in hell, nor suffer thy holy one to see corruption.
>
> Thou showest me the way to life; with joy Thou fillest me before Thee;
>
> At Thy right hand is bliss for evermore.

Dom Philip had not paid attention to Psalm 15 before, but now its words seemed just right. When they finished, they made a profound bow and returned to their places in chapter. With profession completed, all the monks went to church for the conventual Mass.

As he did every profession day, Dom Bonaventure said the conventual Mass. The deacon of the week, Dom Marianus, read the Gospel from Luke with a heavy German accent. Dom Philip listened attentively:

> . . . to the amazement of the bystanders, Elizabeth says that her child is to be named *John*, a name unheard of in their tribe. The bystanders asked her dumb husband Zachariah, "What do you wish to call him?" Zachariah says, "*Johannes est nomen ejus.*" The bystanders were abuzz, saying, "Who do you think this child will

be, for the hand of the Lord is upon him. *Quis, putas puer iste erit?*"

Dom Philip wondered if the hand of the Lord was also upon him. Instead of receiving communion at a private Mass, on this day, Doms Malachi and Philip received the Body of the Lord from Dom Bonaventure's hands, immediately after the deacon received communion. This would not happen again until they made solemn profession.

Doms Philip and Malachi then went, as usual, to serve a private Mass; today Dom Philip served the Mass of Dom Marianus in the Reliquary Chapel. Even though Dom Marianus was very reserved and very pious, he gave Dom Philip a grin at the end of Mass. Dom Malachi served Mass for Dom Emmanuel. With these ceremonies over, Dom Philip was looking forward to reading the letters from his parents. He didn't have long to wait. Before the community meal, Dom Joseph put them in his hatch.

His parents had written on June 11 so that their letters would be waiting for him on the 24. The Novice Master gave him the opened envelope. Dom Philip read his dad's letter first, already sensing his aura, knowing that he would be calling him by his nickname, "Butch," and talking about golf. Dom Philip had started playing golf with his dad when he was three years old, with his mother's cut-down golf clubs. He didn't beat his dad until he was sixteen, by a single stroke on a course in Detroit.

He eagerly read the letter. His father could never quite believe that he had a son like Dom Philip. He had little understanding of his Carthusian life, but he knew that his son had just taken an important step in his life, which, most likely, would never be reversed. In a sense, he found it very difficult to write to someone whose life he no longer understood. Perhaps he felt awkward. Perhaps he was keeping alive the idea that his son would return. In a lighthearted letter, he wrote to the son that he had known for twenty-three years. Ironically, his letter unintentionally catalogued the very things Dom Philip had just promised to deny.

June 11, 1963

Dear Butch:

Today I have been relegated to second position in the batting order, Mom taking over the lead-off spot with the typewriter. However, with my natural speed and ability, I will probably beat out a sacrifice bunt, putting two on the sacks with none out. You will have to bring both runners home with your big hit on the 24th of this month.

I got up this morning at 8:20, full of pep and figuring on paying a visit to the office and making a few calls today, but Mom suggested "why don't you stay home today—your birthday, and all" and, brother, that's all I needed, and minutes after I was back in the hay where I stayed until 11:30. Pretty good, eh? Reminded me of the life at your Monastery—so different.

Mom has already given you all the news, but I'll try and fill in with other comments—as for instance—so far this season I have been out to the Northwestern Golf and Country Club three times, three nine holers (always the back nine) and am glad to report to you that I am in shape, even carrying my own clubs. As long as you must be wondering about the scores, will confess that I have a best ball score of one over par, that is, one over for each hole. Shooting two, and sometimes three, balls, I did manage a best ball of eight over, or a 43 on the back nine. As I played by myself, I won all three games.

Do you know (I'm almost sure you do) that you have a wonderful PR man in Bert Lynch? At Mary's wake, and after the funeral, a great many of the priests present, as well as many friends, inquired about you, your life, when will you be back in the USA etc., which gave us great pleasure in outlining your life as a Monk, and boy, what a job I do on this subject. You'd never recognize your daily life at all.

Boy, did I put it on for you and the Carthusians. Monseigneur Picard (St. Ita's) Kiley, Kealy, McCarthy, as well as Fathers Riordan, Sheridan, Burke, all of St. Catherine's, are especially interested. After the funeral Mass the family and friends congregated at the Cagney's in Wilmette for a buffet lunch, but while everyone was attempting to enjoy themselves, it was not nearly the same without Mary.

Your mother bought us a new tabletop RCA color television, cost a bundle, $495.00. I never miss *Perry Mason* at 9 pm on NBC. Well, kid, must close now. Will be in there pitching for you on the 24th. Best regards to all, and best wishes and love, will now strike out.

Daddy-O

His father's breezy letter was oddly shocking to Dom Philip. It brought him back to his earlier life outside the Charterhouse, and for an hour or so, that life became real again, even though he had just promised to have nothing to do with it. Dom Philip was again nonplussed at his dad's acceptance of his decision to join a Charterhouse of hermits. His dad couldn't have sounded prouder of him if he had been a touring golf pro.

He thought back to his parents' visit a year earlier. The monks allowed fathers inside the Charterhouse, even inside the monk's cell. Dom Philip could still capture the image of his father. Inspired by the incipient visit, Dom Philip had found a broom and swept up the tumbleweeds and food crumbs that had accumulated over the months. His dad appeared fascinated by what his son had called a "cell." He said encouragingly, "And you call this a cell? Your mom and I never had it so good." He prowled around the lumber and fuel room on the ground floor and was amazed at the adjoining room with a workshop. He asked incredulously, "Butch, you know how to use this machine?" He liked the sunny window in the entrance hall, what his son called the ambulatory. He couldn't understand the life, but he wanted to be supportive. When he saw the living room/dining room/study/oratory with undressed wooden paneling, he said with Irish humor, "I wouldn't mind a getaway like this," a place of his own without any women decorating and keeping things tidy, what country people would call a shed. He noticed that the coal-burning stove was next to the oratory; he was glad, at least, that his son would be warm while he prayed.

Most of his mother's letter was about family funerals. Dom Philip's father was the youngest of nine children, and his siblings were dying. His Aunt Mary had just died, and Dom Philip's Uncle Rob, the former chancellor of the archdiocese of Chicago, had died a year earlier. Vivid memories of playing golf with Uncle Rob flooded Dom Philip. Each name in the letter stirred memories. Dom Philip answered his parents' letters the same day, in a style that was part college graduate writing home, part Carthusian-in-the-making:

†

Feast of John the Baptist,

Dear Mom and Dad,

Great to hear from you and to know that Dad is still hitting them down the middle. I got my new cowl this morning at Mass. I've signed up for the next three years of boot camp. Dom Malachi signed up with me.

After two years, I don't even notice the hair shirt anymore, but getting used to the Friday bread and water fast is going to take more time. I've finished my dogma classes and will start Christology soon. I'll be up for minor orders in about two years and need to pass the exams before then.

As you can imagine, nothing new has happened here. I've changed my cell, but except for the gardens, the cells are all the same. Dom Gregory made solemn profession last October 6th, and was ordained five months later. He said his first Community Mass on Passion Sunday. Did I enjoy that! His voice filled the church, echoing all over the place; he wasn't just reciting the words, he was interpreting them; the words "*tremunt Potestates*" were like an opera. Unfortunately for me, now that I'm professed, I'm second cantor on the Prior's side and will be taking over the novices' choir practice. You can imagine how I will love that. I wish I had some of the guys from the major seminary here to help me out. Glad to learn that Otto Gattinger is going to Rome for his final years in the major seminary. Otto is smart and will do well.

I know how important Uncle Bob was to both of you. With Aunt Mary dead, the family is shrinking fast. I put the holy card you sent in my diurnal—"diurnal" sounds terrible, but it's the book containing the parts of the Office we say in cell, the little hours. I will see the card every day.

Look forward to your letters next October 6th. Stay well you guys.

After explaining to his parents that "O Cart." was shorthand for *"Ordinis Cartusianorum,"* Dom Philip took great pride in signing his name, "Dom Philip, O. Cart., St. Hugh's Charterhouse, Sussex." He put the unsealed letter into Dom Joseph's hatch; he, after reading it, would put it in Dom Bonaventure's hatch to be mailed.

CHAPTER 11

Monks Off Pitch (December 18 and 24–25, 1963)

Choir was a battleground. Every night, the monks thrashed out their monastic commitment. The solemns had very differing views on choir, and they never held choir practice. Some cared about how the Office sounded; others were utterly indifferent about the sound and the effect. Some thought that choir should be an aesthetic experience. Others didn't care about aesthetics; they thought that choir should be a pious experience. The monks who tried to sing with one voice praising God considered choir an experience of musical anarchy. The musical barbarians didn't understand the problem of the aesthetically sensitive. Dom Ignatius, for example, thought that hermits singing the plain Carthusian chant together, everyone at his own pitch, was ideal. Dom Philip cared a lot about how the Office sounded. He was trained to focus on producing a particular sound, and the aesthetic experience was important to him.

Pitch and tempo were both contested. How fast should the monks sing? The tradition of the order held that the Office should be sung as slowly as the nerves of the participants could stand. The 1259 Statuta Antiqua required that the monks sing "in a voice as of lamentation so that there be no delight in singing in the heart." But who controlled how slowly they should sing? The First Cantor on the Antiquior's side, Dom Jerome, an Oxford man with a languid and somewhat nasal voice, was notoriously fast. Moreover, when a monk on his side intoned a psalm, Dom Jerome would immediately take up the psalmody at a more convenient (to him or the choir) pitch; Dom Gregory followed his lead. Yet Dom Jerome had a light voice, a fine heady tenor, and was not supported by the rest of the monks on his side, and Dom Gregory had stopped using his normal strong voice in choir. Ultimately, almost no one was singing audibly on one side of the church. On the Prior's side, Dom Ludolph battled to keep the pace slower. Although Dom Ludolph had a strong voice, the Prior sang very lustily, and he didn't follow Dom Ludolph's lead. At times, the Prior's side of choir sounded like a contest between the blithely unaware Prior and Dom Ludolph, a skirmish within a larger conflict. Dom Philip reflected ruefully on Psalm 132: "Behold how good and pleasant it is for brethren to dwell in unity."

Choir was strenuous. Dom Philip, as Second Cantor, had to fill in for Dom Ludolph if he was unavailable. He had to learn how to fight in choir—to control the pitch and speed of the singing on the Prior's side. As he tried to lead the singing, Dom Philip could feel the tension. The greater the seniority, the less pulling and tugging. The tugging came largely from the middle section of choir, where the novices and young monks sat, not from the choir stalls of the older monks. Dom Philip was caught in the middle of the battle. The off-pitch solemns could vote him in or out. How aggressive could he afford to be? How hard dare he push for real Gregorian chant?

On December 18, 1963, the ferial Wednesday before Christmas, Dom Philip steeled his nerves as he walked toward the Novice Master's cell. Wednesday had become the hardest day of the week for him, even harder than Friday's bread and water. It was much worse than the hair shirt and discipline. Ever since Dom Gregory had made final vows, Dom Philip had been in charge of teaching the novices how to sing. Since Dom Columba had made solemn profession in September, and Dom Mark had left in mid-November, there were now only seven novices. A new postulant would be at the novices' choir practice. Dom Philip hadn't talked to him yet. With luck, he was a priest or from a seminary, otherwise he wouldn't know a *punctum* from a *semi-quaver*. Dom Philip walked into the music room, beneath the conference room in the Novice Master's cell, without much hope. He laughed grimly to himself as he remembered how he had thought that the off-pitch monks were sophisticated atonal musicians. The new man was there, looking exhausted, confused, and somewhat terrified. He would be more terrified at the end of choir practice. He didn't know what a *punctum* was, but at least he knew how to sing.

The music for Christmas was among the most arcane, difficult, and longest of the year. For Dom Philip, preparing the novices for this event was a unique and very painful trial. He gathered the men around the antiphonaries—three to a book. The illuminated leather-bound songbooks, with iron-studded corners, weighed thirty-one pounds apiece; the open book was about the length and width of two bed pillows placed side by side, and about five inches thick. The books' size accommodated print large enough so that three monks could read from each book. In the very early centuries of the order, paper was so expensive that the order required the novices to memorize the Office, which was sung in a totally dark church. Later, after paper had become less expensive, the practice of three monks sharing each book started. On this day in 1963, while one novice set up the collapsible carved wooden book stand, another hoisted the book onto the stand. The giant books had the original Gregorian notation: four-line staffs instead of the normal five-line staff, and square musical notes instead of the familiar round notes. Although there were no key signatures, a symbol indicated the position of the semi-tones; for example, E-F or B-C. The problem was, without musical notation, the novices had to understand these intervals. The Christmas liturgy had difficult intervals, even for experienced singers. Dom Philip wished that the Charterhouse had a piano, an organ, or even a pitch pipe.

Dom Gregory had started the novices' choir practice with classical voice training exercises, but Dom Philip simply went through a few scales before tackling the day's work. He first explained to the newcomer that no matter what note he started a scale on, there would be a semi-tone between the third and fourth notes and another semi-tone between the seventh and eighth notes. He looked at the postulant and suspected he didn't know what he was talking about. He already felt frustrated and anxious. He had to cover a lot of ground quickly. Christmas Night Office was a twelve-lesson feast that took nearly four hours of continuous singing.

He didn't have any time to waste in preparing the novices for this marathon. He went straight to the most difficult parts of the week's liturgy. In a full-toned, deeply resonant voice, he first demonstrated how it should sound. The lessons and their responses were sung in a fiendishly complicated, unvarying pattern. Since their beginnings in 1084, the Carthusians had followed an elaborate choreography, repeated century after century, based on the seniority of the monks. What each monk sang depended on his seniority, not on his singing skills. Thus, the least musical monk could end up singing the most difficult music. No matter how badly the monk sang, he sang whatever lesson or antiphon fell to his position in rank. The last novice, for example, sang the first lesson and the second response; the second-youngest novice sang the second lesson and the third response; and so on. The much harder antiphons were sung in descending seniority, so the younger novices wouldn't have to sing antiphons. Dom Philip was very grateful for this because Dom Lorenzo, the last novice, had a beautiful, deep voice that only accentuated the fact that he could never stay on pitch; in fact, he never knew when he was off pitch. Dom Philip worked especially with the senior novices who would be intoning antiphons, trying to help them with the intervals. Unfortunately, Dom Ignatius would intone the most beautiful antiphon, "Pastores." There was nothing Dom Philip could do about Dom Ignatius's hoarse, weak voice.

Dom Philip tried not to hear the lilt and melody in the new postulant's voice—he didn't realize that Gregorian chant was different from show tunes. Dom Philip explained, "Gregorian chant ebbs and flows in all directions, it is all over the place, the pause in the middle isn't a beat," but the postulant kept singing with a beat. Dom Philip interrupted again, "We don't keep time, there is no tempo. We're not listening to a metronome." Dom Philip backtracked and had the group sing scales again. Dom Philip was in despair over Dom Lorenzo; he was all over the place, he didn't get anything right—off pitch, no sense of intervals. Dom Philip knew that Dom Lorenzo was from Calabria, Italy, and had to be used to singing. Dom Philip just had to fit the Gregorian chant to a melody that Dom Lorenzo knew.

After forty-five minutes, Dom Philip was working hard not to make subtly sarcastic comments, but he still had to cover the hardest part of the liturgy. "Now let's look at Midnight Mass again: *'Dominus dixit ad me'* has descending thirds up and down, then a fourth, then a major third." He said, "Dom Lorenzo, you will be singing the second responsory of the first nocturn of Matins, 'He Himself Came.' Remember the intervals in 'What Child Is This.'" Listening to Dom Lorenzo was like falling into musical chaos. Dom Philip's nerves spasmed. "Dom David, you will be singing the third response, *'Verbum caro factum est.'*" Dom David immediately sang it perfectly. An ascending minor third came up next: *"Hodie super nos"* again became "What Child Is This." After another exhausting ten minutes, choir practice ended. As the novices left the music room, Dom Philip reminded them, "Mark the places in your books as soon as you get in choir." The solemns did not look kindly on novices missing an intonation. From the earliest days of the order, the man in the middle more or less handled the switching of books: antiphonary, psalter, and hymnal. Dom Damian loved being the monk in the middle. He always tried to mark the books for the next Office before the monks filed out of church. This was difficult. He had to work very quickly, but at the next Office, he would be ready to rapidly flip books and pages. This required quite remarkable alertness and agility. He used the tip of the ribbon to hold the first place, then flipped to the second place in a flash. There could be no pause or interruption caused by some novice missing his cue at Christmas Night Office—a highly concentrated and major piece of music—that would be like a princess tripping on the way to the altar on her wedding day. Decorum and the glory of God required that the singing be continuous, as a single voice, without a break.

Dom Philip asked Dom Ignatius, who was cantor of the week, to stay for a few minutes. "Rotten luck," thought Dom Philip. Dom Ignatius gave no sign of musicality, and his voice was too weak to keep the monks on pitch. Dom Philip suspected that Dom Ignatius kept thinking about the meaning of the psalms instead of how to sing them. Dom Ignatius had some terribly difficult intonations at Night Office, so although he hated choir practice and was eager to get out of there, to please Dom Philip, he tried to learn the cantor's parts for the Christmas liturgy. Dom Ignatius not only hated choir practice, he especially hated the Christmas music. The simplicity of the Carthusian ferial Offices was a source of joy and contemplation to him. Tonight's music irritated him as much as the elaborate singing of the Benedictines.

After enduring an hour of choir practice and Dom Ignatius, Dom Philip fled to his cell, safe until he had to listen to the novices—who were his responsibility—sing off pitch during Vespers and then again at Night Office. He knew what it was to do a good job in choir, but here at Parkminster, he seemed unable to do it. Dom Philip wasn't used to failing, but he was certainly failing at keeping the novices on pitch.

Although he was in charge, he couldn't get the job done. His voice wasn't loud enough to drown the other monks out, and he seemed unable to teach the novices how to sing. Some of the monks didn't know the difference between good chant and bad chant, and he wondered if some of them just didn't care. He remembered Dom Gregory's comment, "The choral-ignorance of Carthusian simplicity—a choir is wanted but not the necessary means to that end." The more Dom Philip tried to impose his sense of how the choir should sound, the better chance that the solemns might vote him out of the order. But might the monks also vote him out because he failed to create harmony? He was trapped. He couldn't bring musical harmony to Parkminster.

This dilemma tormented him. His nature demanded harmony. He again realized how smart he had been to join a monastery where he had his own house. The solitude of his cell was doubly welcome today as he rejoiced in the glorious weather—one of those great December days with warm southerly winds coming off the English Channel. He was tempted to open the windows but then thought better of it. Once the warm damp got into the three-foot walls of his cell, he would be cold for weeks. Even though the grass was green outside, the cell would be like a refrigerator. Better to go outside and read in the garden.

On Christmas Eve, after a nerve-wracking Vespers, Dom Philip tried to calm himself in cell. He knew he needed a full four-hour sleep to recover before the musical marathon began. At the 10:30 PM bell, Dom Philip hurried to Night Office, thinking about the postulant, hoping he was in the place Dom Joseph had assigned him; Dom Joseph had switched Doms Malachi and Lorenzo so that the new postulant would have a strong voice next to him. The monks more or less sat according to descending seniority, so the postulants sat closest to the altar, farthest from the Prior, who had his own private choir stall abutting the rood screen and facing the altar. Except for the steady red glow of the huge sanctuary lamp, the cold church was dark.

As Carthusian monks had been doing since the time of Bruno, the monks who had already arrived were setting up the beautifully made oak book stands. The center monk of each three-monk team adjusted the flame in the oil lamps (with square metal shades), which were on a swivel and attached behind and to the right of the center monk. With no other light in the unelectrified church, the center monks had to be sure that the soft yellow light falling from the lamp was the same size as the open antiphonary. They then busily arranged the books, putting multicolored ribbons in the places where they had to flip from one passage to another and stacking the books in the right order. The monks all had their cowls up, which blocked their view of everything except the books in front of them. The postulant, of course, still wore secular clothes, a black postulant's mantle, and biretta; he was able to look anywhere. The brothers sat on the other side of the rood screen in the dark, with no books, fingering the rosaries that they carried on their leather belts.

Dom Philip was guardedly optimistic about tonight's singing. The postulant was so tired that he probably wouldn't open his mouth. And all the monks would try harder because it was Christmas; they felt the resonance of the tradition. Most important, Dom Gregory really liked the Christmas liturgy, and when he swung out in his powerful baritone, he more or less pulled his side of the choir with him. He could have drowned out the entire choir, and sometimes Dom Philip wished that he would.

With their thick cowls up and encased in their individual choir stalls, the monks really couldn't hear each other, so the First Cantor always shared a book with the Second Cantor. Dom Jerome, the First Cantor on the Antiquior's side, shared a book with Dom Gregory. Dom Ludolph, with energy flowing out of him and with a strong voice, had Dom Philip as his backup. Doms Ludolph and Philip concentrated on keeping their side on pitch and at a slow pace.

Every Night Office, the four cantors worked at the mechanics of producing the right sound, the right tempo, the right pace of continuous singing. There had always been a right way to sing Night Office. The cantors tried to maintain the transcendence of the occasion, especially at Christmas Night Office. Doms Jerome and Gregory on the Antiquior's side and Doms Ludolph and Philip on the Prior's side put all their energy into keeping the rest of the monks afloat, to keep them from battling each other. Frequently, Dom Philip felt that he was bailing against the tide, trying to keep the most terrible thing from happening—everything would go off track, and the choir would just stop. If that happened, the cantors on either side were expected to keep on singing no matter what support, hindrance, or silence might be coming from the choir. Dom Philip had nightmares over that possibility. As always, there would be the conflict between the singers who were classically trained, like Doms Gregory and Jerome, and those who really liked Gregorian chant.

Dom Philip got ready for the struggle between the musical and the unmusical, the Gregorians and the classicals. As a professional classical singer, Dom Gregory heard the rhythm, and he and Dom Jerome kept trying to keep up the beat, to squash the inherent elongation in the chant. The long pause in the middle of the verse, part of the Carthusian tradition, became a beat for them. Doms Ludolph and Philip really liked Gregorian chant, and Dom Philip could sense Dom Ludolph's frustration when things were not going well. Dom Ludolph's pale eyes, framed by thick glasses, looked at Dom Philip quizzically from the side of his cowl, and they plunged ahead in response. The two of them determined to keep the liturgy Gregorian.

The center of Christmas Night Office is Midnight Mass, which starts exactly at midnight. The Night Office begins with the little hour of Matins (BVM) in cell, then Matins, Midnight Mass, Lauds, and the Angelus in church, and finally Lauds (BVM) before getting into bed—with everything in Latin, of course. For many of the monks, including Doms Damian and Leo, Christmas Night Office was the emotional high point of the year. With everyone in their stalls turned toward the high altar with the lamps lit, the Prior, Dom Bonaventure, at about 10:35 PM, knocked with his key on his choir stall to indicate the beginning of the Office. All the monks prayed silently for the space of three Paters and Aves. Then they all made the sign of the cross. The monks on both sides of the choir stalls turned to face each other with their cowls up. Then, the Prior invited them to prayer. He intoned *"Domine, labia mea aperies"* ("O Lord, open my lips"). All the monks responded, "And my mouth will declare your praise."

Then with their cowls still up, the monks leaned their buttocks against the edge of their misericords and planted their feet on a wooden ramp; putting their hands on their knees, they sang the Gloria Patri: *"Gloria Patri et Filio: et Spiritui Sancto. Sicut erat in principio, et nunc et semper: et in secula seculorum"* ("Glory be to the Father and to the Son and to the Holy Spirit. As it was in the beginning, is now and always shall be"). *"Secula seculorum"* trailed off into thin air. They looked like suppliants. The monks relished this doxology, a short formula of praise to God, singing it very slowly, deliberately, and reverently. After the more or less wandering nature of a psalm, the refrain of this doxology continually came back to what Carthusians were all about. The monks pronounced certain "i's" like long "e's": *princeepeo, feeleo.* The monks got hold of this "e" sound and really sang it. Because of the meter of Latin, the male voices, and the vast church, the effect was like falling waves of sound, especially at a distance. The "n" and "m" sounds hung in the air; and the church became a sound box, filled with the unique resonance of male voices. The monks' church and the chant were made for one another.

As cantor of the week, Dom Ignatius slowly intoned the embellished elaborate, Invitatorium, *"Christus natus est nobis, venite adoramus."* The music disappeared in Dom Ignatius's hoarse baritone, leaving only the words. Dom Jerome, as First Cantor on the Antiquior's side, raised the pitch in a heavy Oxford accent and tried to increase the pace as he took up Psalm 94: *"Venite exultemus Domino, jubilemus Deo, salutari nostro."* As that verse ended, Dom Ludolph, First Cantor on the Prior's side, with energy oozing out of him, raised the pitch for the heavy and sluggish Latin words that came next, *"præoccupemus faciem ejus in confessione,"* then a long pause before the Antiquior's side responded, *"et in psalmis jubilemus ei"* ("Let us come before Him with thanksgiving, and sing unto Him with songs"). Before beginning the first of the three nocturns, the monks all sang the first half of the hymn "Venit Redemptor gentium" ("The Redeemer of the People Has Come").

Tonight, the antiphons started on the Prior's side, then switched between the two sides. After the antiphon and the first verse of the psalm, the monks on the Prior's side could then sit down until the final Gloria Patri. Dom Humphrey, the Antiquior, lowered his cowl and intoned the second antiphon. He simply couldn't hear the notes—the pitch fell by a third. Doms Ludolph and Philip tried to bring it up when they started the psalm, but the Vicar on the Prior's side again brought the tone down at the third intonation. "At this rate, we will be in the ditch by the middle of Matins," thought Dom Philip. Dom Gregory's baritone made a valiant attempt to raise the pitch, but he and Dom Jerome were not Gregorians, so the mood shifted. At the fourth antiphon, Dom Emmanuel sang passionately and breathlessly, as if the

Entrance doors to Parkminster with bell rope to right

Top: Hans Klein and family at White Fathers Novitiate, 1959

Middle: Bernie Shea two weeks before leaving for Parkminster, 1960

Bottom: Chuck Henley's surfcasting team, Summer, 1958

Top: Dave Lynch, seminarian, 1959

Middle: Paddy O'Connell and girlfriend have dinner in Dublin

Bottom: The telegram received by Chuck Henley on board ship

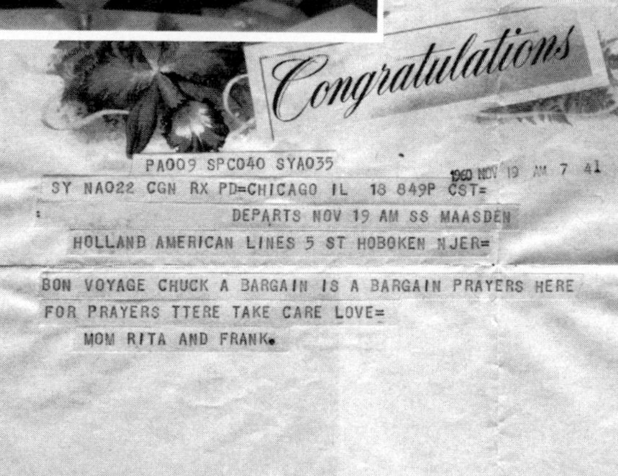

Congratulations

PA009 SPC040 SYA035

1960 NOV 19 AM 7 41

SY NA022 CGN RX PD=CHICAGO IL 18 849P CST=

DEPARTS NOV 19 AM SS MAASDEN

HOLLAND AMERICAN LINES 5 ST HOBOKEN NJER=

BON VOYAGE CHUCK A BARGAIN IS A BARGAIN PRAYERS HERE

FOR PRAYERS TTERE TAKE CARE LOVE=

MOM RITA AND FRANK.

BY WESTERN UNION

Aerial view of Parkminster and the Gatehouse (*Below*)

The Refectory at Parkminster

The monks' cemetery, facing the Great Cloister door

Left: Brother Christopher delivering the monks' meals

Below: Dom Bonaventure at his desk, circa 1957

Left: Dom Joseph (holding Gabrielle, daughter of ex-monk), taken at the Grande Chartreuse, 1987

Below: Dom Philip in upper-story window of his cell, 1964, taken by his father

The Solemns leave the Charterhouse for their weekly walk

Above: Dom Damian and sister Sally outside the Charterhouse, 1963

Right: Dom Philip as novice with mother at door of extern chapel, 1962

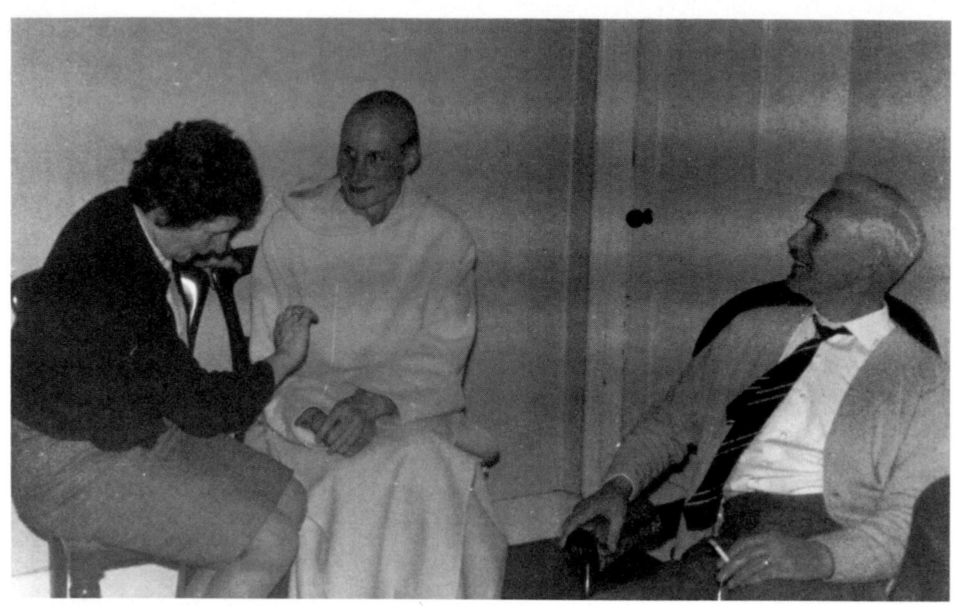

Dom Ignatius and his parents inside the Guest House, 1963

Dom Malachi opening the door of his cell, taken by father, Summer, 1962

Right: Dom Emmanuel, age 90, after more than 40 years as a Carthusian

Below: The burial of a Carthusian monk

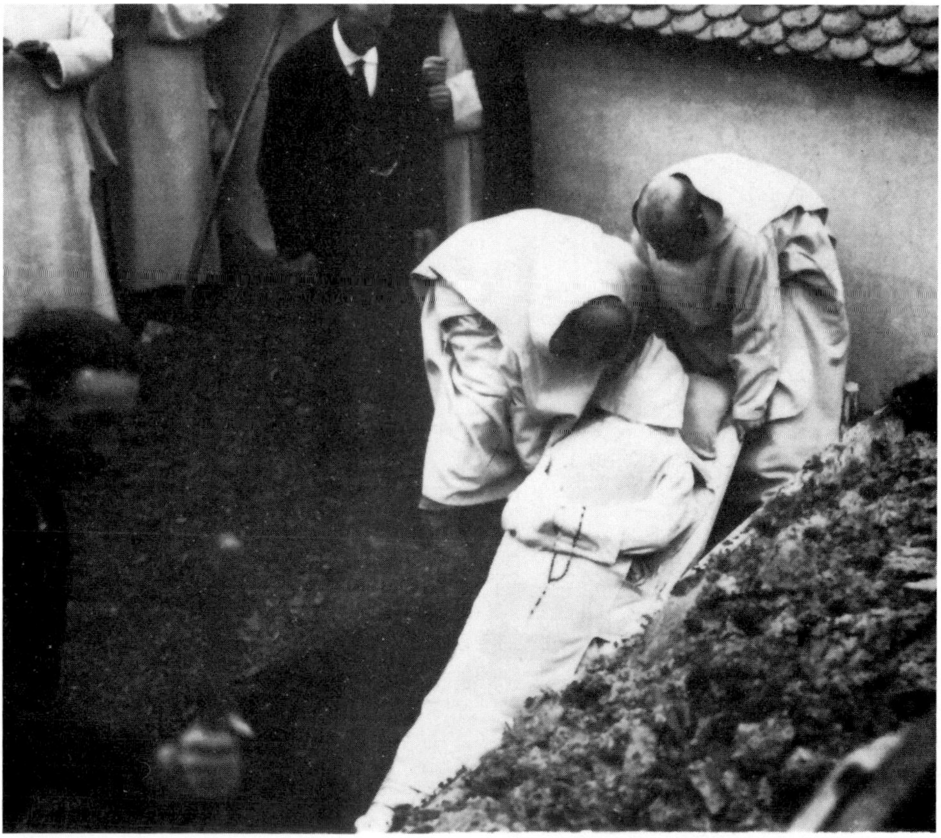

Antiphonary depicting the end of midnight Mass

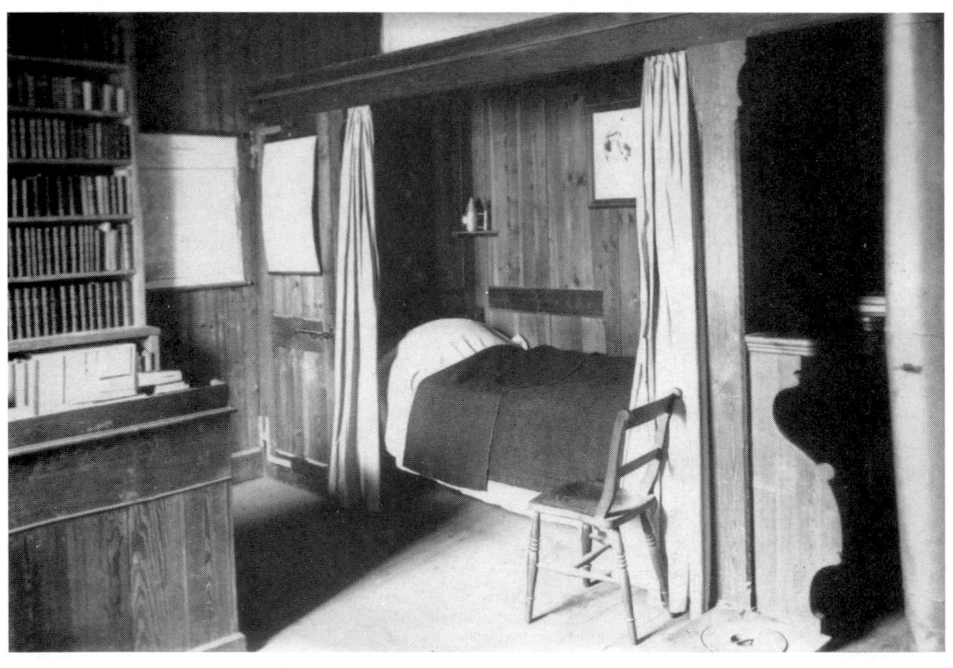

A monk's *cubiculum*

View of the top two floors of Parkminster's library

Above: Dom Columba, September, 2003, age 87

Right:. Hans visits Dom Columba after third stroke, July, 2003

Above: Hans and Dave looking over the walls of the Grande Chartreuse, September, 2003

Right: Hans, Dave, the author, and Bernie at the Grande Chartreuse, September, 2003

Left: Dom Leo, September, 2003, age 70, after forty-three years as a Carthusian

Below: Dom Leo. right, as Novice Master at the Grande Chartreuse, 1975

antiphon were "La Marseillaise." He had a strong voice and hit the pitch right on target, although a French-accented target. Dom Philip felt his neck muscles relax. The monks were temporarily where they ought to be, musically. The exchange continued throughout Night Office, with Latin words slowly but steadily straggling back and forth across the polished wooden floor.

With his cowl over his head, Dom Philip couldn't see anyone, but he suspected that some of the monks, instead of thinking about the music, were actually praying, thinking about the Latin words they were singing. Dom Ignatius certainly would be focusing on the words. He thought to himself, "As always, a few individuals bear the burden of choir and the rest sing, or not, in the way they wish." After the first six psalms of Matins, with an antiphon before and after each psalm, and a silent Pater and Ave, all the monks put their seats down and sat during the reading of the lessons. After only twenty minutes into Matins, Dom Damian started to feel the gradual onset of cold settling into his feet. The monks read the lessons in order of ascending seniority, beginning with the last novice, Dom Lorenzo. Dom Philip was relaxed because Dom Lorenzo was only chanting a lesson, not singing notes. Yet, because Christmas was a very big feast, Dom Lorenzo was more nervous than usual. After walking to the lectern in the center of the church between the two sets of choir stalls, he pulled down and lit the huge brass paraffin lamp that was suspended by three chains. The book at the lectern was smaller because only one monk read from this book. Dom Lorenzo uncovered his head and bowed low toward the altar. He sang, *"Jube domne, benedicere"* ("Pray, Father, a blessing"). Father Prior responded: "*Unigenitus Dei Filius nos benedicere et adjuvare dignetur*" ("May the only begotten Son of God deign to bless and help us"). Dom Lorenzo then chanted the first lesson from Isaiah 9: "The people that walked in darkness have seen a great light; those who dwelt in a land of deep darkness on them has a light shone." Dom Malachi, who would read the fourth lesson, responded by intoning and chanting the verse *"In principio erat Verbum . . . ."* Dom David in his beautiful voice then chanted lesson two, a continuation of Isaiah 9: "For a child is born to us and a son is given to us . . . And his name will be called Wonderful, Counsellor, God, Strength, Fortitude, Father of the Ages to Come, Prince of Peace." The words were glorious, and Dom David was an excellent lector. By this time, Dom Lorenzo had relaxed from the stress of the first lesson and was able to respond calmly and on pitch. Choir practice had worked after all; Dom Lorenzo had got it right. A Christmas miracle. Singing down on each note, Dom Philip himself sang the third lesson, his favorite, echoing John the Baptist, *"Vox clamantis in deserto"* ("A voice crying in the desert"), which then continued "prepare the way of the Lord. Make straight in the desert the way of our God." Dom David then responded, *"Verbum caro factum est"* ("The Word was made flesh and dwelt among us"). Dom Malachi sang lesson four in his powerful and untrained voice. Dom Philip responded and then sang in solo a very slow Gloria Patri: "Glory be to the Father and to the Son and to the Holy Spirit. As it was in the beginning, is now, and will be forever. Amen." The sound, he hoped, could have come from any Christmas Night Office during the last nine centuries.

With the lessons of the first nocturn completed, the monks again stood, starting the second nocturn with the same format. By this time, about 11:00 PM, all the monks were beginning to feel the cold coming through their special cork-lined choir shoes, and there was a lot of coughing. In spite of the cold, for the next few hours, the monks' only exercise would be sitting and standing. The second nocturn alternated between being off pitch and being temporarily almost right. After the monks sang the six psalms, they again began the lessons. Doms Damian, Ignatius, Leo, and Columba did the work of this nocturn. All four lessons were from the first sermon on the Nativity of the Lord by Pope Leo the Great (440–461), Dom Leo's namesake. Pope Leo had successfully confronted Attila the Hun in 452 and later drove Genseric, the leader of the Vandals, from Rome in 455. St. Leo was also the first Pope to assert the Papal Supremacy. To Dom Philip's horror, Dom Damian started singing the wrong lesson in his thin, reedy voice. The Vicar's job was to correct errors, and he loved the job; Dom Bruno knocked on his own choir stall. Dom Damian then sang the right lesson, but when he finished singing the lesson, he acknowledged his error by kneeling down next to the lectern and kissing the church floor. Dom Columba didn't seem to be paying any attention to the notes, but at least he was no longer Dom Philip's responsibility. Dom Ignatius was greatly off pitch, but at least his voice was weak.

Finally, the third and last nocturn. There was, of course, no clock in the church, and monks didn't wear wristwatches, but Dom Philip figured that it was probably about 11:30 PM. The third nocturn had three canticles, or hymns, from Isaiah instead of six psalms. The 150 psalms are a continuous sequence, but the canticles are scattered all over the Bible. Dom Malachi sang especially intensely for Isaiah 66: "Rejoice Jerusalem, and all you who love her, make a feast day." After the canticles, Dom Ignatius, as cantor of the week, sang the verse *"In principio erat Verbum,"* and then the monks responded, *"et Verbum erat apud Deum, et Deus erat Verbum"* ("And the Word was with God, and God was the Word"). Then the lessons.

Dom Philip's stomach unknotted a bit. Until Matins was over, the solemns were now on their own. They were not his problem. A priest always sang the ninth lesson and the Prior the twelfth lesson, but at Christmas Night Office, priest-solemns sang all the lessons of the third nocturn. Each lesson began with an excerpt from one of the three Christmas gospels—of Night, Dawn, and Day—gospels always had to be sung by a priest. Dom Philip could relax. He appreciated Dom Joseph's fine lyrical tenor as he sang lesson nine. To Dom Philip's chagrin, but the other novices' delight, Dom John-Baptist whipped right through lesson ten like a buzz saw. Dom Jerome sang lesson eleven by St. Ambrose in his clipped voice, again too fast by Dom Philip's standards. As always, Dom Bonaventure sang the twelfth lesson, tonight St. Augustine's philosophical, analytical discussion about how the Word could be God: *"Si hoc dicis, quia hoc est verbum Verbi per quod factum est illud."* After thinking about this for a while, Dom Philip decided that this coiled brain-twister sentence probably meant: "If the word of God itself has been made, how can God make everything through the Word." But he wasn't sure; the words played back on themselves. He reassured himself that he wasn't responsible for that sentence.

As Matins neared its end, the monks put their cowls down and as usual sang the twenty-nine verses of the "Te Deum Laudamus," a hymn supposedly composed by Saints Ambrose and Augustine in 387. This was the climax of Night Office; it was what the London Charterhouse monks had sung on their trip to Tyburn Hill to be executed. Dom Damian was ecstatic when the monks sang it more lustily than usual. Dom Ignatius loved its powerful simplicity. Rising from their misericords, with their heads and cowls down, they sang, "We praise Thee, O God; we acknowledge Thee to be the Lord." Then the hebdomadary priest, tonight Dom Bonaventure himself, went to the lectern in the sanctuary and sang the Christmas gospel from Matthew, a continuation of the ninth lesson. A short doxology, *"Te decet laus,"* followed: "Let there be a hymn raised to you, glory to you, God the Father, and the Son, and the Holy Spirit, forever and ever." After a short prayer and two hours of very intense, steady work by the cantors, Christmas Matins ended just a few minutes before midnight.

Now, for Missa in Nocte. The monks were ready for Christmas Midnight Mass. Dom Francis lit two candles. Dom Philip relaxed, as the monks weren't singing antiphonally, and he had less responsibility for this music because the solemns did most of the solo singing. The entrance psalm, or Introit, began with Dom Philip's favorite text, *"Dominus dixit ad me."* Continuing the ascending seniority, Dom Gregory magnificently sang the first lesson from Isaiah, "The people who walk in darkness have great light . . . for a child has been born unto us and a son has been given to us." Then, Dom Gregory sang some great words that Dom Philip would have loved to roll off his tongue, especially with all those "r's": *"Admirabilis, Consiliarius, Deus, Fortis, Pater futuri saeculi: Princeps pacis."*

Continuing the ascending seniority, Dom John-Baptist sang the second lesson from the New Testament. The entire choir responded, *"Alleluia. Dominus dixit ad me: Filius meus es tu, ego hodie genui te. Alleluia."* Then, the deacon of the week, Dom Anselm, who never sang but just sort of recited the words, hacked through the familiar Christmas gospel according to Luke 2: *"In illo tempore: Exiit edictum a Caesare Augusto"* ("And it came to pass that in those days there went out a decree from Caesar Augustus, that the whole world should be enrolled"). All the novices were happy to hear the familiar Christmas story in this strange place, some of them wistfully thinking of their families hearing the story in other churches, in other countries. Dom Anselm ground on:

> And Joseph also went up from Galilei, out of the city of Nazareth into Judea, to the city of David, which is called Bethlehem: because he was of the house and family of David. To be enrolled with Mary his espoused wife, who was with child . . . And she brought forth her first-born son, and wrapped him up in swaddling clothes, and laid him in a manger; because there was no room for them in the inn.

All the monks rejoiced as Dom Anselm concluded: "And suddenly there was with the angel a multitude of the heavenly army, praising

God, and saying: Glory to God in the highest; and on earth peace to men of good will." The whole choir sang with great gusto at the Offertory: "Let the heavens rejoice, and let the earth be glad before the face of the Lord, because he cometh. " Dom Philip relaxed; from here on, until the Communion, the familiar canon of the Mass took over. At the Communion, all the monks sang in awe: *"In splendoribus sanctorum, ex utero ante Luciferum genui te"* ("In the splendor of the saints, I begot you before the morning star"). Dom Bonaventure concluded Midnight Mass by praying that all the monks who celebrated the mystery of Christ's birth would by worthy deeds live with Him. Then he said, *"Ite Missa est,"* and the first Mass of Christmas Day was over.

Dom Philip was unable to suppress a fatigued yawn, but he knew that from this point, he had the stamina to get through Lauds. A rather long interval passed before the monks began Lauds at about 1:00 AM; the break enabled the Prior who had said the Mass and the deacon and Sacristan to return to their choir stalls. The monks shifted in their choir stalls while waiting. They were cold. Dom Damian no longer felt his feet at all. At the sign from the Prior, the weekly cantor, Dom Ignatius, put down his cowl, made a large sign of the cross, and sang the constant monastic prayer, *"Deus in adjutorium meum intende"* ("O God, come to my assistance"). The monks responded, *"Domine, ad adjuvandum me festina"* (O Lord make haste to help me"). The monks again sang a long drawn-out Gloria Patri and the psalm "Deus misereatur nostri" ("May God show us grace and blessing, may His face shine upon us and He be gracious to us").

After this usual introduction, the monks began the part peculiar to Christmas. Still following the descending seniority introduced in Matins, Dom Gregory sang the first antiphon of Lauds, "Today is born a Savior who is Christ the Lord." Dom Philip felt as if he were at the Lyric Opera in Chicago and savored every note. Dom Columba worked hard at staying on pitch for the antiphon for Psalm 99, which he loved, "The angels said to the shepherds, 'I bring you tidings of great joy.'" Dom Leo again rejoiced in his participation in the intricate structure of this ancient hour. He, however, became distracted and got the pitch wrong on the next antiphon. When Dom Ludolph continued the antiphon by starting the psalm, he brought the pitch back to a comfortable tone, and things stayed almost on pitch for the rest of Lauds. Then, Dom Ignatius intoned the "Pastores loquebantur" antiphon, "The shepherds said among themselves, 'Let us see this Word which the Lord has sent us.' Alleluia." After Dom Damian sang the last antiphon precisely and carefully, all the monks sang the canticle of the three young men from Daniel 3: *"Benedicite omnia opera domini, Domino."*

> All ye works of the Lord, bless the Lord, praise and glorify Him forever!
>
> Angels of the Lord, bless the Lord, O ye heavens, bless the Lord.
>
> Waters and all that is above the clouds . . .

Dom Ignatius wasn't finished with his job as weekly cantor, but he was relaxed enough to delight in the canticle. He knew nothing about the music, but he loved the words; savoring the names of everything that blessed the Lord: "Sun and moon, stars of heaven, showers and dews, fire and heat, dew and hoarfrost, ice and snow, lightnings and clouds, mountains and hills, seas and rivers, and even whales." The old monks knew the canticle and the rest of the Office by heart, and they extinguished their lamps one by one. The lights above the antiphonaries gradually disappeared. After the canticle, the novices sensed the end of the long Night Office, and Lauds seemed to proceed quickly. After a couple of verses and responses, the monks sang the conclusion of the hymn begun in Matins: "Venit Redemptor gentium." By this time, the church was nearly dark, with only the novices' lamps remaining lit. Dom Ignatius again sang the verse *"Verbum caro factum est."* The monks again responded, *"Et vidimus gloriam ejus, gloriam quasi unigeniti a Patre."* Then Dom Bonaventure went to the lectern between the choir stalls and concluded Lauds with the same prayer that he had used to conclude Matins. By this time, the church was as dark as it had been when they arrived. Dom Damian felt that this movement from light to dark was the most moving act of Night Office. As the monks finished Lauds at about 1:35 AM, the great bell boomed out the first Angelus of the day.

As the monks filed out of church, the sound of their squeaky cork-lined, tire-soled choir shoes broke into the quiet of the early Christmas morning. Holding his paraffin lanthorn in front of him to navigate the dark cloister, Dom Philip decided that all in all, the Office had come off better than he had feared. It was quite a decent show for early

Christmas morning. As pragmatic as he was, on this night even Dom Philip shared Dom Damian's excitement at being alone in the universe, standing guard while others slept, on duty during the time the devil prowled the earth like a lion. Dom Philip wondered if Dom David was again fretting over Christmas away from his family, without presents or other observances. He had told Dom Philip that during Night Office, he started to get almost visual flashes and smells of home, jumping right out of the Office books. But Dom Philip walked back to his cell, cowl up, holding his lanthorn in his right hand, savoring the cold crispness of this particular Christmas morning. In the midst of all his intense work, Night Office had done its work and produced harmony. God had spoken to him: *Quies.*

CHAPTER 12

The Noonday Demon (April 1964)

⊕

Four months later, the Christmas liturgy had changed to the penitential days of Lent. Nothing else changed at Parkminster. The weekly schedule was always the same—the same in 1964 as it was in the time of Bruno. Like Bruno, Dom Philip thirsted to see the face of God.

During his first two years at Parkminster, Dom Philip had used all his intellectual resources to find God. He craved books. He knew about some of the authors he wanted to read from his theology studies in the seminary, and Dom Joseph introduced him to new ones. Dom Joseph was very cerebral, and he let Dom Philip read the Dutch theologian with the oddly spelled name, Edward Schillebeeckx. On the walks, the novices told him about other writers. Dom Columba talked to Dom Philip about a fourteenth-century contemplative, possibly a fellow Carthusian, who wrote the famous mystical treatise "The Cloud of Unknowing." Dom Philip asked Dom Joseph about the book, and Dom Joseph went to the monastic library and brought Dom Philip a manuscript copy transcribed by a sixteenth-century Carthusian monk. Dom Philip couldn't make much of it. He read:

> For if I can put it in picture language, you are now launched on the spiritual ocean, sailing away from the physical state to the spiritual. Many great storms and temptations will arise at this time perhaps, and you will not know where to look for help. Everything has gone: you experience neither everyday grace nor special. Don't be unduly afraid, even if you think you have got every reason to be so.

He thought, "This is so simple but so hard. I can't analyze this. My mind can't find anything to work on here. Maybe I can read this in another ten years." He was more interested in what the author described as the Cloud of Forgetting, a place to dump all the thoughts that kept him from God.

Dom Philip also learned about the author's female contemporary, Julian of Norwich, whose work revealed her fascination with the concept of the Trinity, a fascination shared by Bruno and his contemporaries. In 1054, varying interpretations of the Trinity caused the Great Schism of the Roman and Eastern churches. The Roman Church believed that the Holy Spirit proceeded from the Father and the Son; the Eastern Church that the Holy Spirit proceeded from the Father alone. In Calabria, the location of Bruno's second Charterhouse, there were many Greek monks who were part of the Eastern Orthodox Church. Bruno achieved the difficult task of bringing Roman and Greek monks together. On his deathbed he tried to relate to both his Roman and Greek monks. Bruno began with the Roman creed:

> I firmly believe in the Father, the Son, and the Holy Spirit; the Father unbegotten, the only begotten Son, the Holy Spirit proceeding from them both; and I believe that these three Persons are but one God.

At the end of his profession of faith, Bruno came back to the dogma of the Trinity, but this time with a direct quotation from the Eleventh Council of Toledo (675), which emphasized the Fatherhood of God, closer to Greek dogma:

> I acknowledge and believe the holy and ineffable Trinity, Father, Son, and Holy Spirit, to be but only one God, of only one substance, of only one nature, of only one majesty and power. We profess that the Father was neither begotten nor created but that He has begotten. The Father takes his origin from no one; of Him the Son is born and the Holy Ghost proceeds. He is the source and origin of all Divinity.

Trying to find some clues about the Trinity, Dom Philip read and reread St. Bruno's deathbed profession of faith.

As a solitary monk, an only child, and an inheritor of Bruno's tradition, Dom Philip's only escape from complete solitude was to get to

God—or "get out." The life in God was complete and total exchange. Dom Philip was looking for a way to get into this interchange. He found the concept of the Trinity, the ultimate mystery, a confounding but hypnotic one. The tides, the ebb and flow, the constant interchange of the Trinity, captivated him: the white-hot interaction of the three persons in one God. He thought about what St. Irenaeus had said in the second century: "All things are known in advance by the Father and then done by the Son in order, in harmony, and in the appropriate time." How, he wondered, does this relationship in the Trinity work? Intensely fascinated, the lure of the unknown made Dom Philip nearly dizzy.

Most novices became engrossed with such complex theological conundrums. Solitude fosters obsession with an idea, and Dom Philip decided that he needed to unlock the puzzle of the Trinity. If he were able to break the code, would it perhaps reveal to him the essence of communicating with God? He attempted to codify the problem, to turn it into an equation that would, once teased out, reveal its inner spiritual logic. First, he listed the reasons for the existence of the Trinity, applying all he knew of philosophy and theology, using the philosophy symbols @ for "but" and ∴ for "ergo" (therefore). He wrote on the back of a letter from his father, carefully marking his † at the top of the sheet. In impenetrable notes, with tremendous intensity, he tussled with the conundrum of the Trinity. And so Dom Philip's formula to understand the Trinity began to emerge:

†

God knows & loves Himself
Divine nature subsists in 3 Persons
∴ twice communicated, i.e. 2 productions
God knows Himself & expresses His Word, i.e. *Pater* communicates fullness of divine nature by intellect
Production=communication of nature production through int.—conceives perfect similitude, but *intelligere=esse*, ∴ in conception *intelligendo*, being subsistent is communicated *(generatio)*
3 Persons in God
∴ distinction
no distinction in absolutes
∴ in relatives

rational relation not sufficient
∴ real relation
all relations founded on either quantity or action
@ not quantity in God
∴ on action, i.e. productions in God
@ action *ad extra* not sufficient for real relation
∴ action *ad intra*, i.e. intellect & will
∴ *Sunt productiones in Deo secundum intellegentiam & voluntatem.*

He paused, as it seemed that some words were beginning to fit. He felt exhilarated. There was an elegance to the notion of productions within the Godhead. The simplicity was attractive. He felt like a dog on the trail. Encouraged, he went back to his intensely wrought notes.

@ not all can be produced, nor can 2 be unproduced
∴ l is unproduced, 2 produced
(intellect precedes will
∴ intellectual procession first)
@ each procession infinite in own line
∴ only 1 procession possible thru each (int.+will)
∴ person produced through will can't produce by int.
∴ person produced through int can't produce by int.
∴ only unproduced person can produce through int. (generation)
@ nothing opposes persons not produced thru will to produce by
@ where no opposition, no distinction
∴ persons not produced thru will produce as one by will (spiration)
∴ 3 Persons in God, 1 generating, 1 generated, 2 spirating, 1 spirated

He thought about the last line—the Father generating the Son, both of them in existence, together they create the Spirit. *Admirabilis.* But then he realized that the Father and Son couldn't create the Spirit since the Spirit was also eternal. And could the Father and Son be in existence before the Spirit? The equations were beginning to confuse him. How could the Father and the Son *become* one God since God is eternal? Something was not right, but he couldn't see where his formula had failed him. The enigma was more difficult than he thought and far from solved. He might even have been expressing heretical ideas.

During the summer of Dom Philip's third year, 1963, his first as a professed monk, the intellectual excitement gradually ebbed. He stopped learning foreign languages and trying to solve the puzzle. A verse from Psalm 138 in Thursday's Vespers articulated his problem: "Thy knowledge is become too wonderful for me, too high, and I cannot reach it." So he stopped worrying about proofs, about what the monks called "ratiocination." Aggressive intellectual work wasn't getting him closer to God; he might even be driving Him away. He didn't know how it had happened or even what exactly was different, but as the months wore on, more and more he sat quietly, waiting. He read less and occasionally tried to write. Lamentations 3:26 echoed around the periphery of his brain: "It is good to wait in silence for the greeting of God." The statutes said: "Intent, then, on the rich substance of truth rather than the froth of words, let us scrutinize the divine mysteries with that desire to know which both springs from love and in turn inflames love." Increasingly adrift in the ocean of the spirit, he had no choice but to allow himself to be moved by its unseen currents.

Dom Philip began to reread Scripture and the early Fathers, especially Origen, a third-century theologian from Alexandria with a speculative turn of mind. Origen was a brilliant theorist and an extraordinarily prolific writer. He was so prolific that various saints argued about his oeuvre: St. Epiphanius estimated that Origen had written 6,000 texts, but St. Jerome assures us that the list did not contain even 2,000 titles. The principal theologian of the early Greek Church, Origen drew much of his intellectual vigor from Plato, but Origen remained sure that God only revealed Himself in the Bible. Dom Philip liked to think about Origen's Pauline dictum: "So happy will they be who see God no longer through a glass, darkly, but face to face, pure of heart, bathed in the radiant light of wisdom." Dom Philip started writing his own commentaries on Scripture on the inside of old envelopes. Origen, after all, had written eighty pages on the "Our Father," besides thousands of pages on other topics.

Dom Philip learned to keep vigil, to wait for the knock, to listen hard for the gentle breeze. Perhaps for the first time, he could sympathize with St. Bruno's question with its hint of despair: "I am so thirsty for God strong and living, when will I see the face of God?" The environment provided no distractions, neither did the daily ritual. Changes in the ritual were so minute as to be invisible. In the fall, for example, drinking apple juice that the brothers made instead of tea was a big event. Holy Week and even Christmas meant a different liturgy, but there was little disruption in the regimen: no extra-long walk, no decorations in church, no family, no visitors, no exchange of gifts, no Christmas tree. The life at times seemed a very mirror of eternity, the sameness of it echoing the unchanging quality of eternity. Dom Philip knew from his philosophy courses that by definition, eternity is unchanging, a constancy.

He felt he was beginning to penetrate the monastic mystery. He wasn't going anyplace. He had already arrived, *hic et nunc.* He was already living the life. He stopped worrying about the future. What difference did solemn vows make? Dom Philip was beginning to realize that he was in a different time zone at Parkminster, and because the monks had no objectives, weren't going anywhere, time pressures didn't exist. As a mortal being, the monk faced eternity every day. Today, tomorrow, tomorrow, tomorrow were all the same. Nothing ever changed. In the face of the vastness of eternity, Dom Philip began to understand his powerlessness and insignificance. He was not in charge of what was happening; his own resources could not help him.

By the end of 1963, Dom Philip merely tried to attend on God, to keep vigil. He became absorbed into *quies.* He realized that God wasn't anything he could imagine or define. God was beyond the sum of his experiences or his ability to conceptualize. And so he tried to stay in God's presence, to wait on God. He spent time meditating, sitting on the fold-down bench opposite his prie-dieu. He found that this was the best place to forget about his body. The Desert Father St. Antony (250–356), whom the monks called the father of all monks, had said, "It is not a perfect prayer if one is conscious of oneself or understands one's prayer." In his hermitage, Dom Philip followed Bruno's advice and "occupied himself in busy leisure and rested in tranquil activity." He hoped that God would reward him and the Charterhouse's other spiritual athletes with peace and joy in the Holy Spirit.

Dom Philip prized his time in cell more and more. His interior silence became louder and only made him want more solitude. The silence of his hermitage was giving him a pure and clean eye to see

God. He felt that his cell was holy ground, a place where, in the words of the most ancient statutes,

> as a man with his friend, the Lord and his servant often speak together. In cell, the soul is united with the Word of God, the bride made one with her spouse, earth joined to heaven, the divine to the human.

His cell became as natural to him as water to a fish. Being alone became natural. He knew from his Scripture studies that God spoke to Jacob, Moses, and Elijah when they were alone. He pondered Exodus 33:11: "The Lord used to speak to Moses face to face, as one man would speak to another." Dom Philip walked in his garden with God as Adam walked in the Garden of Eden. He watched the changing seasons, the liturgy of the natural world.

Quies absorbed everything. By the spring of his fourth year, 1964, Dom Philip didn't read at all. He realized that he couldn't solve the enigma of the Trinity, that reading Scripture merely kept him from being distracted. Without work, his idle mind would reach for whatever he could find—problem solving, speculating, daydreaming, or anticipating the rhubarb pudding at the next meal. Scripture kept his mind anchored, but it didn't get him where he wanted to go. He wanted to journey into God. He stared into the blast furnace of nothing, at Moses' burning bush. He was drawn to the light, but as he drew nearer, he fell on his face in awe. He wondered what it would be like to be an anchorite living on a rock. Easier. No monks singing off pitch. Dom Philip chopped more wood and put on his garden clogs to work in the garden.

Gradually, Dom Philip became more and more aware that solemn profession, a lifelong commitment to this community of hermits, was getting closer. He regularly worried that the solemns wouldn't vote him into the order. He had still not come close to creating harmony in choir, which only increased the normal stress of being a novice under scrutiny. The life became harder. The periodic, relentless grinding of the Friday fasts made Fridays seem longer, and, after four years, he was shaking more by the end of the day. Dom Philip never got used to interrupted sleep 365 days a year. The time for sleep seemed shorter, and four years of broken sleep had made him tired. Although his parents had visited him twice, Dom Philip didn't really remember what life was like outside the walls. He had lost the sense of a world outside. At Parkminster, there was no space for the outside; the inner life displaced the outside. The outside wasn't thrown out, but the life was filled up with other things. The repetitive structure of the life left no core space for anything else. Nothing reminded the monks of life back home.

Then, during this time, suddenly, unexpectedly, the dark force took a more subtle form than it had before. Every day was still the same, but every day began to feel as dry as the dry bread on Friday. Everything was arid. Dom Philip felt that he was wasting his time. Sitting at his prie-dieu, he squirmed, nothing was going on. He struggled with a demon that a fourth-century Eastern monk, Evagrius Ponticus, called the "noonday demon."

> The demon of *acedia*—also called the noonday demon—is the one that causes the most serious trouble of all. He presses his attack upon the monk about the fourth hour and besieges the soul until the eighth hour. First of all he makes it seem that the sun barely moves, if at all, and that the day is fifty hours long. Then he constrains the monk to look constantly out the windows, to walk outside the cell, to gaze carefully at the sun to determine how far it stands from the ninth hour, to look now this way and now that to see if perhaps . . .

The noonday demon tormented Dom Philip with the unchanging routine to which he was committed—today, tomorrow, and tomorrow, and tomorrow: to bed at 7:00 PM, up at 11:00 PM to pray, then to church for Night Office, back to pray, to bed again around 2:30 AM, up again at 6:00 AM for Prime, then to church for the conventual and private Masses, then back to the cell for Sext and reading, dinner at 11:00 AM, manual labor and reading, back to church at 2:45 PM for Vespers, back to the cell for Compline, and then to bed at 7:00 PM. The noonday demon made Dom Philip feel very acutely that the life offered little in return. The noonday demon came and went, but when he was present, Dom Philip felt as if he would never leave. Dom Philip kept conversing with God, but was anyone listening? He wasn't sure; he felt parched. But he took comfort, as did the other monks, in the belief that the harder the life got, the more you were progressing to God.

CHAPTER 13

Outside the Walls (August 15, 1964)

Every man attempting to become a Catholic priest follows an ancient procedure that originally designated actual positions, or jobs, in the Catholic Church, which are today carried out by priests or laypeople. He first receives the minor orders of doorkeeper, lector, exorcist, and acolyte, then the two major orders of subdeacon and deacon. The priesthood is the seventh order. The novices received the minor orders two at a time after they had completed the required ecclesiastical studies. But the novices reacted differently to receiving minor orders. Many of them had not left the Charterhouse since their arrival, and for some, the experience was traumatic. The first time Dom Ignatius thought of leaving Parkminster was when he and Dom Leo went to London for minor orders. The trip to the "world" shook his vocation—intensely—for reasons he couldn't understand.

When it became time for Dom Malachi to receive major orders, he concluded that he didn't have a calling to be a priest. His superiors told him that all Carthusian monks were priests. Yet Dom Malachi simply did not want to be a priest. He wrote a letter to the Sacred Congregation of Rites in Rome, explaining that he wanted to be a hermit monk but that he did not want to be a priest. When he and Dom Guy went outside the Charterhouse on an errand and visited a church, while Dom Guy was praying, he found an old woman, gave her the uncensored letter, asked her to put a stamp on it, and post it. The Sacred Congregation sent a letter to the Reverend Father at the Grande Chartreuse saying that Dom Malachi didn't have to be ordained. Dom

Malachi created a major furor in the order, a disturbance that rippled all the way to the top. This exception was nearly unique.

Dom Philip's first trip outside the Charterhouse walls was on August 15, 1964. With the smell of ripe apples from the garth overpowering him, and the Charterhouse celebrating the feast of the Assumption of the Blessed Virgin, Dom Philip hated to leave the quiet of Parkminster. The statutes say, "We view with horror the thought of going out and traveling about through town and country," and Dom Philip thought, "We've got that right." Yet the trip to London for minor orders meant that Dom Philip was moving closer to ordination.

As he walked through the cloister with his cowl up, sensing the brothers hustling around picking the apples for cider, Dom Philip worried a bit about how he would feel during the ceremony. Would he wish he were still back in the world as a priest? Taking minor orders put him on the same track he was on before he left for the Charterhouse. Would the noonday demon tempt him again? Would he be comparing himself with his former classmates from the seminary? His friends were far ahead of him. They had already been ordained on April 30 of that year. Two who had gone to Rome had been ordained even earlier, on December 18, 1963. His friend Otto and he had been together in the minor and major seminary, and now Otto was ahead of him.

From his cell, Dom Philip went straight to the Chapter House, where he met Dom Guy, the Procurator, and Dom Bede, the Sub-Procurator. They looked odd standing side by side: Dom Guy, at 6 feet 7 inches, had a lot of bulk, weighing about 280 pounds, whereas Dom Bede was slight, the shortest monk, about 5 feet 4 inches. Dom Guy's large-boned and squarish face and his great height and weight made him look like a character from a nineteenth-century English novel. Dom Philip wondered how Dom Guy managed to fit into the choir stall when he prostrated. Without any chatting or small talk, the three monks climbed into a battered black touring car kept in the garage next to the laundry on the north side of the Charterhouse. Eddie, the lay chauffeur who lived in the lodge by the entrance, and Dom Guy sat in the front seat and Doms Bede and Philip in the back; they drove through a green iron gate into the outside world. After three and a half years of moving by foot, Dom Philip was glad to feel a car move under him again. The day was a celebration, a chance to interact with the outside world, a change in the monastic routine.

Before entering the Charterhouse, Dom Guy had been an international lawyer. Brought up Anglican, he converted to Catholicism while in Cairo during World War II. He was educated at Oundle, a private school founded in 1556 by a merchant for the sons of merchants; in 1925, he went on to Wadham College at Oxford, where he was active in debating, and graduated in 1929. His tutor was the famed British academic Maurice Bowra, later Sir Maurice Bowra, vice-chancellor of Oxford. Dom Guy wanted to work in the British Museum, but as he needed to be self-supporting, he got a law degree instead. His partner and friend Eric Fletcher later became a Labor MP and deputy speaker. In 1970, he became a life peer as Lord Fletcher of Islington.

As Procurator, Dom Guy was in constant touch with the outside world, buying cloth, leather, food, oil for the lamps, and whatever else the monks needed. He was also the brothers' Novice Master and in charge of their work. He wasn't supposed to bring worldly news into the Charterhouse (his job was to insure that the monks could live in otherworldly contemplation), but he was very informed about affairs in London. He was curious about what was going on at St. Paul's and wondered what the smart set was doing. Dom Philip had never talked to Dom Guy before, and he found it hard to understand his very thick accent. In his booming Oxford voice, he pointed out the sights to the young American who had been so eager to get to Parkminster that he hadn't taken time to see London. Dom Guy told Dom Philip about his life at Wadham College. He and five or six friends would take off for the weekend with five mystery novels. They each read the same novel, and whoever could figure out the case first, presenting logical arguments, won. Dom Guy confided to him that his dean and tutor, Maurice Bowra, would say in a superior voice, "If I want a religious experience, I look at a painting by Giotto." Dom Philip wondered if Dom Guy's spirituality was hidden deep within him. Dom Bede, from Scotland, didn't say much, but he expressed his concern about Dom Malachi, who was serving his private Mass that week. Dom Bede had noticed that Dom Malachi's hands were shaking at Holy Communion and that he was pale and coughing. He concluded that he had better talk to Father Master about him.

The three monks drove along the south bank of the Thames, heading toward Lambeth Road. Dom Philip was excited by the unaccustomed yet familiar bustle of the city. In contrast to the clean robust lines of Chicago, with its steel-and-glass skyscrapers, such as those designed by Mies van der Rohe, London seemed old and grimy, like an archeological dig revealing layer upon layer of history. London reminded him of Henry VIII and the eighteen Carthusian martyrs.

To his surprise, the Catholic Cathedral of St. George sat at the intersection of major roads and was dilapidated and unattractive. A three-sided roundabout fenced in the church, which was squarish and had neither spire nor bell tower. A large cross stood at the corner where the roads came together, and the exterior of the church, originally yellow brick, was now so covered with soot that it was hard to see the original color. Eddie couldn't find a parking place and decided to risk parking on the playground of Notre Dame school across the road from the cathedral. The monks got out of their old car and headed toward the cathedral. As they went to the corner to cross the street, red double-decker buses, cars, and motorcycles whipped around them. They found it difficult simply to get across. The din of schoolchildren playing soccer adjacent to the church increased the sense of chaos. The noise and mass of rapid movement imprisoned the church like an isolated island. Dom Philip thought, "This is worse than Chicago."

Dom Philip was very aware of the attention the three white-robed monks attracted. As they walked toward the church, people turned to look at them. But Dom Philip felt very comfortable about who he was—and didn't feel like a freak or outcast. The three monks went inside the cathedral, and to Dom Philip's surprise, the interior was quiet and quite lovely. Organ notes from a large pipe organ delighted him—he hadn't heard instrumental music since he'd entered the Charterhouse. He saw tall, graceful columns, an arched white-stone ceiling, leaded and stained glass windows, and rather intricate stone fretwork on both the right and left sides of the altar. Behind the altar, Dom Philip could see an enormous stained-glass window of the crucifixion, depicting Christ surrounded by English saints. The three monks took holy water from the copper-lined marble fount on the wall. Then Doms Guy and Bede went to their seats, while Dom Philip joined the line of young men who were also waiting to receive minor orders.

All the other young men, about twenty-five of them, stared at Dom Philip as he joined their ranks. They wore black button-down cassocks and birettas that resembled the postulants' hats at Parkminster. This scene had been a familiar part of Dom Philip's past, yet he felt no desire to reconnect to it, nor to connect with the men. Dom Philip was the only man in the group who was in a religious order, and if he had been an astronaut, they couldn't have looked at him with more admiration.

Representing the Carthusians, Doms Guy and Bede sat in a right-hand pew off the middle aisle of the church. The young men studying to be parish priests and Dom Philip lined up in the eight-foot-wide middle aisle and moved toward the high altar. The young men took their assigned places in the front pews. The Bishop of Southwark, a small, stout, white-haired man, entered the cathedral and slowly walked straight to the middle of the altar, where he knelt and prayed for a while. Dom Philip felt comfortable in the church, familiar from his childhood and college days, but knew that now it was not his place. When the bishop finished praying, he went to an intricately carved mahogany chair on his left. He had put on special sandals before he entered the church, but at the chair he clothed himself with other elaborate pontifical vestments—gloves and a dalmatic vestment with wide sleeves, marked with two stripes and with a slit on each side of the skirt, which he put on over his long-sleeved linen robe. Kings and queens of England wear a similar vestment at their coronations. Holding his crosier, a six-foot ceremonial staff hooked at one end, the bishop moved back to the altar, where he began Mass. After the "Kyrie Eleison," the bishop went back to the mahogany chair, and the archdeacon, second to the bishop, said in Latin: "Let all who are to be ordained come forward."

Dom Philip and the other young men left their pews and walked to the altar, each carrying a lighted candle in their right hand. They knelt in a kind of semicircle before the bishop. From the *Pontificale Romanum* (a ceremonial book for bishops), the archdeacon then read the prohibitions against being ordained, such as being excommunicated, or illegitimate, or having an extremely bad reputation. Next, the bishop, using a pair of gold scissors, gave clerical tonsure to the men—to symbolize beginning their journey into the priesthood. In order to have enough hair for the bishop to cut, Dom Philip had skipped his last two haircuts; his reddish-brown hair looked like a crew cut with an untrimmed crown of hair. The bishop snipped off some hair with the gold scissors. Dom Philip couldn't help comparing the scissors with Brother Hugh's dreaded long razor. Then the bishop vested Dom Philip with a white surplice as another sign of belonging to the clergy. When all the men were tonsured and vested, the bishop said some more prayers.

The archdeacon finally said, "Let those who are to be ordained to the office of Porter, come forward." The notary called them each by name and each answered "*Adsum*" ("I am here"). Dom Philip felt very pleased that he was receiving minor orders because he wanted very much to be a priest. When all those to be ordained Porters were on their knees before the bishop, the archdeacon instructed them:

> It is the duty of the Porter to strike the cymbal and to ring the church bell, to open the church and the sacristy, and to open the book for the preacher. . . . Study, also, as you open and shut with material keys the visible church, so in like manner study to shut to the devil and open to God, by word and example, the invisible House of God.

Dom Philip wondered if the bishop knew about the noonday demon. He wished that he could be shut out with a key. The archdeacon then gave the bishop the keys to the church. While presenting the keys to each young man to be touched, the bishop said, "So act as about to give an account of those things that are kept under these keys." Then the archdeacon led the entire group to the door of the church. Each man opened and shut the door, then each man gave one stroke on the bell rope. Dom Philip did this every day, so the ceremony was lost on him, but he let it flow over him. Then the archdeacon led them back to the bishop, who said another prayer after the master of ceremonies, the priest in charge of the ceremony, took off the bishop's mitre.

The bishop then said more of the Mass. Dom Philip felt somewhat disoriented because the Roman ritual had become unfamiliar. After a while, the bishop went back to his chair, and the master of ceremonies put the mitre on the bishop's head again, and the archdeacon said: "Let those who are to be ordained to the office of Lector come forward." Dom Philip's name was called again, and the bishop gave an exhortation on the office of Lector. Then the bishop held a breviary in front of each young man; they all touched the breviary while the bishop said, "Accept and be relaters of the Word of God. If you faithfully and usefully fulfill your duties, you will take part with those who have well administered the word of God from the beginning." Dom Philip was used to long Latin rituals, and he rested his mind during the rest of the ceremony. As much as he hated rituals, he wanted to be a priest, so he tried to let the ceremony work on him. Dom Philip would receive the other two minor orders of Exorcist and Acolyte in three months.

The bishop then administered the major orders. When the bishop was finished with the ordinations, he proceeded with the Mass. After the Mass, the bishop gave special instructions to those receiving minor orders: "Say once the seven Penitential Psalms, with the Litany of the Saints, together with the versicles, and prayers." After they indicated their agreement to do this, the Bishop concluded and took off his pontifical vestments. In all, the ceremony had lasted almost as long as Night Office. Dom Philip was glad when it was over, leaving him only with the obligation of praying the Penitential Psalms and the Litany of the Saints. He would pray those later in his cell. Now he was forever a Doorkeeper and Lector.

When the ceremony was over, Dom Guy gave Dom Philip a typically suffocating monkish hug, and Dom Bede said, "Good show." Ordination rituals weren't as big an issue for the monks as profession, but still, minor orders meant Dom Philip was moving along. They were a marker toward the priesthood, but they were not an irrevocable threshold. Minor orders didn't stop you from leaving or even from getting married. Dom Philip wished his father could have been here, but he thanked God his mother was back in Chicago. She would have been canvassing the congregation, letting everyone know that the monk was her son. With the congregation still stealthily looking at them, the three monks left the church and again braved the traffic to meet Eddie on the playground.

As they reached the car, Dom Philip was glad to be going back to Parkminster. In their heads, the three monks were already in the Charterhouse, hidden in the shelter of God. Even Dom Guy talked less. Back in the car, the monks continued their task of praising the Lord, even for London and the strangeness of the world outside the Charterhouse. Only one and one-half miles northwest of St. George Cathedral, Carnaby Street, near Oxford Circus, was the hangout for the young rock-and-rollers who were busy founding the hippie culture that flourished in the anything-goes atmosphere of the 1960s. The monks had never even heard of Carnaby Street. Nor were the monks aware that a week earlier, on August 7, 1964, a joint resolution of Congress approved Lyndon Johnson's determination to commit the United States more deeply to the war in Vietnam.

Meanwhile, Dom Philip felt good about his new status. Psalm 134 sang in his head: "Praise the Name of the Lord, ye servants of the Lord, praise him! Ye who serve in the house of the Lord, in the courts of the house of our God!" He felt so comfortable in his new status that a few weeks later, on the back of a religious card, he wrote to his parents:

†

> For Mom and Dad—9/6/64
>
> "One request I have ever made of the Lord let me claim it still, to dwell in the Lord's house my whole life long, gazing at the beauty of the Lord, haunting his sanctuary." (Psalm 26:4)

As they neared the Charterhouse, Dom Philip made a mental note to talk to Dom Joseph about his concern for Dom Damian—his vanishing sense of humor on the walks, his nervous habit of twisting the stubble of hair above his ear, his quavery voice when he sang a lesson. He would do that tomorrow.

CHAPTER 14

Perseverance (September 16–December 25, 1964)

⊕

A month later, on Ember Wednesday, September 16, 1964, Dom Damian was working in his garden. After four years, from a scraggly patch of weeds, he had created something beautiful. He had asked Dom Joseph for some plants, and Dom Joseph had gone to the brothers' greenhouse to get him some cuttings and pots. Dom Damian fashioned a potting shed in his ambulatory, putting his potted cuttings on the windowsill. Using his lathe, he had built window boxes that cascaded with coreopsis, sweet pea, chrysanthemum, and sweet william. The bare-root roses he'd planted were now climbing up the walls and in full bloom. Delphiniums and gladioli bloomed against his cell wall. Sedum clung to the cloister wall, fronted by showy mallow, lilies, and hydrangea.

Last spring, he had heard of an archeological dig not far from the Charterhouse, and thinking that monks should be capable of anything, he started digging in the heavy clay soil of his garden. The earth in his garden heaped up, and he still found nothing but clay. After he had dug a six-foot hole, he realized that he was not going to find any artifacts, but that he had the beginnings of a pond. He smoothed out his dig and covered it with plastic. He brought buckets of water to fill the pond; then he planted some aquatic flowers in old plastic buckets that he lowered into the pond. A few water lilies were still blooming. The nights were getting cold, but the days were still hot and sunny.

As he worked the soil, carefully pulling any weed infringing on his garden, he thought about Dom Philip's trip to London. Dom Damian had come to the Charterhouse before Dom Philip, but Dom Philip was advancing more quickly. Dom Philip, of course, had taken many of the required courses before he came to Parkminster. Still, Dom Damian idealized Dom Philip and thought that he would be a Prior, at the very least. Still in his mid-twenties, Dom Philip seemed to understand how the world of people worked—he was worldly wise. No one thought Dom Damian would ever be a Prior, but he tried harder and harder to be a perfect monk. At times he thought, "I'm not doing that badly."

For four years, Dom Damian had worked assiduously, observing the rules of the order to bring his body under control. He found that he couldn't meditate if he was thinking about his body and its comforts. So he usually kept his hair shirt tied tightly around his waist, so much so that scraps of his flesh and hair got caught in the rope. Parkminster monks customarily didn't light their stoves until November 1, but no matter how cold it was, Dom Damian rarely lit his stove. He knew that Dom Joseph considered the rate of coal used and the sanctity of the novice inversely proportional. When Dom Damian took his bath every other Saturday, he bathed quickly so that he wouldn't coddle his flesh. Dom Damian read and reread Guigo II, who, in his *The Ladder of Four Rungs,* carefully explains how a monk reaches God. The ladder to God consists of reading, meditation, prayer, and contemplation: "Reading seeks, meditation finds, prayer asks, contemplation feels." After a monk has read about God, "meditation chews it and breaks it down." Dom Damian worked hard at meditation, but he knew that contemplation was a gift, that it didn't matter if he never got there. He did what he could—in his case, observing ascetic practices that prepared the soul for inner prayer. Today, however, the sun was brilliant, and he indulged himself for a few minutes by sitting on a rock in his garden with his face to the sun, letting its brilliance thaw him out. September had just begun—and the evening cold had already started.

Since he came to Parkminster, he had been cold from September to mid-June. He would chronically shiver right to his bones. He knew that his father, a doctor, would be very upset if he knew how cold he was, but after all, Pennsylvania wasn't exactly warm in winter, either. Never feeling warm, however, was difficult. No matter how many layers he put on, he couldn't get warm because everything was so damp. When he put his clothes on in the morning, they were damp. When he went to bed at night, the sheets would be damp. The blankets would be damp. Even his straw mattress would be damp. His muscles tightened as he thought of winter. In the winter, he found it harder to keep clean. When he could no longer strip naked outside to sprinkle water on himself from his watering can, he filled a large tomato juice can with water that he put on the barely warm stove to heat. For six months of the year, using the quadrangular washbasin, he would give himself a sponge bath with the tepid water.

Once the cold got into the three-foot walls of the cells, they acted like a refrigerator. There was no place where he could go to get warm. When the inside cell walls became as cold as the outside, Dom Damian felt as if he were going to turn to ice. He remembered last winter when ten inches of snow had fallen the day after Christmas, then another nine inches three days later. Every evening, there had been a dusting of snow. It was beautiful, but his cell was so cold that he had to stir the water in the toilet bowl to keep it from freezing. At one point the temperature got down to 2° Fahrenheit, which was absolutely unprecedented. Dom Damian couldn't help but grin as he remembered Dom Philip's hapless attempt to use his paraffin reading lamp to unfreeze the water pipe in his bathroom. That year the novices found wooden balls and for recreation bowled them down the cloister. When they could finally leave the cloister, they played ice hockey on the ponds around the Charterhouse. Dom Joseph reveled in the sports, but Dom Columba was scandalized. Dom Damian remembered how depressed he had become when he discovered Dom Leo was a better hockey player than he, even though Dom Leo was older.

Dom Damian could, of course, have put more coals on his stove. But he told himself that real monks didn't worry about the cold. They were oblivious to the needs of the flesh. He thought a lot about his namesake, "Damian," a third-century martyr who had been a physician. He liked the name because it was crisp and sounded Greek: "Dom Damian" had a good ring to it. He reflected that the cold was very minor compared to what his namesake had suffered. In a miraculous way, Damian and his twin brother suffered no injury from water, fire, or being hung on a cross. They were finally beheaded with the sword. Compared to that, the discomforts at Parkminster were minor. It was his home. Dom Damian had felt so out of place in Pennsylvania that he had feared that he was from another planet, but he had always felt at home in the Charterhouse. As he anticipated the next Monday walk, he thought to himself that he was where he was supposed to be. At only twenty-four years old, he firmly believed that he had found his place in life.

As he worked in his garden on this sunny day, he was preoccupied with his extraordinary luck in getting inside the monastic library. Dom Damian agonized about whether he should tell the other novices about his adventure into forbidden territory. As far as he knew, he was the only novice who had been there. It was a fluke really. He wanted to read the writings of Guigo, and they were in Migne's Latin *Patrologia Latina*. Dom Damian didn't know why Dom Joseph let him go to the library. Since Migne's work was in 222 volumes, perhaps Dom Joseph simply didn't want to locate the right volume himself.

As Dom Damian climbed the ornate spiral stone staircase to the library, he could see aerial views of the grounds through the small windows cut into the walls. He gasped when he opened the double doors. Books, books, books: books climbing the walls to the tall ceiling, with a center aisle case of more books. The library was about as wide and high as the Chapter House below, but longer; he guessed about eighty feet. A crucifix hung at the far side above a white Madonna and child. The crisscrossing thin wooden joists of the ceiling created intricate intersecting horizontal and vertical lines. All he could see was glorious old wood and books. He felt overwhelmed with excitement.

The solemns could visit the library between None and Vespers on ordinary days, but today no one else was in the library. Dom Damian climbed the metal staircase to the top level, enclosed by a carved wooden railing; stacks of folios were below the steps. Some thoughtful monk librarian had put a makeshift table and chair under each window so that the solemns could read their books by sunlight in the unelectrified library. He looked out of the first window and saw the graveyard of the monks, bordered by a low stone wall, then by the monk's garth, then by the cells—perfectly symmetrical and so beautiful. He went back down the stairs and opened the old wooden card catalogue and saw yellowing cards with handwritten, spidery script, clearly very old. With immense pleasure, he looked again at the walls—solid bookcases all the way up to the intricate ceiling. He noticed that long ago, some monk librarian had designated different areas of the library with white wooden signs with large black Latin letters: *S. Scriptura, Christologia, Cartusiana, Theol. Ascet.* . . .

He opened the glassed-in bookcase opposite the front door and found nearly a hundred rare books and manuscripts. He opened one—a manuscript missal, circa 1325. A glorious illuminated capital letter in the middle of the page jumped out at him; the Blessed Virgin with a halo of solid gold and the Christ child formed a large letter "C." Dom Damian estimated that a monk must have spent all his recreation time for six months creating just that one intricately lined capital letter. In the bookcase, Dom Damian found twelfth- and thirteenth-century antiphonaries. It pained him to see the rot and mildew on the covers. Under the bay *Cartusiana*, he discovered a whole series of diurnals, from the very first printed copies to the present; there were a lot from the sixteenth century. He went back to the glassed-in bookcase and found some *incunabula*, books printed before 1501. Then he saw a rare choir book, about the size of an opened newspaper, about two inches thick, chained to the top of the center aisle.

He pulled himself together and realized that he had been told to look at *Patrologia Latina*, not to survey the entire collection. He did not allow himself the pleasure of going to the bottom floor. He hurriedly found the row of Migne volumes on the bottom shelf of the center bookcase. What he wanted was in volume 153, column 639. He looked about once more, then reluctantly but obediently took volume 153 and went down the circular stone staircase. Going back to his cell, he thought, every minute, about how he would go to the library every day when he was a solemn.

Every part of his body craved to tell the story of being in the library. After agonizing about it, he decided he really couldn't brag about this to the other novices. Dom Joseph had said he could go only if he "were discreet. If you tell the others, they will want to go too." If all the novices pestered Dom Joseph to go to the library, Dom Damian would lose any chance to return.

And so his thoughts drifted back to his gardening. He deadheaded some coreopsis and waited for the church clock to chime the three-minute alert for Vespers (BVM). In the meantime, Dom Damian reflected on John Cassian (360–430), who had introduced the Psalter as the most important text for a monk to read. Every novice knew that true monks should read Cassian. Ever since he had entered the novitiate, Dom Damian had yearned to read Cassian. Yet last spring, when Dom Damian asked Dom Joseph for a copy, he refused; Dom Joseph had suggested that his only reason for wanting to read Cassian was to impress the other novices. When eventually Dom Damian did read Cassian, it bored him. Cassian advocated moderation in all things, and Dom Damian wanted to be a perfect monk, and quickly.

But his dislike of Cassian worried Dom Damian so much that he confided in the Prior at his yearly conference. He found Dom Bonaventure sitting behind his massive desk, which was covered with papers and books. Dom Bonaventure scrutinized Dom Damian carefully. He asked him how he was doing. Dom Damian said, "Just fine, but I'm worried that I really don't respond to Cassian at all. I know that I should." To Dom Damian's amazement and relief, Dom Bonaventure said that he didn't like Cassian either. The usually reserved Prior visibly relaxed and said he read Origen most of the time; he told Dom Damian that Erasmus had said, "one page of Origen meant more" to him than "ten pages of Augustine." He drifted back in time, telling Dom Damian that he had been in cell without an official position for four years, and he had enjoyed reading a thirty-volume commentary in French on Thomas Aquinas's *Summa.* When he had finished reading Aquinas, he found everything else he read very loose; Aquinas was so clear, orderly, and logical. Dom Bonaventure glowed when he remembered those years in cell. It was nearly sunset, and the whole room with all its highly waxed wooden surfaces reflected the golden sunlight. For all the mellowness of the moment, Dom Bonaventure seemed so far above human conditions and desires that when he came to think about it later, Dom Damian realized that talking to him about Cassian had not relieved any of his anxiety.

The church clock chimed at 2:27 PM. Dom Damian dropped everything, as the rule required, took off his garden clogs, and went into his cell to pray. When the church clock chimed 2:42, he immediately put on his choir shoes and choir cuffs and waited by the door to his cell. As soon as Dom Francis rang the bell for Vespers, he left his cell and hurried to church. He got there a bit early, so he checked the notice board in the *tabula* and saw that this week he would serve Dom Emmanuel's private Mass. While his own chapel was being repaired, Dom Emmanuel was saying his Mass in the Reliquary Chapel on the top floor, next to the library, which pleased Dom Damian greatly. He deliberately let himself think about the treat in store for him. He would have to confess this distraction at the next Chapter of Faults, but he didn't care. He imagined himself climbing the forty-odd stairs to the chapel. He could already pick up the musty smell of the chapel. He remembered every detail. Although he knew that he would have to confess, "I failed to keep custody of the eyes," he would revel in the gloriously ornate detailing of the most beautiful room in the Charterhouse.

Sublet had painted another mural in the back of the chapel, above the paneling, in warm shades of gold and brown and white; shaped like a half circle, a copy of his *Gloire Celeste*, which had won the Grand Prize of Rome in 1870, depicted the triumphant Christ with his parents on either side. The entire body of St. Boniface resided under the altar. Every year, the new novices irreverently hooted when the older novices told the story of St. Boniface's arrival. In 1895, the priest who represented the monks had found the saint's bones and a vial of his blood in an Augustinian convent in Rome; the monks paid 1,000 francs for them. The Carthusian Procurator General in Rome had a wax body made for the bones, purchased a casket, and ensured that all was carefully sealed. But he had to get the casket back to England. The French ambassador to the Vatican sealed the casket with his ambassador's stamp so that customs officials would not open the casket. If anyone broke the seal, the relic would no longer be certified as authentic. The Prior at this time had the responsibility of seeing that the English customs officials didn't open the casket unless he was present. When he received the telegraph telling him that the casket would arrive at Charing Cross, the Prior left for London. But there was no package for him. He was advised to try the other station. Nothing there either. The officials told him that the package was probably late. Because the Prior wanted to return to Parkminster the same night, he went to the customs officials but had difficulty explaining the contents of the very large package. He finally decided to tell the customs officials that the package contained the bones of a famous person to which the monks attached great value. The dumbfounded officials promised that no one would open the casket and that they would forward it as soon as possible. St. Boniface arrived at the Charterhouse the next day. Because the monks knew nothing about him except that he had been martyred in some unknown way, they called in a local doctor, Dr. Rymer, who, after inspecting the saint's teeth, concluded that he had been about sixty-five years old at the time of his death.

Dom Damian loved choir from the moment he arrived at Parkminster. As the years went by, choir continued to support him. He was aware of the choir battles, but they seemed to him a gentle, necessary evil. He was aware of Dom Philip's ever-increasing stress over the lack of musical harmony, but Dom Damian enjoyed choir. He wondered sometimes if Dom Philip would care if the monks sang from the Chicago telephone book, as long as they kept on pitch. He didn't know anything about pitch, and he knew that he was just one more hair in Dom Philip's hair shirt, but he liked to sing lustily. When he first came to Parkminster, Dom Ludolph had been the choir instructor, and he encouraged everyone to sing loudly. He would say, "Competence gives confidence," before each choir practice. Dom Damian liked being part of this ageless group of men trying to reach God through prayer. The physicality of the Office appealed to him: standing, sitting, kneeling, inclining, prostrating together. Dom Damian listened hard, and he could hear the strong young voices mixing with the older and more fragile ones.

Dom Damian looked forward more and more to the Divine Office. He loved the progression of the liturgy; the Office followed natural time, completely integrated with the seasonal year. The Old and New Testament texts, composed hundreds of years apart, were like stanzas of the same song, whose mood would swing with the season. After a few years, Dom Damian could anticipate the Divine Office, looking forward to particular texts. The Carthusian liturgy was simpler and closer to the Old Testament. Few feast days distracted the Carthusians from the inevitable, relentless progression of the liturgical year—from Christ's birth to his death to his resurrection. Dom Damian loved the liturgy leading to Christmas. On the first Sunday of Advent, it began with the book of Isaiah: "Hear, O heavens, and give ear, O earth, for the Lord has spoken: 'Sons have I reared and brought up. But they have rebelled against me . . . '" (1:2). Then, "a child is born to us, a son is given to us" (9:6). As the monks prepared for the birth of Christ, the Old Testament application to Christ mesmerized him. Night Office in particular was his joy, his sustenance. For Dom Damian, Night Office on Christmas Eve was the most important event of the year.

This year, 1964, he had prepared particularly hard for Christmas, eating less bread on the Friday fast, putting less coal on his stove, preparing for the miraculous birth of Christ. He felt a certain inner nervousness that he hadn't felt before. His father's concern that he was too temperamentally fragile for the Carthusian life kept slipping around in his thoughts. Dom Damian couldn't entirely eradicate his father's fears from his own mind even after four years at Parkminster. When he was ten, he had become obsessive about stamp collecting and got stomachaches; when his father forbade stamp collecting, he recovered. He had stomachaches again when he was seventeen and had to take a long bus trip to school. Now, at age twenty-five, he seemed to be struggling again—he thought to himself that there was not only a Cloud of Unknowing but also a Cloud of Undoing, and he was in that cloud.

Yet Dom Damian felt the power of the liturgy sustaining him throughout Advent, allowing him to put his father out of his mind. The night of Christmas Eve, 1964, was particularly cold, and the monks were in the unheated church for nearly four hours. When Dom Damian got back to his cell, he tried to light his stove but found he was shaking too hard to strike a match. He was terrified that the cold would keep him from staying at Parkminster. Was his shaking a sign that the dark force was trying to keep him from solemn vows? Was it another temptation, or just the sheer frigidity of the place? The idea that he might have to forgo his calling was the most terrifying thing imaginable to Dom Damian. He could conceive of no other place he wanted to be, no other life he wanted to lead. With overwhelming anxiety, Dom Damian wondered, was this a trial from God that would bring Him closer, or was he going mad?

About 3:00 AM on Christmas Day, he went to Dom Joseph's cell. This intrusion was totally unprecedented. Dom Joseph looked at him quickly before sending him back to his own cell. Dom Joseph then went straight to Dom Columba's cell, now on the solemns' side, burst in, and said, "Who do you think is the latest to break down?" Having explained the situation, he asked Dom Columba to "go over and see what you can do for him." Dom Columba found Dom Damian in his ambulatory in a state of acute distraction. He was slowly and unsteadily pacing in his ambulatory, twisting the stubble of hair above his right ear. He didn't acknowledge Dom Columba's arrival but finally said in a low, unsteady voice, "I feel that if something is not done for me at once I'll go off my head." Dom Columba took him upstairs to his *cubiculum* and talked to him a bit about his obsessional thoughts, stoking the stove until the *cubiculum* glowed with heat for once, and also heating a brick to warm the bed. Then he gave him a sedative, which he readministered the next two nights. As a medical doctor, Dom Columba was concerned that the temperature in Dom Damian's cell was less than 50°, but he had no control over it: According to the usual rule, he wasn't even allowed to talk to the novices. Yet he put his hands over the frightened novice's hands and said, "I'm sorry that you are so cold. It is my fault. I should have been watching you more closely." With Dom Columba's comforting hands over his, Dom Damian fell into a sound sleep, allowing Dom Columba to return to his cell and write a medical report for the use of a psychiatrist if one was needed.

CHAPTER 15

Togetherness and Warmth (December 25–26, 1964)

CHRISTMAS/ST. STEPHEN'S DAY

After the long Night Office of Christmas morning, Christmas Day was a special day of meditation between the monk and God, set aside for the monks to speak individually to God from their hearts. No classes, no conferences, not even any recreation time. As on Ash Wednesday, there was no social contact at all between the monks; they had no shared festivities or celebrations until the following day, St. Stephen's Day. The monks even ate their Christmas meal alone in their cells. Doms Leo, Ignatius, Damian, and Malachi had had their first Carthusian Christmas in 1960, but none of them remembers much about it. On December 25, 1960, however, Dom Ignatius had written very enthusiastically to his parents in Germany:

> You perhaps cannot comprehend how we celebrate Christmas over here; on the first Christmas day we stay in Cell all day, except for the Office in church, occupied with nothing but contemplating what had happened in the stable near Bethlehem. No Christmas carols, no crib, no Christmas tree (not even a little branch of it), no presents, no candles—nothing, quite nothing save what happened at Bethlehem. And yet I can assure you quite honestly that I never experienced such a merry Christmas. Not that the

celebrations with the White Fathers, and especially those at home, had not been beautiful—indeed they always have been the most beautiful days of the year—but over here the joy is more deep.

In Cell PP, on Christmas 1964, Dom Damian was sleeping off the sedative that Dom Columba had given him. Thanks to Dom Columba's stoking his stove, his cell was very warm. During the Mass at Dawn, the sun had began to filter into the refrigerator-like church. The cold and damp had settled in like a fellow monk. The morning was cloudy. The monks went back to their cells until the Mass of the Day, said before Sext at 11:00 AM.

Two cells south of Dom Damian, in Cell SS, Dom Lorenzo had returned from the Mass at Dawn and Dom Bruno's private Mass. Newcomers had come and gone, leaving Dom Lorenzo again the last novice. From Calabria, Dom Lorenzo looked like a typical Southern European, short and swarthy, with a stocky build, a rather square face, and dark, happy eyes. He had a perpetual beard shadow. Dom Lorenzo had, of course, seen St. Bruno's second Charterhouse in Calabria and hoped to return there when he was solemnly professed. As a young man, he had immigrated to England and worked in a hotel, then took a vacation to India where he became a Buddhist. Returning to England, he studied nursing with the dream of returning to India. Then, like Hans, he decided to help India by a life of prayer. He was interested only in God, *Soli Deo.*

For him, Parkminster and the very fact that he had such an opportunity to become a *Certosino* overwhelmed him, time and again. Dom Lorenzo went his own way and didn't pay much attention to the others. He didn't like to talk on the walks; on some days, he wouldn't talk at all. He did not have any inner struggles, even though he had great difficulties with academic study. All he needed was his simple religious faith: Mary was his mother, and the incarnate Jesus was in the host. He was not drawn to theological disputes over the Trinity and Redemption. Questions such as, "Is all of humanity redeemed?" eluded him. This Christmas Day, he sat at his semicircular table facing the garden. The sun had already reached his east-facing window on the upper floor, but the cloister wall still blocked the sun from reaching his garden. He could glimpse the dead stalks of flowers in the shade-covered garden. As he looked out, he thought, "In a few months, I can work the garden again. I might graft new stock on those old espaliered pear trees, maybe plant some miniature box hedges in front of them."

This year, as the last novice, Dom Lorenzo had an important job—building the fire in Dom Joseph's cell for St. Stephen's Day. Dom Lorenzo reminded himself to gather some pine boughs that afternoon to throw on the fire, but he tried to put this distracting duty out of his mind. He still missed the sights and smells of Christmas, though he had come to like the quietness of Christmas Day. He eagerly anticipated St. Stephen's Day, when he would get his Christmas mail from his family, which he'd read again and again once Dom Joseph had given it to him. He tried to find ways to get Dom Joseph to give him his mail before Christmas. He sometimes felt angry when he had to wait for it. He often felt angry for reasons he didn't understand.

Perhaps an hour later, by the time the sun climbed over the walls of the gardens on the north side of the cloister, a brother had just rung Dom Philip's bell to announce the special Christmas dinner. Dom Philip opened the *gamelles* with pleasure, knowing that this would be the best meal of the year. Dom Guy, the Procurator, always tried to put on a good Christmas meal. He was an excellent provider for the monks and always had special food for Christmas. This year, young Brother Hugh's father, a Scottish lord, had sent a crate of fresh salmon caught on his own estate. Dom Guy had enthusiastically taught Brother Christopher how to prepare it, along with a Christmas pudding smothered in his own favorite white sauce with brandy. Dom Guy had recipes for a hundred sauces and some were quite good, others barely edible.

In Cell S, south and next to Dom Lorenzo's cell, Dom Ignatius sat in his garden. In spite of the cold, spring didn't seem very far away to him. In the church year, spring was already happening with the birth of Christ. Looking at the dead roses, he knew that they would soon be alive again. He thought about the birth of Christ, and how Christmas was the beginning of a cycle. Christ was born so that He could die. Christmas Day set the liturgical clock ticking. The sun on this Christmas Day had finally cleared the wall of the neighboring Cell R on the south side, and the bright sun burned off the chill of the morning haze. At this time of day, the air outside in the garden was warmer than the inside of his cell. With walls on all four sides, the gardens were microclimates, and Dom Ignatius could usually keep his roses blooming until early December. He had moved into Cell S two years ago after simple profession. He now felt quite at home.

Dom Ignatius loved the familiarity of this day, the predictability of what each Christmas would be like. He had lost none of the enthusiasm expressed in the letter to his parents four years earlier. He loved the simplicity of Carthusian life, the routine that never changed, the "plain food" of the psalms. Dom Ignatius reflected on Psalm 2:7: "You are my son; Today have I begotten you." He felt great comfort as he again delved into the mystery that he and all the monks were beloved children of God, beautiful in the eyes of God. He took out the notes he had taken from a 1960 sermon that Dom Emmanuel had delivered in the Chapter House.

> Thus the joy of Christ is won by sharing in a kind of great cascade of love which starts from the Father, reaches the Son who prolongs it in our direction and that we in turn ought to prolong in that of others, until the unity between us is realized. "That all may be one."

Dom Emmanuel had always been his favorite monk. While struggling with the doubts stirred up when he received minor orders in London, Dom Ignatius had asked the Prior if he could talk to Dom Emmanuel for spiritual direction. After their meeting, they sent notes back and forth for a while. Dom Ignatius looked at the last typewritten note he had received. In it, Dom Emmanuel had taken back his earlier affirmation that contemplation was possible only in the solitary life. He said, *"Mon affirmation . . . est évidemment trop absolue."* Dom Ignatius felt relieved. He also thought about the cascade of love. He remembered Isaiah 9:2:

> The people that walked in darkness
> Have seen a great light;
> Those who dwelt in a land of deep darkness
> On them a light has shown.

During the last four years, Dom Ignatius had also seen a great light. His goals had changed.

When Dom Ignatius had joined the Carthusians, he had planned to become perfect, a saint. He had had a clear-cut view of right and wrong, of perfect and imperfect. Over the years, he became content with remaining a fragment, an unfinished saint, a saint that the life would carve from his own spirit. Today, on his fifth Christmas, he thought that he had become much more tolerant, more easygoing, more concerned with the other monks. He had developed a sensitive, wordless awareness of them. He knew how tense Dom Philip had been last night, although he simply couldn't understand why he had become so overwrought. The singing had inspired him, and the liturgy continued to amaze him—surely that was enough? Dom Ignatius had also been sensitive to Dom Damian's growing distress. His awareness had another consequence that surprised and worried him. Since August, he and Dom Philip had been taking a class in moral theology from Dom Anselm. Their supplemental textbook, *De Castitate,* discussed homosexuality, a concept new to Dom Ignatius but one he instinctively recognized because he had never felt any attraction toward women. The book reiterated that any homosexual activity was a mortal sin.

To distract himself, he thought about St. Stephen's Day, one of his favorite days in the Charterhouse. His Germanic soul loved everything about Christmastime, especially Christmas carols and warm fires; for him, St. Stephen's Day was a very joyful event. As the sun started to go down, his garden became chilly, and he went inside before getting ready to leave for Christmas Vespers. His cell, Cell S, was the farthest from the church, and if he didn't leave at the first sound of the bell, he would keep the other monks waiting.

Dom Columba was on the other side of the cloister, in Cell I. When he returned to his cell after Vespers, the sun flooded his garden over the lower wall on the south side of the cloister. This was Dom Columba's sixth Christmas at Parkminster, his first as a solemn, a professed monk for the rest of his earthly life. He had looked forward all year to this day when he could keep his mind clear and open to God. He didn't read or even pray in the usual sense. He just knelt in his oratory, filtering out all the thoughts that might keep him from God, putting them into the Cloud of Forgetting. Sometimes God spoke to him, sometimes God was quiet. Dom Columba was content either way. He kept his mind quiet, brushed away distractions as if they were flies, and kept focused on the mysterious reality that the monks called God.

In Cell NN, in contrast to Cell I, there was no sun at all. After Christmas Vespers, Dom Leo could see the sun on the roofs of the Charterhouse, on top of the cloister and his ambulatory, but because of the direction his cell faced, there was no direct light for him at all after three o'clock. Dom Leo would have liked to go down to his workshop to work on his lathe, but the statutes forbade manual labor on Christmas Day. He didn't tolerate much physical inactivity. He needed to move so he could keep meditating. He paced around his dark ambulatory—back and forth, back and forth, faster and faster. He tried to maintain a really prayerful awareness of God's presence. He thought not so much about the birth of Christ as about Christ's life. He liked to enter into the spirit of the liturgical season, carried along each year, ever deeper. He theorized that Christmas really started on March 25, the feast of the Annunciation. The virginal conception of Jesus shouted that the birth of Christ was wholly God's work.

He too enjoyed the idea that the liturgical year was beginning again. He realized that the solemnity of Christmas, as with all the great feasts, was most apparent not in the community Mass but in the Night Office. He loved the grand sequences of the Christmas liturgy. This year, the solemn, familiar readings had acquired new meaning for him; they impressed themselves on him in a different way. The eccentric chanting voices of the senior monks pulled him into the depths of this ancient feast. Dom Leo settled into his chair, put his hands on his table, and became very quiet, letting the liturgy of the Mass of the Day sink into him—*"Puer natus est nobis. . . . Cantate Domino canticum novum."*

He had, however, an unexpected distraction that he could do nothing to quell. Dom Leo had had a very upset stomach all afternoon; he felt nauseous. The Advent fast had included abstinence from milk products. The sudden return of dairy products, especially in the form of rich white sauce, was too much for the stomachs of many monks. Dom Leo thought about tolerating his discomfort, but word had gone around the novitiate that if you felt ill on Christmas Day, you could go down to Father Master for a "medicinal" slug of "Elixir Vegetal," an original concoction of the Chartreuse liqueur, 71 percent alcohol, 140 proof. Before Compline, with some self-reproach, Dom Leo went to Cell OO, Dom Joseph's cell, for some "Elixir Vegetal."

Next to Cell NN, in Cell MM, Dom Malachi was coming to the end of the worst Christmas he had ever had in the Charterhouse. He tried not to kick the iron box on legs that the monks euphemistically insisted was a stove. It had been going out all day. Each time he returned to cell from church, the fire was out, and the cell was freezing. By Vespers, the stove had filled the place with thick acrid smoke. Dom Malachi had spent Christmas with legs numb from the knees down, trying to clean up the mess and keep the fire going. Before Compline, the fire started burning properly, and Dom Malachi could finally concentrate on praying. Dom Malachi had been distracted at the long Night Office, but he had discovered that while chanting the psalms, he could consciously give himself permission to continue to think about his current project for a few minutes. Then, he could return his full attention to the Office.

As he sat in his oratory, he thought about what his Carthusian life meant to him. He didn't feel called to be a priest. He knew that he wanted to be a hermit monk, but he argued with himself about the Church's position on priests: On the one hand, the Church needs priests and therefore emphasizes the "glory" of the priesthood; on the other hand, the Church proclaims with ardent faith that God saved mankind by the sufferings of the Lamb, "*Agnus Dei qui tollis peccata mundi.*" And when Dom Malachi thought about the world he left, it was clear to him that there were many suffering lambs that Christ unites to himself. So why does the Church need monk priests, especially hermit monk priests? The questions frustrated him, making him feel rather angry with the Church and perhaps also with God. After having asked him to follow Christ into the desert, God had not sent him any Fathers of the Desert to advise him. He always had to look within himself for the monastic tools; to develop a fine ear, if not for music, for listening to the voice of God.

On Christmas Day, Dom Malachi looked back and tried to see what the Lord Jesus was doing with him. He thought about the extreme anxiety he had felt right before he took simple vows and the pain he felt now. His life in this damp cell seemed odd, and he again realized how much he loved to nurture people. It was Christmas Day, and he had no human contact at all. He couldn't even write to his parents. It was painful to him. Dom Malachi had a great faith, but he also had a great heart. After Vespers, Dom Malachi had climbed up onto his windowsill so that he could look over the Charterhouse wall. He could hear the children of the neighboring farmer playing with their new toys on the other side of the wall. He thought again about his first Christmas and the letter he had received from the young lady he had met on the *Mauretania.* To convince himself of the righteousness of the Carthusian life, he focused on the verse from Scripture, "If you love me, I will turn all things to the Good."

⊕

The liturgy on St. Stephen's Day was much as usual, only a little longer due to the feast being within the Octave of Christmas, and so having extra *memorias* and various other prayers. About 12:30 PM, after Sext in church, dinner in the Refectory, and None in church, the novices moved toward Dom Joseph's corner cell. Leaving None quickly before the other monks, Dom Lorenzo hurried to the novices' conference room and went straight up the short flight of stairs. The fireplace, on the east side of the room, was made of some sort of gray-black stone with a smooth finish. During his morning manual labor break, Dom Lorenzo had laid the fire very diligently, hoping it would light with only one of the Charterhouse matches. He had started out with shavings from his lathe, then some pine boughs, then he carefully built a layer of wood that he had chopped very thin, in even pieces; then he laid on some whole logs. He had put a pile of pine branches next to the fireplace to toss on the fire. Right now, he lit one match, and the fire started quickly, with little need for tending.

By this time, Dom Joseph and the other novices were coming up the steps to the conference room. Eager to soak up the once-a-year warmth that was starting to fill the room, they took their places at benches facing the window and the church. As always, Dom Joseph sat at his table facing west, with the large window behind him, with his back to the church. Although Dom Joseph could easily have preached without notes, he took pains to read his sermon as custom required, without any rhetorical flourishes or dramatic intonations. The presentation was, in fact, dull. He read about St. Stephen, the first deacon and martyr, and how appropriate it was to have his feast on the day after Christmas. St. Stephen, a Greek-speaking Jew, had preached that the new Christian religion was the fulfillment of the Jewish tradition. The Jews hated him for this belief and stoned him to death. Saul of Tarsus, later St. Paul, ordered the stoning. Dom Joseph explained that the purpose of Christ's birth was his death, as was St. Stephen's.

After he finished reading the sermon, Dom Joseph got up from his table, and with considerable gusto said, "Merry Christmas," in eight different languages. The novices knew that he was showing off a bit, but since it was Christmas, that seemed all right. Then Dom Joseph distributed Christmas cards and letters. The novices would read the letters later in cell, but they passed the cards around before putting them on the mantelpiece over the fire. Dom Ignatius still found putting Christmas cards on the mantelpiece a strange English custom. Dom Joseph also gave the novices Christmas presents from their parents. These they opened right away. Many of the presents were sweets that were immediately shared with the other novices. The novices had a good laugh over the Christmas present that Dom Ignatius's father sent him—a box of cigars. Monks never indulged in such luxuries. The Prior would keep them and give them to Dom Ignatius's father to smoke on his next visit. Dom Ignatius commented, "I wish they had been chocolate cigars."

Whenever the novices got together, they would tell stories, and Dom Ignatius, of course, had a story about the Christmas menu. The monks never ate meat or poultry of any sort. But apparently, due to some quirk in the medieval taxonomy of fauna, moorhens—small ducklike birds that seem to spend quite a lot of time feeding underwater—did not count as poultry. Some benefactor had heard this and donated a box of the nonprohibited birds for Christmas dinner. Everyone got very sick. The hens were exceptionally bony and made the monks, who were not used to meat, feel quite queasy. From then on, salmon was the preferred Christmas entrée. Dom Leo commented, "That was the punishment for eating meat." They all talked about the year, 1960, when Dom Damian was the last novice and overdid building the fire—he almost burned the Charterhouse down. Besides having built an overlarge fire, he had forgotten that his job was also to put it out, and a coal had escaped and burned into the wooden floor. Dom Malachi liked to tease Dom Lorenzo from Italy. He knew how much he hated the cold and asked him if he was going to keep his cell as hot as he had last winter. Dom Lorenzo had put too many hot coals in his fire bin (a cut-down Esso drum); the tin became hot and burned the paint, setting off noxious fumes. By the time the monks missed him at Night Office, Dom Lorenzo had become partially asphyxiated and was unconscious. None of the novices let him forget it.

After more stories, the novices started singing Christmas carols, with no accompaniment, of course. Dom Philip disliked this celebration, but he had had great fun all week planning what carols to sing and in what order. He had copied out the lyrics on half sheets of blank magazine pages. Although he hated the familial environment, he wasn't being judged by the solemns, so he wasn't very anxious. With only five novices present, his strong baritone could easily hold the group together, even with Doms Lorenzo and Ignatius grating on his nerves. And he had the help of Dom Joseph.

Dom Philip had chosen all of his favorite carols. He decided to have the group begin with "Joy to the World" as an easy starter—they were used to this carol from choir practice. In deference to the origins of the order in France, he followed with the French "Les anges dans nos campagnes" and "Il est né, le divine enfant." At this point, Dom Bonaventure arrived. The novices all stopped singing, and Dom Joseph said, "Thank you for coming, Father Prior." In heavily accented French English, Dom Bonaventure said, "Merry Christmas" to the group. As a sign of respect for the Prior, Dom Joseph and all the novices knelt on one knee and kissed one of the bands of his cowl. The Prior was very humble and seemed to be embarrassed much of the time. He waved his hand and said, "Go right on." Then he added, "Would you mind if I join you?"

Dom Philip handed Dom Bonaventure a copy of the lyrics, and the singing continued. Dom Bonaventure had a strong voice and was a help with the carols, especially the French and Italian ones. Because two of the five novices were American, Dom Philip had thought it fair to include "Go Tell It on the Mountain" which Dom Malachi sang with great gusto. "In the Bleak Mid-Winter" suited Dom Joseph's Irish tenor. With a bow to Dom Ignatius, the group sang the fourteenth-century German carol "In Dulci Jubilo," which Dom Ignatius sang lustily. Dom Philip especially liked "All Through the Night," which he sang beautifully. The other novices pestered him to sing "All Through the Night" in solo, but he refused—although he would have loved to sing the song again. The novices continued, eating sweets while they sang. Because they were in England, Dom Philip had included "God Rest Ye Merry Gentlemen"; Dom Leo interrupted to correct Dom Philip because he was not singing a perfect fifth between "rest" and "ye." Dom Philip didn't bother to respond. Dom Lorenzo liked singing "Gesu Bambino." Dom Philip had, of course, included "Veni Veni Emmanuel" and "Adeste Fideles." He concluded the singing with a carol about another St. Stephen's Day: "Good King Wenceslaus." The novices sang it so well that they insisted on singing it again.

When the caroling was over, the novices chatted for a while. Dom Bonaventure, looking as exhausted as usual, moved around the room talking amiably to them. He was a very gentle man whose round reddish face and round horn-rimmed glasses gave him an owl-like demeanor, although his lumbering movement was anything but birdlike. He was always jovial. He talked to Dom Ignatius about a book he was reading, and he again urged him to read Origen. He complimented Dom Malachi on his renovated garden that had produced a great profusion of flowers for the altar the previous fall. He asked Dom Philip about the American Christmas carols that he hadn't heard before. He was particularly interested in "Go Tell It on the Mountain"—he became even more interested when Dom Philip told him that the carol was a Negro spiritual. He talked to Dom Leo about the very proficient work he was doing on his lathe, making monastic presents, and suggested that he add wooden candlesticks to his repertoire. Later, he saw Doms Malachi and Leo talking together and moved over to join them to discuss how this Christmas differed from a Trappist one.

When Dom Bonaventure left, the novices chatted for a few more minutes. After a short while, Dom Joseph said, *"Benedicite";* the novices responded, "*Dominus,*" and, except for Dom Lorenzo, returned to their cells until Vespers at 2:45 PM. Dom Lorenzo cleaned up and extinguished the fire.

Back in their cells, the novices all felt the sharp contrast: warmth and togetherness on December 26, damp, cold, and solitude for the rest of the year. They responded in very different ways to St. Stephen's Day. Ironically, with its intent to please, to lessen the rigor of the life for the novices, with all its color and warmth, especially because of its color and warmth, St. Stephen's Day created a challenge for some of them.

Dom Malachi found it especially hard to manage the transition between singing Christmas carols in a warm place and the solitude of his chilly cell. He felt slightly dizzy, slightly disoriented. The contrast was almost too much. The pain was intensified, in part, by a renewed sense of guilt about the woman from the *Mauretania.* He felt guilty both because he had left her abruptly, a woman he loved and who trusted him, and also because he had postponed his entrance to the

Charterhouse. He had hesitated after promising God to live for Him alone.

Each of the other four novices responded in different ways. Dom Ignatius basked in the afterglow of the celebration. The occasion had met his need for human companionship; he felt better about his ability to continue. He looked forward to reading his parents' letters. He also looked forward to the afternoon's manual work. The Reverend Father had introduced a new notation that had to be written by hand in the huge antiphonaries. Since Dom Ignatius had an interest in calligraphy, Dom Joseph had given him the job. Dom Jerome would be stopping by to instruct him. Doms Leo and Lorenzo had particularly enjoyed singing the Christmas carols, each being reminded of other, very communal Christmases they had experienced with their families in Dublin and Calabria.

Dom Philip had thoroughly enjoyed the singing and the chocolates. He even admired Dom Joseph's sermon, but he hated the festivity, the togetherness, the unmonastic feelings that it had aroused. The celebration made him remember all the phony family get-togethers with required rituals that he had grimly endured at home. He decided to block out the memory of the day until the next year. He had survived St. Stephen's Day for three years. He had just two more to endure before solemn profession would bring him the kind of solitude that blanketed even the festive fires of St. Stephen's Day.

CHAPTER 16

Monks Disappearing (Winter 1965)

In nine months, between May 1964 and March 1965, at least seven novices left, some because of Dom Joseph's brusqueness, which in the confines of Parkminster could prove very destructive. As early as 1961, Dom Joseph had forced Dom Edward, an English novice, to leave. He had grown up in Africa, becoming a Catholic at age eighteen. His conversion infuriated his father, who threw him out of their house, giving him only £20 and plane fare back to England. His father died while he was at Parkminster. Before he entered the Charterhouse, he had been a member of the Royal Air Force, and he prided himself on self-discipline. Dom Edward, supposedly, had been asked to leave because he wasn't eating even the one Carthusian meal a day. Dom Bruno had told him to lose weight because, he said, "If you get fat, you can't pray," and he gave him intricate and complicated directions on what to eat. At this point, Dom Joseph arrived. What Dom Joseph did not realize was that, in part, Dom Edward hadn't been eating because of the unbearable confusion and stress he felt over the feud between his former Novice Master, Dom Bruno, and Dom Joseph.

Dom Edward's craggy British face became pinched and tense. Dom Joseph would ignore him for weeks on end, not even walking with him. He then would spend three hours in his cell, haranguing him about Dom Bruno. Dom Edward had the audacity to tell Dom Joseph in his very deep, gravelly voice that he had met with more charity in the barrack room of the Royal Air Force. Dom Joseph made sure that Dom Edward left the next day—for the hospital in Cheam. When he returned two weeks later, he was told to leave for good. In fact, Dom Joseph was still so angry that he had the Prior himself tell Dom Edward to leave. The Prior told Dom Edward, not unkindly, that a vote on him would have split the house apart. He also suggested that some people have a vocation to the Carthusian life for a limited time, for four or five years, not a lifetime. The Prior instructed him to leave during Vespers so that none of the other novices would see his departure. Dom Edward couldn't understand why he was being asked to leave. He didn't know what he had done wrong. He felt unbearably lonely in the Guest House without saying good-bye to anyone except Dom Columba.

Ten years after Dom Edward left, Dom Columba, who had become Prior by that time, called him, and said, "We've decided to be Christians. Why don't you come for a visit?" Theo Faber returned to Parkminster with his two children. Only after the visit did he stop having a recurrent nightmare that had persisted since he left. The nightmare depicted people tearing his habit off when he was out in the world. He believes that his Carthusian experience immeasurably affected his life afterward, and he considers it one of his life's "most influential experiences. In spite of the pain towards the end, I have never regretted those years . . . the experience gave me an ease and need for solitude." He concludes that at a purely psychological level, "it was important simply because I did it. I suppose that it is a bit like someone who has managed to run a four-minute mile. They may not have got a world record, but they achieved something."

Dom Joseph had been intemperate at other times. When Dom Columba was still a novice, he had been impressed at a Sunday conference and wanted to hear more about the sermon. After Vespers, he went to Dom Joseph's cell and said enthusiastically, "Benedicite," before eagerly jumping right into the topic: "I want to talk about the conference this morning." Dom Joseph anticipated criticism, especially from Dom Columba, who was an experienced monk. He jerked upright in his chair and snapped angrily, "Well, what about it?" Dom Columba didn't know what to say. He felt as if he had been electrocuted. He couldn't respond. He couldn't even move. He finally mumbled something and left. He went back to his cell and sat slumped over on the bench in his oratory. After some time, Dom Joseph came to his cell, perhaps feeling guilty for his defensiveness. Dom Columba just said, "I have never seen that side of you."

The statutes instructed the solemns that "to continue to keep a candidate when it is manifest he lacks the necessary qualities, is false—we almost said cruel—compassion." The solemns had voted Dom Paul out in 1963, against the recommendation of the Novice Master and the Prior. Before leaving, Dom Paul wrote to a newly professed solemn, "Thank you for all your kindness over the years. A great pain hit me when I was told I had to leave. The life meant everything to me. Dear Father, in the midst of all this grief, I offered up all my pain for your health. I plan to go on to the priesthood." Because the solemns never spoke to the novices, and only saw them in choir and at the Sunday Chapter, this vote is difficult to understand. In earlier years at Parkminster, the solemns had accepted the Novice Master's recommendations almost without question. Shortly after Dom Joseph had become a solemn, Dom Bruno, then Novice Master, had recommended that a particular novice, an American priest, be voted out. This novice had been in the novitiate with Dom Joseph, and they were good friends. Dom Joseph lobbied the other solemns to allow the novice to make solemn profession. When Dom Bruno made his recommendation, Dom Joseph challenged him, and the solemns voted the novice into the order. The new solemn caused Parkminster more trouble than any other monk. Perhaps the solemns had reason to distrust Dom Joseph's judgment.

Dom Bonaventure decided that Dom Mark should leave and "get married." After four years, Dom Mark could hardly sleep at all. He was so nervous that on one occasion, Dom Joseph sent him to Dom Ignatius's cell, where he kept talking about what had happened to him the night before he left for the Charterhouse. The conversation left Dom Ignatius very disturbed. The novices were supposed to talk to the Novice Master if something troubled them, but Dom Joseph was not always available to them. He was cavalier about their personal problems and had no understanding of psychology—nor the desire to learn. Dom Mark left in November 1963, completed a Cambridge doctoral thesis in early Italian literary history in 1973, was elected to the Australian National Academy in 1985, and gained a personal chair in 1987. He now has four daughters and two grandsons. He visits the Charterhouse when in England and has recently built a new home in Western Australia containing a replica of a *cubiculum.* For him, "Those four or so years at that juncture of the post-war period were crucial to my life and later career." His memory is of "the brief intense companionship of the novitiate with those gifted, slightly older men, their range of backgrounds, and a common serious intent" and of how it is "comforting, even touching, to think that men we knew forty years ago still nurture good memories of that period and experience."

In early April 1965, Dom Joseph wrote to the Reverend Father asking to be relieved of his job as Novice Master. The two Monk Visitors appeared at Parkminster, came to Dom Columba, and confirmed, "There's trouble in the novitiate. Some of the novices feel that Dom Joseph is totalitarian; we'll have to appoint you as Novice Master." Dom Columba protested that he was recently professed, "not even two years out," but the Visitors insisted: "You have the capacity for helping people think through their problems. You are a healer." Without more discussion, the Visitors dismissed Dom Joseph and appointed Dom Columba as Novice Master. Assigned to the Charterhouse in Pisa, Italy, Dom Joseph was happy to get back to being a full-time monk. Dom Columba did not want to be Novice Master. He worried that the novices might not respond well to having a Novice Master who had been a fellow novice. Would they trust a newcomer as a spiritual guide? Dom Philip missed Dom Joseph because they shared similar backgrounds and a theoretical bent, but he trusted Dom Columba. But Dom Columba didn't find that out for sure until thirty-four years later.

As Novice Master, Dom Columba had to advise the novices on whether they should stay. As a medical doctor, Dom Columba knew that most men would have difficulty with the cold, the fasts, and the broken sleep. Did the novice have the physical strength to bear the burdens of the order? Dom Columba had to decide whether the novice could live on his own resources for the rest of his life. Did he have the maturity, the balance? Nothing came from the outside. Had the novice stored up enough emotional resources to last for sixty-odd years? Could he get that energy from books, which Guigo called, "the imperishable food of our souls"? The novice obviously had to have an aptitude for solitude, but Dom Columba believed that the novice also had to be able to live in community. Dom Columba thought that monks had to be tolerant, even easygoing, to survive. Some of the novices developed very clear-cut ideas of what a monk should be and do, and they thought that the other monks should share their ideal. In Dom Columba's view, these men would get into trouble.

Dom Columba also worried about how the solemns would react to a Novice Master whose decision-making rule was: "If you have reasonable doubts about the life, you should leave." Dom Columba was convinced that every person was unique, that individuality was the gift of God. He thought that his job was to discover the true calling of each novice and to encourage it, to respond to the way God was moving in each individual. He believed that not every Christian was meant for the radical Carthusian life, but he also knew that the monks, and the novices, defined success or failure in terms of their ability to persevere in cell.

The remaining novices were unsettled by the change of Novice Master and the exodus of novices. The departure of a solemn, however, was even more of a threat; the novices worried: If a solemn left, might they also leave, even after solemn profession? Dom Ludolph left in 1964. Through their secret grapevine, the novices heard that after sixteen years in the Charterhouse, Dom Ludolph left the very night he received a letter telling him that his father, a sports writer for a large New Zealand newspaper, had died. Rumors proliferated. Dom Ludolph didn't even wait to get secular clothes, he just walked out of the Charterhouse gate before Night Office and was never seen again. One novice thought that he had joined relatives in Ireland. Another novice heard that first he was in the hospital, but that he was then assigned as a parish priest. He could not become a layperson because he had been ordained—but he had no experience or training to be a parish priest. He couldn't cope—he just left and went to London, where he got a job doing the index for the English Jerusalem Bible. After that, he met a nurse and got a job in a shoe factory. Dom Ludolph has chosen not to comment on the stories. But less than six months after he left Parkminster, he visited Rome, when Vatican II was still in progress. He was not welcomed by the Procurator General of the Carthusian order, but his former teachers, the Marist Fathers, arranged for him to say Mass on St. Peter's tomb.

The first novice to leave of the five who had arrived between July 1960 and March 1961 was Dom Ignatius. By Christmas 1964, he found himself struggling with serious doubts about his vocation, and in early February, he left, less than a year before he would have made final vows. The moral theology classes had taught him that he might be homosexual. He agonized about it. According to Catholic moral theology at that time, homosexual acts were much more sinful than a heterosexual rape, even of a young girl. He was terrified by the discovery, and to try to relieve his tension, he endlessly cut wood until he was exhausted. He couldn't talk to any of the priests in the Charterhouse. Talking about a "sin" so stigmatized, within the monastic community especially, would have grave implications for his chance to make solemn profession. He asked Dom Bonaventure for a confessor from outside the Charterhouse. As he had for other monks, the Prior called in a Jesuit priest who was also a psychologist specializing in helping priests. Faced with what he was learning about himself, in confusion and fright, Dom Ignatius finally went to Dom Columba, whom the Prior, on Dom Ignatius's request, had already made his confessor. Nothing is worse for a monk than sin, and wishing to reassure Dom Ignatius, Dom Columba, in the language of the era, insisted that homosexuality was not a sin but "a disease." The July 27, 1964, issue of *Life* magazine carried a fourteen-page report titled, "Homosexuality in America," referring to it as a "social disorder." Many doctors such as Dom Columba saw homosexuality as a disease. Dom Ignatius was relieved that he was not committing a sin. Before God, he was innocent. Dom Ignatius continued to see Dom Columba, who encouraged him to go forward with solemn profession. But he reminded him that in the eyes of the Catholic Church, taking solemn vows was permanent, until death, and to go forward having doubts was risky. With that in mind, and still in doubt, Dom Ignatius decided to leave.

He wrote to his parents, "My nerves suddenly could not measure up to solitude. This has been a very common thing here. Of about thirty-six applicants since 1960, thirty-two did not stand up to it, adding myself, and the American with the recent nervous breakdown, and of the remaining . . . I have my doubts for three." Dom Ignatius wrote a request for dispensation:

Reverend Father in Christ,

I ask for a dispensation from my religious vows, which in the normal course of events would expire on December 8, 1965.

Reasons for this petition are:

1) According to the judgment of my confessor, notable change of circumstances which could in no way have been foreseen; had I foreseen it, I would certainly not have taken the temporary vows.

2) Spiritual and nervous deterioration as a result of 1).

In Christo,
Fr. Ignatius [N].

Dom Leo had found out about Dom Ignatius's decision and left a note in Dom Joseph's hatch: "Dear Father Master, Please give this to Dom Ignatius." Dom Leo had written the note on the back of a letter from one of his sisters. Dom Joseph read the note and gave it to Dom Ignatius:

†

Dear Dom Ignatius,

Goodbye is too final a word—just "au revoir" . . . It makes the Patria so much the more desirable to know that we will meet there again. I make few friends, I never lose them. Besides it is in Xt [Christ] that we are most together and I know you are as much in him as ever. Bald heads, long habits have never meant anything to me. I thank you for the book, only regret I have nothing at all to give in return. But I have my prayers and my love in Christ, maybe a little for your own sake too. It has been a real pleasure to have had you as companion for this part of the road, the place will be so much duller without you. God bless, in Xt fr. Leo [N]

Remember me in your prayers too!

PS: Have an address somewhere. I might be looking for a job in London myself!

Like all the novices, Dom Leo didn't know if the solemns would vote him into the order. They would decide his fate in eight months and he knew that he might indeed be looking for a job. Dom Ignatius was scheduled to leave on Saturday, but since Friday was the *rasura* day,

Dom Joseph insisted that he leave a day early so that the other novices wouldn't notice that he wasn't having his hair cut. The Prior gave Dom Ignatius, now Hans again, £20 but asked that he sign a note saying that he would pay it back; Hans's parents repaid the Prior as soon as Hans wrote to them. Three weeks earlier, Dom Joseph had alerted another ex-novice, Romilly Pitt, an upper-class Englishman who had left four months earlier, to meet him. Romilly met Hans at Victoria Station. The sun had been shining brilliantly when he left Parkminster, but by the time he got off the train, London was enveloped in fog, as was Hans. Romilly met him waving a German magazine with a picture of a nearly naked woman on the cover. Romilly took Hans for a steak dinner at the Hilton in Park Lane by Hyde Park, close to the site where the eighteen Carthusians were hung, drawn, and quartered centuries earlier. Hans was horrified and repelled by the London of 1965: men with long hair, women in pants suits, and worse yet, women in skirts so short that their knees weren't covered. Romilly said they were called miniskirts and had been invented by Mary Quant, who had a shop on Carnaby Street a half mile away.

Alone in a foreign country, Hans went back to the White Fathers, who gave him a place to stay. He wrote to his parents, "Had to leave a day before planned because Fr. Master didn't want other novices to know: Fr. Master didn't want trouble and questions, didn't want distractions." His parents had been so proud of him. How could he face them and his other relatives? Hans was too uncomfortable to go home right away, so he stayed with the White Fathers in London for several weeks and visited a woman who had been his nanny in East Berlin before the war. He felt totally out of place in the world he had left five years earlier. The students at the White Fathers kept hearing someone getting up at midnight to chant the psalms. When the rector of the seminary heard the rumor, he decided that Hans should leave and get acclimated to the outside world. When Hans did return to West Berlin, his first purchases were the records of the famous contralto Kathleen Ferrier. He was accepted to a very competitive medical school and successfully returned to his plan of being a missionary in Africa. Yet he spent years questioning doctors and priests in an attempt to accept his own homosexuality. The openness introduced by Vatican II gave him courage that lasted even when the conservative church returned.

⊕

To the present day, Dom Damian remembers very little of what happened between Christmas Day, 1964, and the day he left the Guest House before Easter week, April 11, 1965. Much of the following information comes from the other novices and from letters written by Doms Joseph and Columba.

On February 2, 1965, Dom Damian celebrated his second anniversary as a professed monk. A year from now, he would ask the solemns to vote him into the order for good. Dom Joseph felt that Dom Damian was tough and would soldier ahead. Dom Columba, the doctor, felt that he had learned that he needed to keep his cell warm and that he would make it to solemn profession. Dom Columba had given strict instructions to Dom Damian that he keep his cell above 65°. But as the winter went by, Dom Damian couldn't keep warm. Nothing seemed to warm him. His fingernails were always white. His hands were swollen with chilblains from the cold. He couldn't sleep. He obsessively thought about Dom Ludolph, whose mysterious disappearance shortly before Christmas tormented him. He thought about his father's criticisms. In late February, he went to choir again, the first time since his collapse on Christmas morning.

The first day he was back, he had a lesson to sing. Dom Philip noticed that Dom Damian was again twirling the stubble of hair above his right ear—the typical indication of his distress. Dom Damian was so anxious that after he started singing the lesson, his voice just trailed off. Monks weren't supposed to look at anything but their books, but Dom Damian felt Dom Philip's concern and rage. In fact, Dom Philip was thinking, "How dare they ask him to read a lesson in his state?" Dom Philip had talked to Dom Joseph about Dom Damian, but to no avail. Dom Damian kept struggling to get better; he desperately wanted to stay. Dom Columba told the brothers to leave a half bottle of cider in his hatch to help him get to sleep after Night Office.

Toward the end of Lent, Dom Damian, his fingertips cracked and raw, again started shaking uncontrollably. He could not face life in cell. This time, a three-day sleep had no effect. Dom Joseph came to him and said, his fine features tensely knitted together, "I'm no longer going to take responsibility." Dom Damian didn't know exactly what that meant, but Dom Joseph immediately moved him to the Guest House. Dom Damian would not talk to his fellow novices again, even to say good-bye. He, like the other disappearing monks, would just vanish. In spite of his wretched health, he didn't want to leave. And he didn't want to face the disgrace of having gone to the most rigorous order in the Catholic Church and then failed. He looked again at the telegram that his Aunt Rita had sent from Chicago four years ago: "Bon voyage, Chuck. A bargain is a bargain. Prayers here for prayers there."

The following day, Dom Guy drove Dom Damian to the American Embassy in London to get a passport. The passport depicted a shaven-haired, intense, but tired and anxious young man in a white hood. At the time, Dom Damian looked so scared, so terrified, that Dom Guy took him two miles south to the Tate Gallery (the Tate Britain since 2000) to cheer him up. They drove south from the American Embassy in Mayfair, past Victoria Station, and down to the river Thames. Dom Guy had delivered a paper on art history at Wadham College and was familiar with this world. The Tate Gallery is an imposing neoclassical building, located on the north bank of the Thames, not far from the Houses of Parliament. Built to house the art collection of the sugar tycoon Sir Henry Tate, the museum opened to the public in 1897 and houses the national collection of British art from 1500 to the present day, the largest and most comprehensive collection of British art in the world. Both monks, Dom Damian in particular, looked intently at the painting of Sir Thomas More standing by his prison window in the Tower of London. His daughter Margaret is visiting him, and both are looking out at the group of Carthusian monks being led away to their deaths. Later, in 1535, Henry VIII also beheaded More. Dom Damian was greatly attracted to the picture, but the excursion into the secular world made him unbelievably anxious. During the four and a half years he had been in the Charterhouse, London and the way people dressed had changed a lot. He felt that he had stumbled into unreality. He reached in his pocket for the Librium pills that the local doctor had given him for emergencies. But he remembered that the statutes said, "We should be careful not to use medicines in an abusive degree with damage to our quest of spiritual perfection." Dom Damian didn't want Dom Guy to see him taking the pill. He became so nervous that he dropped the bottle. Pills spilled all over the black-and-white checkerboard marble floor of the Tate Gallery. Everyone turned to stare at the pill-popping monk. Dom Damian tried not to pass out and only wished that he could be dead. Dom Guy looked at him, sad and puzzled, and hurried him back to the car. When they returned to Parkminster, Dom Guy told the Prior that he thought Dom Damian could not make it back to the States alone.

When they returned to the Charterhouse, Dom Guy took him to the tailor shop. Brother William found his original suitcase and secular clothes in the Porter's Lodge. For two weeks, while he waited for his father to come to take him home, he stayed in Room 6 of the Guest House. It felt much lonelier than his cell. He missed seeing the monks in choir. One day he walked eight miles to a small town in his civilian clothes and visited the local pub. He felt somewhat better. Dom Joseph agreed that he already looked better and that he seemed quite calm. He saw nothing emotional and thought it a very calm affair, almost a "reasoned" breakdown. Dom Joseph tried to be reassuring: "I am quite sure your health will pick up with time—it always does once one gets back into normal conditions of life." He often came to the Guest House to talk about his own troubles: "I have a hard time with Dom Leo, we're so much alike." But Dom Damian, again Chuck, found it hard to think of Dom Joseph having a hard time with anyone. Dom Joseph gave him *The Practice of the Presence of God.* He inscribed, "*ad usum D*" on the title page in pencil. Chuck also read and reread a paragraph he had translated from *Écrits spirituels* and had copied on the back of an old magazine.

> For the soul is, in the last resort, but a mere capacity. It has nothing from itself and in itself. It is in God it must draw to fill up the void, and this it does by the union with Him developed in prayer. It ought, therefore, rather receive than take. Consequently the perfect state of prayer consists in this, that the faculties of the soul are united in a contemplation marked by silence, calm, and expectancy. This being so, the soul's cooperation (in the work of sanctification) consists in consenting to the gifts of God and in receiving them. . . . This silence and this expectancy of the soul before God must constitute a state of dependence on the Author of all Gifts, of annihilation before Him and of adoration of His greatness.

Chuck accepted his annihilation, but for years after leaving Parkminster, he had Charterhouse dreams. He dreamed he was somehow back there, doing really well and thinking that he might just make solemn profession this time, but deep down, he knew that it simply wouldn't happen. As he waited for his father in the Guest House, he was still living in the Charterhouse psychologically. He worried about the plants abandoned in his cell. He wondered if his large Christmas cactus would survive until someone else used his cell.

Chuck also wished that he could have said good-bye to the other novices. He knew they would have noticed his prolonged absence and would be worried about him—and about themselves. He particularly wished he could have said good-bye to Dom Philip, who was the only one who had worried about him all along. Dom Philip's chuckle would have comforted him. Chuck went to see Dom Bonaventure before he left. After telling him how privileged he was to have had the experience of being a Carthusian novice, Dom Bonaventure told him that the dispensation from his vows would come from the Reverend Father in a few weeks. He asked him to sign and date the dispensation within ten days of receipt and return it to Parkminster for the archives. As usual, he advised him to read Origen: "I always read Origen, my boy, Origen solves everything." As his interim doctor, Dom Columba was also able to visit him. He looked into his anxious eyes and said in a compassionate but quiet, reasoned, and factual voice, "Don't worry. God is over it all."

Chuck's father, a physician, was afraid of flying, but he came within two weeks, before the Easter solemnities in the Charterhouse had begun, the week of April 11. He asked the Porter, Brother Raphael, for his son. Brother Raphael went to get Dom Joseph and mentioned that the father looked ten times worse than the son. Chuck went to meet his father by taking the longest way to the Gatehouse. He went back into Prior's Hall, through the cloister, past the *rasura* and Refectory, and down the wide, black-bricked path to the Gatehouse. Brother Raphael said "*Benedicite*" to him and opened the gate. Chuck went to his left to the North Parlor, where his father and the secular world waited for him. They took the bus to Horsham and then the train to Victoria. They did not spend the night in London but went straight to Heathrow, then to Pennsylvania, and a long car ride home. He and his father spoke little on the trip back to the States via bus, train, cab, plane, and car. They both had a lot of suffering to do. There were no rest stops from the time Chuck left the Charterhouse until he returned home on a day when the sun wouldn't set. He had left the States a hero and now, a twenty-five-year-old man, he could not return without his father.

⊕

In October 1960, when Dom Philip had applied to Parkminster, the twenty novice cells were full, and he had to wait for an empty one. Now, in 1965, there were only four novices—Doms Leo, Malachi, Philip, and Lorenzo. Tellingly, in four years, Dom Philip had seen only two novices make it to final profession, Doms Gregory and Columba. Five months from now, Dom Leo would be permanently voted in or out of the order. The novice under simple vows has to convince the solemns that he will be able to live as a healthy Carthusian monk for the rest of his life. Dom Philip hoped that he and the other three novices would make it to final profession. Probably at Dom Columba's request, and the Prior's agreement, a psychiatrist interviewed all of them and assessed them "in order for the life."

The monks who survived had learned to keep their balance—at times to give in to some of their needs for physical and psychological comfort, to bend a bit. Over time, to keep his balance and his sanity, the monk makes peace with some unmonastic desires. Dom Malachi, for example, found that when he tried to pray when the grace was not there, he got a headache. He slowly recognized that thoughts about his family or other mundane happenings were good and proper at times. Like listening to music or hitting a golf ball correctly, he learned to feel when the sound was true and the vibrations harmonious. Dom Malachi reflected that Dom Anselm, the novices' professor, had found a way to cope with solitude, allowing him to maintain a human balance and not to be overly concerned with what the other monks thought. Dom Anselm lived the familiar life of a Benedictine as much as he could. Against the rules and spirit of the Carthusian order, he had a clock ticking in his cell, a roaring fire waiting for him when he returned to cell after the cold hours in church, and books spilling over in his *cubiculum.*

Those who could survive, stayed. No one wanted to leave. They only left when they began to crack or were asked to leave. They believed the biblical parable: "The kingdom of heaven is like a merchant seeking good pearls, who, when he had found one of great price, gave all that he had and bought it." Those who survived to burial were particularly suited to the Carthusian life. Some were balanced people, some weren't, but they had the faith and the inner resources to live out the logic of their faith. If there is a God, they thought that a reasonable person would seek a relationship with Him and only pay attention to Him. As Dom Leo would say on the walks, "It's very simple."

CHAPTER 17

Monks Dying (February 6, 1962; Fall 1965)

FERIAL DAY

Dom Philip had been in the Charterhouse not quite a year when he experienced his first monk death. He saw the black-bordered announcement on the notice board in the *tabula* when he went to Night Office:

> **OBIIT**
> Venerabilis in Christo Pater
> Dom Hugo-Maria Plein,
> sacerdos, professus Cartusiæ,
> hospes in Domo Sancti Hugonis
> Parkmonasteriensis,
> Professionis suæ anno 37°
> Die 6° Februarii 1962
> Post completorium
> fr. Guy Thackrah,
> Procurator.
> REQUIESCAT IN PACE!

Dom Hugo-Maria had been ill for a very long time. He was eighty-seven years old, and his death was no surprise. Dom Hugo-Maria had been a monk for over sixty years; he had been a professed Carthusian for thirty-seven years. He looked leathery and hard. As he grew older, even though an invalid, he looked more energetic, more eager—like someone who knew he was finishing the very end of a race, breasting the tape on the last lap. For some time, he had been moving in and out of the portal to eternity.

Dom Philip wondered if the Prior had given him the last rites. Had Dom Hugo-Maria been alone when he died in his cell? Then he remembered a Sunday when the Vicar, Dom Bruno, had read the statute about "Dying Monks" in the Chapter House. Sitting on wooden benches, the monks had listened to the details of a Carthusian monk's death. The novices were especially happy to learn that "a plenary indulgence should be given to the dying monk. It is a ceremony of its own before the anointing." A plenary indulgence takes away the entire temporal punishment due to sin; if the monk was truly sorrowful for his sins and determined to struggle against his bad tendencies, a plenary indulgence would take him straight to Heaven, bypassing Purgatory. They were further comforted by the other rituals surrounding monk death.

The Vicar continued:

> As long as he remains in imminent danger of death, there should always be one or more of his brothers to watch over him. When he seems to be on the point of dying, a signal is given so that all may pray that he has a holy death. The Prior hastens to his bedside with some of his brothers. When assembled all say the *Credo* so that by this profession of faith the dying man's faith is strengthened and his hope encouraged. Those present pray for the dying brother.

Dom Philip felt a comforting ray of sunshine fall on him from the high arched windows as he listened to how the other monks help the dying monk. He had heard rumors that the monks were buried naked, so he was surprised and somewhat disappointed to learn that:

> Those present remain praying until the community can be summoned. The dead man is clothed in habit and cowl, hair shirt and

cincture as well if he is a choir monk. This applies also to novices. All garments should be in good condition. The body is placed on a bier and covered with a suitable cloth.

Remembering this statute, Dom Philip thought that Dom Hugo-Maria probably had not been alone. Perhaps Dom Guy, the Procurator, or a brother had been checking on him and was with him at the end. Dom Philip had only seen Dom Hugo-Maria once, when Dom Joseph had sent him to deliver some books to the invalid monk.

After Dom Bonaventure notified the solemns of the death, Dom Joseph instructed the novices to join the solemns keeping vigil in Dom Hugo-Maria's cell. Dom Hugo's dead body was in his *cubiculum.* The brothers had tied a white cloth around his face to keep his jaw from hanging open. As soon as the brothers had washed, dressed, and laid out Dom Hugo-Maria in his cell, the monks watched two by two, reciting psalms and praying until the whole community escorted the body from Dom Hugo-Maria's cell to the church. The brothers had sewed the hood of his cowl shut from ear to ear and laid the body on the planks from his straw bed. They loosely wrapped both board and body in a white cloth. The monks all had their cowls up and sang the psalm, "Beatus vir, qui non abiit" ("Blessed is the man that followeth not the counsel of the wicked") and other psalms until they reached the church door. Then the chanting stopped. The monks laid Dom Hugo-Maria between the choir stalls on a wooden bier made of parallel slats of wood. The body stayed in the church throughout the night as the monks sang Night Office as well as a special Office of the Dead. Two monks alternated keeping vigil until the funeral Mass in the morning.

Dom Bonaventure said a simple requiem Mass, and then the entire community—solemns, novices, postulants, and brothers—assembled on either side of the bier. Vested in church cowl and stole, Dom Bonaventure sprinkled the body with holy water and incensed the cross and body. As cantor of the week, Dom Marianus intoned with his guttural German accent, "*Credo quod Redemptor meus vivit*":

> I believe that my Redeemer lives and on the last day I will be resurrected and I will see him in the flesh. And in my flesh I will see God my Savior. I myself and no other will see him with my own eyes.

After again sprinkling the body with holy water, Dom Bonaventure continued to pray, "You who love souls take the soul of your servant who kept the faith while he was in his body." Against the background of the monks' continual chanting, they processed to the graveyard from the church doors opening onto the cemetery and garth. With their cowls up, they continued to antiphonally sing Psalms 50, 41, 131, 136, and 85. Although Dom Humphrey, the very frail Antiquior, did not usually sing very loudly, he bellowed out the psalms. Dom Philip thought that he looked like an old English bulldog—stolid, although he was not even strong enough to pull the bell rope. Opposite the church, the brothers had dug a six-foot grave in the grassy graveyard walled off from the garth. A tall wooden cross, perhaps fifteen feet high, stood at the graveyard at the far end from the church. The apple trees beyond the graveyard were still dormant, and the sun outlined the intricate cross on top of the church spire.

Holding a six-foot wooden cross in front of him, Dom Philip, at that time the last novice, led the procession to the cemetery. When the monks arrived at the grave site, Dom Philip stood at the head of the grave, so close that he could feel his toes inside his choir shoes gripping the edge of the hard clay soil. Dom Philip made sure that the body of the crucifix faced the grave. Dom Leo noticed that the hard clay soil kept its sharp ridge and that Dom Philip's feet were right at the edge of the grave, like a military sergeant. Dom Bonaventure stood on the right side of the cross. The senior monks, Doms Anselm and Francis, carrying the censor and holy water, stood on either side of Dom Bonaventure. At the foot of the grave, Dom Humphrey held the large candle. He and Dom Hugo-Maria had been monks together for a long time, and tears streamed down his face. In this time of grief, he remembered their weekly conversations and Dom Hugo-Maria's courage in helping people who had suffered under the Nazis. When the brothers laid the body near the grave, the singing stopped, and Dom Bonaventure sprinkled and incensed the grave while the monks sang: "We are expecting a Savior, the Lord Jesus Christ. He will transform the body of our humiliation so that it may be conformed to the body of his glory." Dom Philip thought of Dom Hugh's worn-out body and imagined the body conformed to the glory of Jesus. He found it a satisfying moment, completely uncompromised.

After Dom Bonaventure again sang the "Kyrie Eleison," the monks sang more psalms, then were silent, then more psalms. Finally, the monks sang three canticles, ending with the canticle of Simeon, "Nunc Dimittis":

> Now dost Thou dismiss Thy servant, O Lord, in peace, according to Thy word; Because mine eyes have seen Thy salvation, Which Thou hast prepared in the sight of all nations, A light of revelation to the Gentiles and the glory of Thy people Israel.

While the monks sang the "Nunc Dimittis," Dom Bonaventure incensed the grave. All the monks then prayed in silence for a while.

After the Prior finished the graveside prayers, two brothers lowered the wrapped body into the grave, where Dom Hugo-Maria joined the other forty-some anonymous monks in the Charterhouse's graveyard. The Prior threw the first handful of dirt on the old, unembalmed, and uncoffined body. When the first clods of clay hit the body, Dom Philip thought that if any of those solid clods of clay fell on his nose, they would break it for sure. He thought he could hear a *plunk* or *plop* as the clods hit against the dead monk's stomach. The monks then chanted psalms until the brothers had entirely filled the grave with the heavy clay soil of Parkminster. The brothers would later mark it with a wooden cross without name or date. There would be no flowers.

After every burial, the monks went to the Chapter House for a brief sermon and a meal in common. After Dom Bonaventure spoke briefly about Dom Hugo-Maria, life in the Charterhouse resumed its course. To alleviate sadness, the monks always got an extra evening meal on burial days; otherwise, death scarcely interrupted the Charterhouse's routine. No one publicly rejoiced that Dom Hugo-Maria had run the good race, that he had survived the rigors of the life, that he was now at Christ's right hand. Dom Philip had thought that perhaps there would be a "Te Deum" sung, but there was no community celebration; neither was there any grief or lamenting. Dom Hugo-Maria had succeeded in his role of being a living sacrifice acceptable to God. There was nothing left of Dom Hugo-Maria—God had consumed him. It was a quiet passing. Dom Philip felt odd, perhaps a trifle disoriented, but he felt no sadness. After he thought about it for a while, he felt that this was probably the way it should be, that this was a natural process, and that monks should go out the same way they came in, without anything. Dom Hugo-Maria's cell would stand empty on the solemns' side of the cloister, probably until the next novice made solemn profession—perhaps himself or Dom Malachi.

The memory of the death of Dom Hugo-Maria recurred more frequently as Dom Philip's own solemn profession approached. In late September 1965, the Prior allowed a priest friend, Dick Schmidt, to visit Dom Philip. This in itself was extraordinary. Another friend, who had just been ordained in Rome, had tried twice to see Dom Philip, the second time to give him his first priestly blessing, and had been told, "We do not allow visitors" before the Porter pulled the wooden partition shut. Dom Philip's mother had arranged Dick's visit. She wrote to the Prior twice, finally obtaining permission for Dick to spend the entire day with Dom Philip. How she achieved this apparently impossible task isn't known, but she was a very shrewd woman and contributed generously to religious orders. Did she sense that Dom Philip was unhappy when she read his four letters a year? Or, just before he made a monastic commitment for life, did she reconsider whether she wanted to lose her only son forever?

Dick was very nervous that Dom Philip wouldn't want to see him; that he would be too busy talking to God. But when Dom Philip entered the North Parlor, he rushed over to Dick and hugged him. For the first hour or so, he just asked Dick questions, about what was going on outside, about Vatican II, about their old classmates. Then he told Dick that the graveyard made sense of the life. He explained, "Last Thursday, around 2 PM, I went by an open cloister door and looked out. The cross in the center of the graveyard was right in front of me, about fifteen yards away. The graveyard wall, the garth, and the cells framed the cross. The graveyard gives you the best sense of the place—for seeing all of the Charterhouse, the church behind, the garth, all the cells. The Charterhouse came into focus for me. As I stood there, with the afternoon sun hitting the wooden crosses that mark the graves, I thought, there is only now and death. There is nothing else, *hic et nunc*. And, as a monk, every day I am deliberately moving toward death. The monastic structure keeps me focused on what my life is about." He then told Dick about his troubles with the other monks in choir. Dick, after looking at Dom Philip for a long moment, hesitated, then slowly asked: "Dave, if you're unhappy, why do you stay?" Dom Philip responded without hesitation, "I've come here to be alone with God, and I'll pay the price."

Later, the image of fresh earth piled over Dom Hugo-Maria's body recurred. Dom Philip looked out of the window toward his garden. Dom Hugo-Maria had lived the same day every day for nearly forty years. Dom Philip had been in the Charterhouse not quite five years, and he knew how difficult it was to get up in the middle of every night, he knew how hard it was to fast on dry bread and water on the coldest winter days. Above all, he knew the hardness of a life that never changed, that would never change, when every day looked like every other day. Dom Philip would continue to be the Second Cantor on the Prior's side of the choir, but the off-pitch monks had already stressed Dom Philip so much that at times even his voice failed him. Last week, his voice had trailed off when he intoned a psalm. On some days, he couldn't get a word out. Yet his voice was fine on the Monday walks. Dom Philip didn't need a doctor to tell him that laryngitis was not the problem.

The days would continue to draw on until he too was dropped into a grave. Yet monks were notoriously long-lived; legend has it that St. Antony lived for 105 years. Dom Philip had perhaps another sixty years of making the same rounds every day. Could he keep going for sixty years? Notwithstanding the rumors of Vatican II, no one in the Charterhouse believed that an order that hadn't changed since 1084 would change now. And how long would the dark force keep him from communing with God? The dark force usually came and went, but Dom Philip now felt that the dark force had become a permanent part of him. Would the monks continue to be inharmonious? Would he be the only monk singing? In five months, he would make final profession, committing him forever to this life, yet he would continue to fail at keeping the monks on pitch. He feared he could become increasingly interested in watching the mice in his garden.

Dom Philip knew that there was no life on earth like this one: No other life had a structure that allowed, even forced, minute-by-minute attention to God alone. He reflected on St. Bruno's advice to a friend: "Only those who have experienced the solitude and silence of the wilderness can know what benefit and divine joy they bring to those who love them." He considered even harder Bruno's comment to his monks in France, "Also my brothers, take it as certain and proven; no one, after having enjoyed so desirable a good, can ever give it up without regrets, if he is serious about the salvation of his soul." Then he thought of the Latin inscription on the door of one of the cells: *"Qui perseveraverit usque in finem, hic salvus erit"* ("The man who stands firm to the end, he will be saved).

CHAPTER 18

Solemn Profession (September 29–October 6, 1965)

WEDNESDAY, SEPTEMBER 29, 1965

At the same time that thoughts of death absorbed Dom Philip, Dom Leo was about to step through the Carthusian door to realize the final passing of Paddy O'Connell. Unlike the other three novices, he was not struggling or agonizing about the decision. Dom Leo had already made the complete commitment—he was calm and steady. But he was also very aware that he was crossing an irrevocable line and experienced the anxiety that goes with that decision. As Novice Master, Dom Columba proposed Dom Leo to the community, yet he realized that Dom Leo had not told him much about himself.

Dom Leo had been at Parkminster for over five years. For five years, he had been trying to absorb its rhythms. He thought that he finally understood how to be a monk. In another week, he would make solemn profession, which would irrevocably bind him to this particular group of hermit monks for all the days of his life.

The Carthusian statutes admonished every monk to "sit down and consider whether he really wants to yield himself to God forever." Dom Leo had done that, and he felt settled in his mind. Dom Leo would be subjecting himself to the Prior as God's representative. He knew that submitting his will to that of another man would be difficult. He knew what the Carthusian life was about; he had been living it for five years. He knew about the noonday demon and the occupational hazards of the life: The lack of communication made it impossible to get the facts; the absence of critical discussions made rash judgment a serious hazard; solitude could foster self-absorption, laziness, selfishness, absorption with the body, and imaginary ills and slights. He knew that he could allow himself too easy a life in cell; wasting time is the worst sin of the solitary. He could also allow himself too hard a life and go the way of Dom Damian. Carthusian life could foster a sense of elitism—the hubris that precedes self-destruction. He remembered the legendary Irish monk Aedh, who fasted so immoderately that he saw visions, then jumped to his death from a mountaintop. Dom Leo knew that he had to make the most out of every small human experience to grow in his humanity, to keep his balance. For him, solemn profession was a profound and calm act of faith.

Dom Leo knew about the factions, the waves at the surface, but he knew that the liturgy had supported him for five years. He knew that he wanted to search for God in the solitude and silence of Parkminster. He thought that he could survive—with God's help and the prayers of the other monks. For better or for worse, the life at Parkminster was his life. He knew about families, and he hoped that God would use him to hold this family of hermit monks together. He would settle here forever in mind and in body. He was thirty-two years old—he could be here for another sixty years. He thought about the old Irish saying, "You will be a long time dead." Between today and the day of his death, he would be living in monastic time: Every day would be a time of dying, but every day would also have in it something of eternity.

In preparation, Dom Leo made the customary eight-day retreat. Dom Columba had given Dom Leo a book on the meaning of clerical celibacy. Dom Leo thought that the author twisted and turned trying to find the answer, but he knew that clerical celibacy was a hard topic. During his retreat he thought more about Psalm 62, especially verse 4. *"Melior est misericordia Tua super vitas."* Dom Leo translated it literally as, "Better is your mercy than lives." Remembering his successful life outside the Charterhouse, Dom Leo thought: "It is better for me that God's mercy is leading me along His way than it would be for me if I could choose a successful life in which my talents were recognized; where I was good in an easily seen way. I could choose so many 'lives' for myself perhaps, all so very good. And yet: *'Melior est misericordia*

Tua super vitas.' It is Your guiding and leading that means everything to me. *'Labia mea laudabunt Te!'"*

After the retreat, he confessed all the faults he had committed during the previous year. The monks did this every year on the Sunday closest to their profession day. This year that Sunday was October 3. Dom Leo was grateful for this custom. He knew that the faults were small things, but he knew that they weakened the spirit of the family.

Dom Leo prostrated before the novices and confessed his faults in order to beg their forgiveness and prayers. He had written his faults on the back of a 1964 Carthusian calendar. He read:

> I accuse myself of all my faults committed against monastic poverty, charity, and obedience during the past year.
>
> *Poverty:* keeping clothes in poor repair, neglecting the pear trees in my garden, leaving an ax in the snow, leaving a hoe outside for the entire year, leaving a roller outside for 4 months, not returning a pen knife borrowed from Father Master, breaking a lamp glass in choir, tearing my habit through carelessness, not cleaning walk boots, forgetting my diurnal in the Guest House, breaking a walking stick, causing soot in chimney to smolder, leaving Charterhouse in shabby habit, pouring cider which was left over out the window so that it ruined a patch of grass.
>
> *Charity:* forgetting schedule changes frequently, forgetting bath time 3x, went to wrong chapel to serve Mass 5 times, forgot choir practice twice, passing in front of Fr. Prior at lectern, showing disgust for other's errors, ringing another monk's bell too loudly, being impatient when instructing a postulant, allowing someone to ring a sick person's cell, climbing over a neighbor in choir, being late passing things on, making patronizing comments, making remarks about laggers.
>
> *Obedience:* Being out of cell frequently, insufficient knowledge of statutes, leaving a gate which is always shut open, showing ambition, doing things to compete, stating views too strongly, speaking to brothers unnecessarily once, failing to observe custody of the eyes frequently, infidelities to time schedule, altering my time schedule 2 times, not weeding garden, not preparing adequately for Office and classes, late for bed habitually, sending notes without permission 5x, slow in delivering a message.

> Besides these faults, I have failed to show monastic spirit: not admitting myself wrong, arguing to assert myself, having a superior attitude in class, criticizing someone's outlook, asking for special types of reading, questioning acts of superiors, making disrespectful remarks to a superior.
>
> I accuse myself of these and all the many other faults that I left out. I ask pardon for anything with which I might have hurt Father Master or my companions and ask for your prayers for my correction in the future.
>
> In Xt,
> Fr. Leo [N].

Dom Leo got up and returned to his place. Dom Columba then read a short sermon especially written for him.

> Dom Leo's work is now only paying attention to God. His role is not that of a priest or an administrator or a builder. As the years flow by, everything in Dom Leo's life is reduced to this unique occupation of wanting God and his Holy Will, for to him these have now become one, as they are in God. . . .

After the sermon, the novices said good-bye to Dom Leo, as their conversations with him would end when he became a solemn. Even when they had been novices together for five years, the novices never talked to the solemns. The next time they would talk to Dom Leo would be when they also became solemns. They promised to pray for Dom Leo in his quest for God.

Once Dom Leo had made final profession, only three novices would remain. They wondered about their future. Doms Malachi and Philip would be up for final profession in eight months. They thought about the world on the other side of the wall. They knew that the Carthusian coat of arms over the main door of Parkminster symbolized the order's mindset. The words below the cross and orb were: *Stat Crux dum Volvitur Orbis* ("The cross stands firm while the world moves on"). For 900 years, Carthusian monks had not cared about the world moving on. The Carthusian monks focused upward, into the Cloud of Unknowing; they tried to forget all that they thought they knew, to dump that pseudo-knowledge into the Cloud of Forgetting. Dom Leo was ready to do that forever.

On the following Wednesday, October 6, Dom Leo dedicated himself to the inheritance he cherished and was claiming. He was pleased that his solemn profession would take place on the feast day of St. Bruno. Dom Bonaventure, the Prior, said the solemn High Mass, with the community's most important relics on the altar in twelve brass-bound caskets of varying sizes. Some of the caskets contained three large relics, other caskets many more. Dom Leo was glad that the Charterhouse's bones of St. Bruno (encased in brass) were among them. Among the thirty or so other relics, the brain and skin of St. Rosaline were in one casket; in another, there was the richly embroidered stole of St. Hugh that the Grande Chartreuse gave to Parkminster in 1895 to celebrate the dedication of their Reliquary Chapel.

In the unlighted church, Dom Francis lit a candle on the altar. When the Prior knocked on his choir stall, the monks all bowed for silent prayer. After making the Carthusian sign of the cross, Dom Bonaventure chanted, "Place, O Lord, a guard on my mouth." The other monks responded: "And place a door to my lips." The Prior then sang the community's confession of sins: "I confess to God and to you my brothers that I have sinned exceedingly by my fault through pride, in my thoughts and in my words, in what I have done and in what I have failed to do." The Carthusians fear the sin of pride—the pride of observing seemingly impossible monastic discipline, of climbing Mount Everest, of being the Catholic Church's Green Berets. Then, singing "*Adjutorium nostrum in nomine Domini*," Dom Bonaventure went to the inlaid altar steps and bowed profoundly while saying a Pater and Ave, a custom exclusively Carthusian.

The Mass for St. Bruno's feast day was the Mass for Confessors, with some parts written especially for St. Bruno. The entrance hymn advised the monks to "meditate on wisdom." Dom Bonaventure read the first prayer. Dom Leo thought it especially appropriate for a solemn profession:

> Almighty and Eternal God who prepares mansions in heaven for those renouncing earth, we humbly implore Your immense clemency, that through the intercession of our father Bruno, we may faithfully fulfill the vows which we make.

Dom Malachi, the cantor of the week, read the special epistle for St. Bruno in a loud, strong voice: "The Lord leads the just in the right ways and shows to them the kingdom of God and gives to them the knowledge of the saints . . . Wisdom is stronger than all." Dom Leo prayed fervently that he would gain wisdom while living the life initiated by St. Bruno. The deacon of the week, Dom Emmanuel, passionately and breathlessly blasted out the gospel from Luke 12, which warned the monks to be faithful, to be prepared. Jesus said to his disciples, "Let your loins be girt and bright lights in your hands so that when the Lord comes and knocks on the door, you can quickly open it." Dom Emmanuel had been a monk for twenty-nine years, and everyone felt that he was serious about getting prepared. The monks spent their lives getting ready for that knock.

Today, because it was a major feast day, Dom Emmanuel incensed the altar. Holding the chains in his left hand, with his right hand, he swung the long length of chain with the censer of incense at its end. With their heads down and their cowls over their heads, the monks listened to the chains clanking and inhaled the smoky, sweet odor of incense filtering through the church. After the Offertory, Dom Leo went to the center of the sanctuary steps, bowed profoundly, and sang the Latin verse *"Suscipe Me"* in his soft Irish voice:

> *Sustain me, Lord, as you have promised, that I may live;*
> *Disappoint me not in my hope.*

The other monks, in their choir stalls, but facing the altar, repeated the verse. Then Dom Leo sang the verse again, and the monks again repeated the verse. Then again. After they finished, all the monks, leaning against the edge of the raised misericords, bowed low, with their hands on their knees, and sang the "Gloria Patri" extremely slowly, with a long distinctly Carthusian pause in the middle of the verse, after *"Spiritui Sancto,"* until the words disappeared. Then they prayed in silence.

As soon as the monks had begun singing the second half of the verse "*Sicut erat,*" Dom Leo stood erect and went down the Prior's side toward the first stall, knelt before the monk in the stall, and said, *"Ora pro me, frater."* He did the same for all the monks on the Prior's side, and then went to the Antiquior's side and did the same. Dom Philip felt uncomfortable about this obeisance, but Dom Malachi felt deeply touched and honored to be asked to pray for Dom Leo. Dom Philip, thinking and hoping for his own solemn profession, felt that Dom Leo would need all the prayers he could get to live this life for another sixty or so years.

Dom Leo then went back and faced the altar. Dom Bonaventure blessed the new cowl of the solemnly professed with holy water. Doms Francis and Guy then removed Dom Leo's cowl and replaced it with the wide-banded cowl of the solemnly professed. During this time, all the monks stood with their cowls down facing the altar. Continuing to face the altar, Dom Leo moved to his right, toward the epistle side of the altar; the Prior also went to the epistle side. Every monk listened as Dom Leo very precisely read the Latin formula of profession in his Irish voice.

> I, Dom Leo, promise perpetual stability, obedience, and conversion of my life, before God, his saints, and the relics belonging to this hermitage, which was built in honor of God, the Blessed Mary ever Virgin, and Blessed John the Baptist, in the presence of Dom Bonaventure, Prior.

He had written this formula on parchment and signed it. After he finished reading, he kissed the altar and put the parchment on it as an offering of his life to God. Dom Bonaventure would later sign the parchment, add the date and year, and deposit it in Parkminster's vast archives. In a sense, any trace of Paddy O'Connell also disappeared into the archives; Paddy O'Connell had irrevocably become Dom Leo. Solemn profession was a kind of death, a free and conscious entry into the mystery of the death and resurrection of Christ. While holding onto his self by faith alone, Dom Leo physically felt death come over him—the death of totally abandoning himself to the will of God. Dom Leo then prostrated before the Prior's plain wooden chair (one that the Sacristan had brought from one of the cells), and Dom Bonaventure blessed him while the monks again bowed low, leaning against their misericords. In his full-voiced baritone, Dom Bonaventure sang a prayer in Latin with his right hand extended over Dom Leo. He prayed for the conversion of his life:

> Our Lord Jesus Christ, you who are the only Way to the Father, we beg your great kindness and mercy for this your servant: that you may free him from all disordered desire, and lead him along the path of monastic observance. Grant that the voice of your

invitation so graciously calling sinners with the words, "Come to me all you who are heavy laden and I will give you rest" may so exert its attraction over him that he cast away the burden of his sins, and tasting how good you are, be ever strengthened and refreshed by your hidden nourishment. As you spoke concerning the sheep of your flock, may you acknowledge him and number him among them, and may he so acknowledge you that he never follow another, and never heed the voice of strangers, but Yours alone, as you say: "If anyone would serve Me, let him follow Me." You live and reign ever and ever.

Dom Bonaventure then sprinkled Dom Leo with holy water. After that, he went back to the middle of the altar and incensed the altar in the normal way. Dom Leo then returned to his choir stall and sat, as did the rest of the monks, until after the Prior had finished. The profession ceremony over, Dom Leo remained in his choir stall until communion time. After a five-year trial in the novitiate, Dom Leo was now a solemn.

Before the consecration, Dom Emmanuel lit a second candle, not only to solemnize the act, but also to assist the Prior in the dark church. Before raising the large brown wafer, Dom Bonaventure genuflected on one knee without touching the ground. When he bent over the wine, changing it into the blood of Christ, he bowed profoundly. In a uniquely Carthusian custom, all the monks, with their cowls completely over their heads, *ex toto,* first flipped the front panel of their cowls in front of them, then lay on their sides on their cowls, resting on an elbow with their hands together and their knees bent. Dom Bonaventure raised the chalice unseen. The monk closest to the bell rope again rang the church bell. Dom Bonaventure mentioned Dom Leo's name during the Eucharistic prayer so that the offering of his life would be joined to that of Christ. When the consecration was over, he distributed communion only to Dom Leo. At the end of Mass, he simply said, *"Ite Missa est."*

After serving the private Mass of Dom Columba, Dom Leo went back to his cell. On this solemn feast day, the little hours of Sext and None would be prayed in church, so he wouldn't have much time in his cell today. He was very hungry: The day before solemn profession was a fast day. He still clearly remembers eating two portions of bread to give him courage—one white and one brown—whereas usually a monk ate one or the other. Yet his cell looked particularly bright to him that morning, and the late fall flowers in his garden seemed to be standing straighter. He already sensed a growing consciousness of daily living. Tomorrow, he would move to a cell on the solemns' side of the cloister. He read his letters. He was happy to see a congratulatory letter from Hans. His mother sent congratulations from his University College, Dublin classmates, and greetings from his siblings, aunts, uncles, cousins, nephews, and nieces. Although they weren't allowed to be physically present at Parkminster, October 6 was a big day for the O'Connell family. Dom Leo immediately wrote to his mother and siblings; his brother Brendan and his wife, Helen, visited him shortly afterward.

Dom Philip was starting to have nightmares about choir. In the nightmare, he was the First Cantor on the Prior's side, and the pitch kept going down and down and down until the monks simply stopped singing—like writing with chalk on a blackboard until your hand goes down so far it hits the chalk tray. As a cantor, he would have to keep singing no matter what. He would be singing all alone in choir. Dom Philip was frightened and prayed, "I cry unto Thee, O Lord, hear me! Harken to my voice, when I call upon thee." He got out of bed and wrote a note: "Important not to be afraid of the future, either staying or leaving. Important to hold onto obedience to the Spirit who leads into the desert, maintains or leads out of the desert."

But in mid-October, a week after Dom Leo had made final profession, Dom Philip decided to leave the Charterhouse. He still thought being a hermit monk the best life on earth, but he doubted that he would be able to survive. He had earlier told Dom Malachi, "I want to walk out, not be carried out." Dom Columba had repeated his formula to help him decide: "If you are in doubt, leave." When Dom Columba talked to him thirty-four years later, he said, "You were right. You didn't belong here. Your talents belonged elsewhere."

Dom Philip prepared well in advance for his departure. A month before he left, he and Dom Guy went to the American Embassy to renew his passport. On the way they stopped at Hampton Court, about fifteen miles southwest of London. Dom Guy was determined to show this young American one of the greatest historical monuments in England. Dom Guy loved architectural history, and Hampton Court contains some of the finest examples of Tudor architecture. Henry VIII had been its most famous occupant. Cardinal Wolsey built the palace in 1515, but four years after its completion, he gave it to Henry. Under William and Mary, Christopher Wren further enlarged the Tudor palace. The buildings cover six acres and the gardens another sixty, bordering the north bank of the Thames. Doms Guy and Philip spent about an hour wandering the gardens. Dom Philip was particularly fascinated by the holly and yew maze originally planted in the late seventeenth century. He was even more amazed that the tourists circled around the two monks and took pictures, thinking that they were part of the historical reconstruction.

For the next month, Dom Philip continued to live as a Carthusian novice. Some of the solemns knew he was leaving, but he told none of the novices. He wrote to the parents of Dom Malachi and to Chuck to let them know he would be flying into New York and would visit them in November. He wanted to be home for Thanksgiving. He left the novitiate on a Thursday before the Friday haircut and stayed in the Guest House for a week, letting his hair grow out a bit. He was again Dave Lynch. The tailor returned his clothes, which revealed a small problem; he had gained twenty pounds while at Parkminster. During the week in the Guest House, he went to Mass in the Visitors Loft and continued to pray the day hours of the Divine Office from his diurnal. He read a lot. The brothers brought him his food.

He didn't want to worry his parents or make them think they had to come get him. He wrote to tell them that he would call from New York and asked Dom Bonaventure to post the letter after he had left the Charterhouse. During their visit, Dom Bonaventure returned the money Dom Philip had left in safekeeping with him when he became a novice—$5,000 from his farewell party over four years earlier. As Dave left his office, Dom Bonaventure urged him to continue reading Origen.

Dave was calm about leaving Parkminster, hugely relieved to have the tensions in choir behind him. On an early November day, Dom Columba came to say good-bye, and late in the afternoon Dave walked out of the gate and down the road to catch bus number 107 for Horsham. Then he took the train back to Victoria Station and spent the night at the Victoria Station Hotel. The next morning he took a cab to Heathrow and boarded a plane. On the flight back, he looked forward to meeting Dom Malachi's family and to seeing Chuck again. He landed at Kennedy Airport and took a cab to Brooklyn. He visited the family of Dom Malachi and spent the night with them. He gave them news of Dom Malachi and the other monks. He felt relaxed and on familiar ground with this family. Dom Malachi's mother reported to her son that Dave was a very well-brought up young man because he had brought a gift. Dave called his parents, but Dom Bonaventure had forgotten to post the letter, so his parents were not expecting to see him outside the Charterhouse in this life. To Dave's surprise, they were very matter-of-fact about his presence in New York. They did not miss a beat. His dad said simply, "Terrific, when will you be home?"

From New York, he went to see the only man in America who could understand his state of mind—Chuck Henley. While the two ex-monks played various sports, they talked about their experience in the Charterhouse. Dave, of course, told Chuck about Dom Joseph's departure. They talked about what they would do next; Dave thought he would probably join another monastery, perhaps the Camaldolese. Talking to Chuck was a safe place for Dave to reflect on his recent experience and current uncertainty. He learned about what Chuck was doing and how he was adjusting. They talked about the war and, the draft that President Johnson had announced just three months earlier, but most of all about Parkminster.

Then, Dave went back to Chicago to meet his parents, who were in their late sixties by then. They met him at O'Hare Airport. He hugged them both in a matter-of-fact way, and they got into their green Oldsmobile and drove back to their apartment on the north side of Chicago. There were no heavy emotions. Dave had been gone too long, and they had never been an emotional family. They had been proud of him when he was a monk, but they were glad to see him back in Chicago. They were all somewhat ambivalent. They could not understand where he had been; he was remote to them. He was not able to speak of his journey to God. They unconsciously agreed to act as if he had never been away. They talked about his trip and asked about Chuck and Dom Malachi's family. Thanksgiving was a few days away, and they asked how he wanted to celebrate it. The following week, still revisiting his decision to leave the Charterhouse, Dave went to sign up for the draft, but at age twenty-seven, he was rejected.

Of the five who arrived in 1960–1961, Dom Malachi was the second to make solemn profession. On June 24, 1966, on the same day that Dave would have made solemn profession, Dom Malachi committed himself forever to the Carthusian life. He moved to the solemns' side of the cloister; he was disappointed not to move into Dom Ludolph's vacant cell, a corner cell with a new lathe. On August 9, 1966, Dom Columba wrote to a former novice, "Dom Malachi sends his thanks and prays for you. He is in his honeymoon ecstasy which will last, I believe." In his first year, Dom Malachi remembers a growing intensity of daily living; the days weren't long enough for all the things he wanted to do. Yet Dom Malachi never really settled into the order. When the time came for him to be ordained, he felt very strongly that he didn't have that calling, yet, as we have seen, he was able to remain in the order without being a priest.

One evening three years later, as he tried to get out of bed for Night Office, he found that he could not move at all. After some time, with great determination, he managed to get out of bed and attend Office. When the same paralysis occurred several days later, he could not recover his ability to move. He was unable to respond in any way to the outside world. It was as if he had lost contact. He thought, "If this is what you want Lord, I am all right with being institutionalized." He heard the Prior, then Dom Guy, come into his cell, and recognized the fear in his voice when Dom Guy realized that he couldn't communicate with him. The hospital could find nothing wrong. The order eventually sent him to London to sit in the opulent waiting room of a Harley Street psychiatrist, who put Dom Malachi through hypnosis and psychotherapy. Dom Malachi recovered, but as he learned how to live an ordinary life, something had altered. The specific grace that enabled him to live in cell was removed.

The order sent Dom Malachi, then thirty years old and once again Bernie, to an old folks' home in Brighton that had a retired priest in residence. Dom Bruno asked a parish priest to visit him, and Dom Guy wrote to Hans in Germany, asking him to visit Bernie. Hans and Manfred, his partner, immediately came. Bernie said to them, "I'm a bit strange, aren't I." Manfred responded, "Everyone's a bit strange." A member of the old folks' home put Bernie in contact with another parish priest, who gave him a room in his rectory, and his voyage back into the world began. He went to the States to visit his family and to California to see the young woman he had met ten years earlier on the

Mauretania. Although their feelings for one another had not changed, she told him he was "too late." She was married with two children: Their opportunity had passed. But their correspondence has continued uninterrupted ever since.

Bernie Shea's departure completed the extraordinary experience of the five young men who rang the Charterhouse's bell in 1960–1961. All five came with the intent of seeing the face of God, of stretching the limits of human spiritual experience, to live for God alone in solitude. Three of them survived the harshness of eleventh-century Carthusian life until almost the moment when they would commit themselves forever to the Carthusian order. Two of them made solemn profession. Of these two, only one was able to continue the voyage in perpetuity.

The price of failure for the others was high. They found the isolation in the world much worse than in their cells. Secular humans felt remote to them, and they were remote to others. They had staked their lives on the dream of being a Carthusian monk. They had no other dreams, no other ambitions. They had been living in monastic time for five years, but secular time had not stood still for them. While they were in the Charterhouse, the world had changed, mores had changed, even the Catholic Church had changed. Like Rip Van Winkle, they awoke to a foreign world. Their position in their families had shifted. Their classmates and friends had married, become professionals, or just moved on in other ways. They were alone; they could not have imagined their separateness from the rest of the human race. Their own families had no idea, or desire to know, of their life in the Charterhouse. Even their parish priests could not understand their lives as Carthusians. They could talk to no one. They were alone, suffering the very harsh price for leaving the Charterhouse.

EPILOGUE: LATER

⊕

OCTOBER 6, 2005

And so, of the five young men ringing the Gatehouse bell, only Dom Leo remains in the order. When Dave Lynch watched the cardinals marching into the Vatican to elect Pope Benedict XVI in April 2005, he commented: "If Paddy O'Connell and myself would have become secular priests, I might be one of the Cardinals, and I would be voting for Paddy O'Connell."

Now seventy-two years old, ordained a priest in July 1968, Dom Leo remained at Parkminster for six years. The Reverend Father then reassigned him to the Grande Chartreuse, where he was well-respected; after teaching Scripture for about three years, in April 1975, he became the Novice Master. In 1976, he wrote to Chuck Henley, "I am still in the fight." As Novice Master, he brought a Paris psychologist to La Grande Chartreuse to teach him and the other Novice Masters to help the novices adjust to the life. In December 1990, the Reverend Father appointed Dom Leo as acting Prior of Parkminster for six months. After this time, the community voted him Prior—although the vote was not unanimous. At the customary party after the election, one solemn said to another, "Did you ever see such a party—like a wake."

Immediately after the election, Dom Leo opened the cloister door separating the monks and brothers and said, "This door is to be kept open, never to be closed." A monk asked, "What about our 900-year tradition?" Dom Leo responded, "If you take that line, we're finished." Dom Leo still looks forward. When Hans and Bernie visited Parkminster in 1995, Dom Leo, still Prior, took them high up on the scaffolding as he explained how he was spending a "million pounds sterling" (received from the English Heritage) to reconstruct the Charterhouse. During the 1961 long walk, Dom Leo had asked Bernie who Jesus Christ was to him. Now Bernie asked Dom Leo, "Who is Jesus Christ to you?" Monks don't forget.

Although Dom Leo says, "I lost my history somewhere along the road. I never think of the past," even he doesn't completely forget. On March 25, 1994, Dom Leo, still Prior, in a sermon to his monks, told them that he had received a letter from a young woman the day before. Her mother, Thérèse, had been an intimate friend of Paddy O'Connell's; in fact, he had been courting Thérèse and would perhaps have married her. Throughout the years, Thérèse had kept him informed of the events of her life; more significantly, she entrusted her family to his spiritual care. Dom Leo admits to his monks, "the news of her death both brought back a whole part of my life and also a sort of picture of how it could have unfolded in its beginning and in its end." He reflected that if he had married Thérèse, her daughter writing to him might also have been his daughter. He concluded, "The Lord had other ideas, and I made a radical turn around and entered monastic life."

Does he regret his radical turn? In August 2005, he responded, "Of course not! One sets out in life with a few rudimentary ideas taken from someone else; the whole beauty of it is the learning, the entering into the mystery that envelops us, a process that does not and never will end. . . . In this life we experience this mystery in the darkness of faith, yet for me it is an inexhaustible reality into which each day I try to enter, letting go of every image and concept in a naked reaching into God as He is in Himself. The immense love that God is has humbled me. I believe in God, I hope in and for God, I want to love God and all that is in him. Each day I start again to try to live these basic truths of the penny catechism. That's it. I am profoundly grateful for the opportunity my life as a pretty poor monk gives me to do so." After forty-five years in the Charterhouse, Dom Leo is "as thirsty now, thirstier, as I was on setting out."

The monks have different opinions about Parkminster's future. Dom Leo believes that the order needs to adapt to the twenty-first century. He thinks that every monk who makes solemn profession has a vocation; it is the order's responsibility to figure out ways for them to live out their commitment. Until June 10, 2001, Dom Leo functioned as Prior, Procurator, and Novice Master. Under his Priorship, Parkminster became more comfortable. The cells now have flush toilets and showers and hot water in the winter. He zealously promoted the rights of the brothers and created a very sophisticated Web site. He always believed in the future. In radical contrast, Dom Columba believes that if God wills, the order will survive; if He doesn't, the order will have completed its mission. In 2001, German monks, the strictest in the order, made the Monk Visitors' biennial visit to Parkminster and reported themselves "shocked" at what they found. Some changes at Parkminster were effected immediately. At the General Chapter in 2001, Dom Leo and six other Priors received *misericordia* and were removed as Priors. The politically correct monks refer to Dom Leo as "controversial. That is why he got into trouble." The more straightforward Dom Columba says, "Dom Leo is no monk." Clearly, different definitions of monk prevail at Parkminster. In 2003, Dom Leo spoke of the shift from a liberal movement in the order toward the original conservatism, remarking philosophically, "I had a run of 15–20 years, now the other side has a chance." But he still thinks Christmas Night Office feels like five minutes instead of five hours.

What are the "golden horde who returned home" doing? Where are they now? The story of the five young men ringing the Gatehouse bell is history, and perhaps the life I describe has itself become a reliquary. Initially, I had doubted that these men would be willing to talk to me. But I had two things in my favor: The monks tend to idealize women, and that was certainly a help, as was the reassuring fact to them that I had married an ex-Carthusian. I could, it was clear, cope with Carthusians. They proved willing to share an experience that fundamentally shaped their lives, and they were as eager to talk about it as most veterans. Except for Bernie, all the monks responded immediately to my formal letter and invitation to talk—Bernie responded weeks later with a forty-page letter. I have been struck by repeated comments like these: "I did not expect this gift," "the chance to make contact again has been an unexpected gift. It feels very good, thank you for stirring this up." Hans described an "unforeseen opportunity to return to ourselves some forty years back."

When Hans, Chuck, Bernie, and Dave left Parkminster, they respected the solitude of their comrades. Yet when I first wrote to Hans in 1999, he immediately replied, "They are all in front of me, the companions of 1960 to 1965." Forty years later, Hans still remembers the faces of those who came and went in the Charterhouse. Now a retired physician, he lives in the small German town where his family has lived for three generations. He has a picture of Mount Everest on his desk, still admiring Edmund Hillary's ascent of Everest and still climbing mountains himself, particularly those in Czechoslovakia. He continues to study Hebrew so that he can read the psalms in their original language. Since he left Parkminster, he has kept up a nearly one-sided Christmas correspondence with Dom Columba. Bernie did not return to live in Brooklyn. He lives in France with his wife, where they started a school for teenagers unable to learn in traditional settings. His two children, Timothée and Gabrielle, now aged fourteen and twenty-two, have written to Dom Columba since they were able to write. Hans is the godfather of Timothée.

In 1969, Chuck's Christmas cacti were still alive in Cell PP, although, in Dom Columba's words, "looking somewhat withered. They haven't been watered since you left." In 1975, Dom Columba gave one of the cacti to Chuck's wife. After not being watered for ten years, the cactus was still alive. A retired university librarian, Chuck still loves Night Office and during his job as librarian had collected monastic books to read in his retirement. In spite of his illness in the Charterhouse, he believes that "I was incredibly lucky to have been so naive and receptive at Parkminster." Chuck believes that Dom Joseph was the most formative influence in his life and treasures the Carthusian experience. He feels he was cheated of being a solemn father, but in his retirement he has returned to many monastic practices and hopes to succeed this time.

In a December 1965 letter, Dom Columba urged Chuck to remain in touch with Dave; he wrote, "Your years together have forged lasting bonds—and with us also, because we feel very united with our brothers who have been called elsewhere in God's mysterious designs." The ex-monk search put Chuck back in contact with Dave, who had become chief executive officer and president of a small national consulting firm after being senior vice president of personnel for a large Chicago bank. He is currently a consultant for people and companies in transition. Three days after his wedding in 1967, Dave took his wife to visit Parkminster. As the newly wed couple walked down the winding drive, a brother saw them. He rushed out to greet Dave and said, "Dom Philip, I knew you would come back." His wife was not pleased, and not surprisingly, Dave did not visit the Charterhouse again for thirty-four years. Then, he talked to Dom Columba for three days, feeling as if he had been talking to him for all the intervening years. For Dom Columba it was "as if I am talking to a brother."

The five men, now old men, do not speak with bitterness of their experience. Some, until they read this book, considered their departure from the Charterhouse a personal failure. They were, and are, incredibly generous and idealistic. Like Theo Faber, who had been Dom Edward at Parkminster, they consider their stint as Carthusian novices the defining moment of their lives. Hans is grateful for the life that made him more tolerant of himself and others; he is especially grateful for having learned how to nurture a prospering thirty-three-year friendship with Manfred. When Bernie left in 1969, he had wanted to reform the order, to stop the nonessentials from becoming sacred—in his words, to purify "that ancient ship that had picked up the barnacles of every century." He wanted to go back to 1084, before Bruno's ancient order had been layered over with antiquated and irrelevant customs. Yet he admits a profound gratitude to "the life." He is grateful that "the Lord led me in and led me out." For Dave, "to have had the opportunity, for five years, to seek God in a quiet and fundamental way has been a lifelong gift." Yet the memories stirred by my queries have left some ex-monks ambivalent; they discovered that their idealized Charterhouse belonged to them alone. Many were not aware of the waves at the surface, of the politics that determined young men's futures, or of how some of the solemns learned to make the life more comfortable.

By September 2003, I had been e-mailing my monk characters for over four years, but I had not met most of them. Before completing *An Infinity of Little Hours,* I needed to meet them in person. They were perhaps even more curious about me. As Bernie pointed out in an e-mail before the trip, "You have managed to get us talking like old soldiers. And though you have made us each, I am sure, feel very at ease with you, there remains the question and the mystery as to 'who is Nancy?'"

The reunion began on the grounds of the Grande Chartreuse itself. On the evening of September 13, 2003, five of us crammed into Hans's Mercedes camper. I had met Hans and Manfred that morning at the Hotel Richemond in Geneva, as had Dave en route to the Grande Chartreuse. Bernie was meeting us there. I had never met him, but I had seen pictures of him and thought he looked like God on the Sistine Chapel ceiling. Hans and Manfred stayed in their camper; Dave and I checked into the local auberge. When I left my room, I saw Manfred standing at the door of the next room. I looked in and saw Bernie in his underwear. I knew him immediately. We looked at each other, and then hugged for a very long, quiet time, as if we had shared much pain, as if he were my brother. I thought to myself, "I have hugged God in his underwear." Manfred didn't know what to make of it. He said, "Bernie only shook Dave's hand."

For five or so hours in the crowded camper, time stopped. We continued a conversation that had no beginning. The monks' printed-out e-mails are fourteen inches high, about 6,000 pages, and they had all read the then current draft of this book. I kept my tape recorder going, and Manfred cooked and fed us as we talked without stop, as if from a continuation of yesterday's conversation. The monks mainly talked about what happened to them—the difficulty of leaving the Charterhouse, and how hard it was to adjust. Hans remembers that it took him months. These years were painfully solitary. Bernie agreed, explaining that one of the ex-monk's sufferings is that he looks like everyone else yet has been radically transformed. He admitted that "an ex-monk is not an easy person to live with." His wife agrees, as I do. When Bernie is meditating instead of working for the school, she says, "Lofty words without concrete acts are empty words." Dave made a superficially easy adjustment, starting work almost immediately with a large Chicago bank. His intention was to keep busy while he planned what to do next, but he stayed at the bank for twenty years, while repeatedly revisiting his decision to leave Parkminster.

As the evening in the crowded truck wore on and the wine bottles emptied, the talk turned to how they had stayed in touch with the Carthusian life. Living out their personal myths, these men are integrating the most important experience of their life as they go forward to old age and death. In Bernie's words: "I believe with all my heart that the 'ex-doms' have drunk from the fountain of St. Bruno and the graces received have changed something deeply within." They now live in the world but are still, in Hans's words, "struggling like a postulant on his first day in the Charterhouse, trying to hide in the Cloud of Unknowing for five to ten minutes a day." Hans, Chuck, and Dave meditate in the Carthusian manner each morning. Bernie lives a contemplative life—his son Timothée says, "The fact that he works by himself allows him to meditate and contemplate most of the time." The monks still inside the Charterhouse consider "perseverance" as continuing life in cell; from my perspective, all these men have persevered in the goals of their youth. Except for Hans and Bernie, these men will probably never see each other again. No one talked of planning another reunion. Their comment was, "This was the gift. This experience is sufficient for years." They are happy to know that they are not alone, that the others are at their proper posts in England, Germany, France, the United States, and elsewhere in the world. I noticed that all of them treasure domesticity; even Bernie talks about missing his son when he is at boarding school. He says, "I am becoming human."

We spent the next day together, exploring the mountains around the Grande Chartreuse, getting as close to the Charterhouse as we could with our cameras. Bernie left to return home, and in late afternoon, Hans, Manfred, Dave, and I left for Ittingen, a Carthusian Charterhouse-museum in Switzerland. Then on to the small town in Germany where I met Hans's indomitable mother; Hans had told me she was very formal, so I had practiced how to greet her in German, but she immediately said, "Call me *Oma,*" which means "grandmother." Hans translated the journal of his years in the Charterhouse and showed me the small notes the novices wrote to each other. Bernie called us a few days later and suggested the word "*surnaturelle*" for the reunion. All Hans's brothers and their wives got together to meet the American lady who was writing a book about Hans's experience in the Charterhouse.

The next day, I flew to England. Before meeting with Theo Faber, Romilly Pitt, and the former Dom Gregory, I revisited Parkminster. Dom Columba and the new Prior had read a draft of the book. The Prior's initial comment was, "Doms Columba and Leo haven't changed in forty years." I asked if there was anything he wanted me to change, and he only requested that I change the names of the monks still in the Charterhouse. Dom Columba liked the book so much he stayed up until Matins to read it a second time before my visit; he claimed he considered taking it to church to read during Night Office.

When I first met Dom Columba in the fall of 1999, he was still excited over how he had seen St. Bruno's picture in a Dublin bookstore as a youngster and then again in the brothers' choir at Parkminster. I had expected to meet a formal, reserved monk. I met a human being who overwhelmed me with empathy and intuitive understanding. Now eighty-nine, he has not left Parkminster. After his stint as Novice Master, he was Prior from 1979 to 1991. Following the continuing changes of Vatican II, Dom Columba was the first Prior to be elected rather than appointed. He buried ten of the monks during his eleven-year watch. As requested by the Reverend Father, he resigned his office as Prior in 1990 and was happy to resume being a choir monk, happy to keep to his cell. Dom Columba now lives at Parkminster in a special cell for elderly monks. He has his own shower, and there is always hot water, which he describes as "too much luxury for a monk." He had a stroke in 2002 and felt immense gratitude, not the slightest fear. He commented, "If death is anything like this, fine." After his third stroke in 2003, he asked the Prior if Hans could come to visit. The Prior agreed, and Hans came immediately. He saw him again the next year for his fortieth anniversary as a Carthusian monk and reported that Dom Columba "is happier to be a hermit than he ever was."

Dom Gregory, the professional singer from the Royal Academy of Music, stayed in the Charterhouse for nineteen years. After not singing from the time he left for Parkminster, at age sixty-five at his parish retirement party, he sang as if he had never stopped. He still delights in music and still sounds as he did on the records he made before entering the Charterhouse. He has a great zest for life. Now a retired diocesan priest in the north of England, he keeps a very Carthusian schedule. He has plenty of time to study, think, and pray with almost no preoccupations. He believes that he is continuing his basic vocation. A convert to Catholicism, he still delights in Catholic teaching and is trying to love God as a contemplative priest.

I have not been able to locate Dom Lorenzo. He made solemn profession in 1967 and was ordained in September 1970, in the presence of six family members who were delighted that the bishop addressed them in Italian, their own language. In 1971, the Reverend Father assigned Dom Lorenzo to the Charterhouse of Farneta. Beginning in 1973, the Reverend Father gave him a series of authorizations of absence that lasted until June 1975. On June 13, 1975, Dom Columba wrote that Dom Lorenzo "has left the order and the priesthood without permission and is now a hotel waiter." On November 27, 1975, an ex-Carthusian hermit wrote to a monk at the Grande Chartreuse, "For many months, Dom Lorenzo has not been here at the island of Elba because he was too disturbed by the tourists. It seems to me that he went to Italy toward Modena." On November 28, 1980, Dom Lorenzo applied for laicization.

⊕

Not much changed for the Carthusians between 1084 and 1965, but a lot changed after December 8, 1965. Three years later, in 1968, the Catholic Church required every member of a religious order to put their criticisms of the order in writing. The Carthusians refused to do this at first—they feared it would disturb the silence that was essential to their lives. Unlike their earlier experiences, Rome insisted. At the command of Vatican II, in 1971, the General Chapter approved changes to the order's statutes that were later brought into conformity with the 1983 Code of Canon Law and approved by the General Chapter in 1989. In the 1960s, there were thirty-five monks and only twelve brothers. In 2005, twenty-one men live in a Charterhouse that had housed nearly a hundred monks at the turn of the twentieth century: six solemnly professed monks, five novices, five solemnly professed brothers, three brother novices, and two donates. Since 1965, four choir monks have made solemn profession at Parkminster.

The brothers have become a more dominant force. The new regimen allows the brothers, if they wish, to take part in choir and to live in cells. They wear the same cowls as the monks, and their beards are no longer obligatory. They participate in classes and only work six hours a day, instead of eight. The order has instructed the Priors to take into account the desires and feelings of both the brothers and monks before giving commands; in a sense, they negotiate their schedules. Together, they elect their Prior, who now has more authority. Yet continuities remain. Monks entering after the changes of Vatican II do not consider the changes "substantial." One of them comments, "The substance, the life, the attraction, the ideal is still the same. It is the accidental that changes. We still offer what St. Bruno offered his friends: to seek God in solitude."

There are only five spots left in the graveyard. Dom Joseph died in 1994. He had a successful monk career as Vicar for the Carthusian nuns at the Certosa di San Francesco, hearing confessions and giving conferences. In October 1965, while still at the Charterhouse of Pisa, he wrote to Dom Bonaventure, "It is worthwhile having had a job to enjoy the next afterwards by contrast." In October 1968, in a letter to Chuck, he wrote, "I have never been so happy in my life. . . . I have discovered that I had to hit the 50s for the really happy years to start." He met Dom Columba at a bi-yearly conference at the Grande Chartreuse and referred to "a cloud over Parkminster." Dom Columba said to forget the past and received him warmly. Dom Joseph continued to correspond with the novices who had left.

In 1965, the Visitors recommended that Dom Bonaventure be reassigned to the new Charterhouse in Vermont to oversee its construction. Shortly afterward, he was diagnosed with Alzheimer's disease and died on February 6, 1968. Because Dom Guy had very successfully directed the brothers, the Reverend Father appointed him as the next Prior. Dom Bruno welcomed him as "the Devil you know is better than the Devil you don't." Dom Guy died at Parkminster on September 4, 1995. Dom Columba had been saying Mass in the extern chapel; every Sunday, he asked those attending to pray for Dom Guy. This went on for weeks until someone said, "We should stop praying for Dom Guy because it's time he died." He wasted away, nothing but skin and bones, but was very patient. In spite of what many monks considered Dom Guy's worldliness, he died a very edifying death, but took forever to do it. Mountaineers die because they don't quit, and perhaps the same unrelenting logic applies to the Carthusian monk. Dom Bruno's nervous breakdown after forty years as a monk supports this view. He died on August 24, 2000, at Parkminster. When Dave left, Dom Jerome also left for a two-year leave of absence, which became perpetual exclaustration; he is still a Carthusian, but he lives outside the Charterhouse. He does not perform parish duties, but he says Mass every day and visits the Charterhouse yearly. Dom Anselm died at Parkminster on June 15, 1971. Dom Ludolph, now seventy-seven, has three grown children. He remarked in September 2004: "My admiration for the life has never diminished from the moment I first learnt of it."

When I last met with Dom Columba, he explained that when he rereads Theresa of Avila's *Interior Castle*, he stops to pray: "Because she makes you see that God loves you—the whole point of Carthusian life." Then, from memory, he quoted St. John of the Cross: "What will take place on the other side when all for me will be overturned into eternity; I don't know. I believe, I believe only that a great love awaits me." As most old people would say, he commented, "It's not hard to die when everyone you know is dead." In his words, he is "so old and coming to an end." I walked with him from the extern Guest House to the Gatehouse door, where forty years earlier five young men had rung the bell. When we parted, he shook my hand and said very factually and unemotionally, "See you in another place."

APPENDIX

Dramatis Personae*

NOVICES

Dom Edward [Theo Faber] (Apr. 21, 1935), England, professed Dec. 8, 1959
Dom Gregory [Geraint Clerke] (May 17, 1931), England, professed Oct. 6, 1958
Dom Columba [Patrick McCormick] (Apr. 19, 1916), Dublin, Ireland, professed Sept. 14, 1960
Dom Paul [Paul Ryan] (Sept. 1, 1927), Boston, Massachusetts, professed Dec. 8, 1960
Dom Mark [Vincent Pirera] (May 27, 1939), New Zealand, professed Oct. 6, 1961
Dom Leo [Paddy O'Connell] (July 6, 1933), Dublin, Ireland, professed Oct. 6, 1962
Dom Ignatius [Hans Klein] (Sept. 12, 1938), Berlin, Germany, professed Dec. 8, 1962
Dom Damian [Chuck Henley] (Feb. 29, 1940), Philadelphia, Pennsylvania, professed Feb. 2, 1963
Dom Malachi [Bernie Shea] (Feb. 21, 1939), Brooklyn, New York, professed June 24, 1963
Dom Philip [Dave Lynch] (Mar. 2, 1938), Chicago, Illinois, professed June 24, 1963
Dom Lorenzo [Alessandro Sansone], Calabria, Italy, professed Oct. 6, 1964
Dom David [Peter Zeffert] (Nov. 29, 1940), Melbourne, Australia, clothed Oct. 6, 1962

*Not everyone living at Parkminster during this time is listed. I list the monks in descending order of their date of profession.

SOLEMNS

Dom Humphrey Pawsey (Sept. 22, 1898), England, professed Nov. 7, 1922, Antiquior
Dom Hugo-Maria Plein (1875), Germany, professed Feb. 2, 1925
Dom Bonaventure Cretton (Nov. 16, 1904), Switzerland, professed June 24, 1930, Prior
Dom Francis-Xavier Gomez (Dec. 14, 1909), Kerala, India, professed Aug. 15, 1935, Sacristan
Dom Bede Rose (Feb. 15, 1911), Scotland, professed Mar. 20, 1937, Sub-Procurator
Dom Anselm Stoelen (Sept. 11, 1887), Belgium, professed Mar. 20, 1937, philosophy and theology professor
Dom Emmanuel Galante (May 15, 1887), France, professed May 26, 1938
Dom Bruno Sullivan (Aug. 8, 1923), England, professed June 24, 1947, Novice Master until 1960, then Vicar
Dom Guy Thackrah (Mar. 31, 1907), England, professed Aug. 15, 1948, Procurator
Dom Jerome Down (Sept. 4, 1920), England, professed Sept. 8, 1950, First Cantor on Antiquior's Side
Dom Ludolph Matheson (May 25, 1928), New Zealand, professed June 24, 1951, First Cantor on Prior's Side
Dom Joseph Hannan (Mar. 20, 1916), Australia, professed Mar. 25, 1954, Novice Master 1960–1965
Dom Marianus Marck (Apr. 5, 1921), Saxe-Meinigen, Germany, professed Feb. 2, 1956
Dom John-Baptist Hamilton (July 22, 1913), United States, professed Mar. 25, 1957

POSTULANTS

Hyacinth Objidja, Nigeria, arrived after March 1961, left July 31, 1961

BROTHERS

Brother Bruno Holden (Nov. 22, 1892), England, professed Dec. 8, 1922, Infirmarian, bookbinder
Brother William Gillett (Jan. 17, 1901), England, professed Nov. 17, 1928, tailor
Brother Hugh Bones (Jan. 7, 1898), England, professed Oct. 29, 1930, haircutter
Brother Raphael Dennett (Sept. 12, 1906), England, donation Aug. 14, 1933, Porter
Brother Christopher Ciszewski (Sept. 7, 1901), Poland, professed Aug. 15, 1950, cook
Brother Peter O'Donovan (Dec. 27, 1939), England, professed Nov. 1, 1972

APPENDIX

A Note on the Sources

The Carthusian *lingua franca* is monastic Latin. The monks follow St. Jerome's Latin (Vulgate) translation of the Greek Septuagint rather than the Hebrew text. This creates some confusion regarding the numbering of the psalms. In the Greek Septuagint, Psalms 9 and 10 are one psalm, Psalm 9; in Hebrew, the same psalm is divided into Psalms 9 and 10. The following psalm, therefore, is Psalm 12 in Hebrew (and in modern translations) and Psalm 11 in the monastic Vulgate. The discrepancy, of course, continues throughout the rest of the psalms. Various Carthusian monks translated the Latin Vulgate for this book. Sometimes they disagreed with each other's translations. Dom Ignatius, for example, thought Dom Philip's translation of the Mass for John the Baptist too loose, too colloquial. But that is what Dom Philip heard.

Because most of my sources are personal correspondence, such as e-mails, faxes, and letters, or are from books unavailable to the public, I have not included endnotes in this text. The words, thoughts, and actions that I attribute to various monks come from my archive of monk correspondence.

Little has been written for a general audience on Carthusian life before Vatican II. The most useful and authentic is Serrou and Vals's illustrated *Au "désert" de Chartreuse: La vie solitaire des fils de St. Bruno,* cited below.

PUBLICATIONS ON CARTHUSIAN LIFE BEFORE VATICAN II

Bösen, Willibald. *Auf einsamer Strasse zu Gott.* Freiburg: Herder, 1987.

Boutrais, Cyprien Marie. *The History of the Great Chartreuse by a Carthusian Monk.* Translated from the French by E. Hassid. London: Burns, Oates & Washbourne, 1934.

Catholic Encyclopedia. On-line edition, 2003.

"The Chartreuse of St. Hugh." In Sussex, *Littell's Living Age,* set. 5: 175 (Oct.–Dec., 1887), 24.

Chauncy, Dom Maurice. *The Passion and Martyrdom of the Holy English Carthusian Fathers: The Short Narration,* 1570. Unique manuscript, edited by Rev. G.W. S. Curtis. London: The Church Historical Society, 1935.

Degand, A. "Chartreux (Liturgie des)." In Fernand Cabrol and Henri LeClercq, eds., *Dictionnaire d'archéologie chrétienne et de liturgie,* III:I, cols. 1045–1071. Paris: Letouzey et Ané, 1913.

Hogg, James. "Dom Edmund Gurdon: A Memoir by James Hogg." Dr. James Hogg, ed., *Analecta Cartusiana.* Salzburg: Institut für Anglistik und Amerikanistik, 1988.

Hogg, Dr. James, et al., eds. *Analecta Cartusiana.* 231 vols. Salzburg: Institut für Anglistik und Amerikanistik, 1970–1996.

Laporte, Dom Maurice. *Aux sources de la vie cartusienne.* 8 vols. Saint-Pierre-de-Chartreuse: La Grande Chartreuse, 1960–1971. Available at the Library of Congress.

Ravier, André. *Saint Bruno: The Carthusian.* Translated by Bruno Becker, O.S.B. San Francisco: Ignatius Press, 1981.

Serrou, Robert, and Pierre Vals. *Au "désert" de Chartreuse: La vie solitaire des fils de St. Bruno,* with 100 illustrations. Paris: Éditions Pierre Horay, 1955.

Sheppard, Lancelot C. "How the Carthusians Pray." *Thought: A Quarterly of the Sciences and Letters* (September 1929) IV:2, 294–311.

"St. Hugh's Charterhouse, Parkminster." *Catholic World* (Apr.–Sept., 1940) 151:901–906, 102.

Thompson, Margaret E. *The Carthusian Order in England.* Published for the Church Historical Society. London: Society for Promoting Christian Knowledge, 1930.

INFORMATION ON THE PRESENT-DAY ORDER

A Carthusian. *Carthusian Novice Conferences.* Kalamazoo, MI: Cistercian Publications, 1993–1999. 5 vols.

A Carthusian. *The Spirit of Place: Carthusian Reflections.* London: Darton, Longman and Todd, 1998.

Hogg, Dr. James, et al., eds. *Analecta Cartusiana.* 231 vols. Salzburg: Institut für Anglistik und Amerikanistik, 1970–1996.

Lockhart, Robin Bruce. *Halfway to Heaven: The Hidden Life of the Sublime Carthusians.* New York: Vanguard Press, 1985.

Nabert, Nathalie. *Les larmes, la nourriture, le silence: Essai de spiritualité cartusienne, sources et continuité.* Paris: Beauchesne Éditeur, 2001.

North, Richard. *Fools for God.* London: Collins, 1987. Chapters 2–4.

Paillard, Thierry. *Le jour où j'ai sauté dans l'infini.* Paris: Presses de la Renaissance, 2004.

Skinner, John. *Hear Our Silence: A Portrait of the Carthusians.* London: Harper Collins/Fount Paperbacks, 1995.

USEFUL WEB SITES

www.chartreux.org and www.parkminster.org.uk.

APPENDIX

*The Carthusian Horarium in the 1960s**

11:00 PM Rise
11:10 Matins of the Blessed Virgin Mary (BVM), meditation
11:45 Matins and Lauds—Angelus**
About 2:00 Lauds (BVM)
About 2:15 Sleep

5:50 AM Rise
6:00 Primes†
6:30 Angelus, meditation
7:15 Litany of the Saints, Conventual Mass
About 8:00 in the chapels: Terce, Private Masses, Communion
9:00 Terce (BVM), a little relaxation in private
9:30 Theological Studies
10:15 Manual Work
11:00 Sexts, dinner, recreation in private

*The English Charterhouse has not kept copies of their 1960s horarium. I compiled this schedule from that of the Grande Chartreuse, a novice's letter to his parents, and the memories of eight monks of that time.

**Bold type indicates activities the monks performed together.

†In plural Offices, for example, "Primes," the monks prayed both the Little Office of the Blessed Virgin and the Divine Office.

12:00 PM Spiritual reading, theological studies
1:30 Angelus, Nones
2:00 Spiritual reading
2:30 Vespers of BVM
2:45 Vespers
3:15 Study
4:30 Manual work
5:15 Examination of conscience, prayer
6:00 Supper (summer schedule), recreation in private
7:00 Angelus, Complines
About 7:20 Sleep

On Walk Days:
Earlier dinner
Angelus and None of BVM on walk

GLOSSARY OF RELIGIOUS AND MONASTIC TERMS

Ambulatory entrance hall inside the cell, a passageway about forty feet long.

Antiphon a short piece of music in plainsong sung before and after a psalm or canticle. The words illustrate and enforce the meaning of the text.

Antiphonary one of two very large books containing antiphons, one for Night Office, the other for the remaining hours, compiled in the twelfth century.

Antiquior title of the third senior in the house. In the absence of the Prior and Vicar, the Antiquior presides and does all that the Vicar does when the Prior is absent. He should be a solemnly professed monk with whom the Prior and members of the community can usefully consult. He often is the most senior monk.

Archdeacon an ecclesiastic who ranks next below a bishop and has administrative responsibility for a diocese.

Biretta black quadrangular hat worn by diocesan priests.

Breviary a book containing the canonical hours of the Divine Office.

Brother a nonclerical male member of a religious order who intends to make or has made solemn vows. A brother does not aspire to the priesthood and, in this case, does manual labor in the monastery.

Canon a secular priest in the Middle Ages who lived either in a community or was associated with a cathedral.

Canticle songs and hymns scattered throughout the Bible, such as the "Nunc Dimittis" or the "Magnificat."

Cassock black, floor-length, form-fitting robe that buttoned down the front, worn by diocesan priests.

Cell the individual house and garden where a hermit monk lives.

Chapter House a building attached to a cathedral or monastery where meetings of the chapter are held; in this case, the monks comprise the chapter.

Cincture a girdle or belt, originally a flat band, secured with a clasp or buckle and, in this case, made of painted white leather.

Charterhouse the English name for a Carthusian monastery.

Church cowl flowing garment, made of white wool, with sleeves and an attached hood.

Cloister the enclosed walkways connecting the cells to the church and the other communal buildings.

Commemorations mainly the antiphon of Our Lady after Lauds and Vespers; during Mass, the commemoration of the living and the dead.

Compline (see **Divine Office**).

Consecration the part of the Mass where the priest changes bread and wine into the body and blood of Christ.

Cowl a sandwich-board, sleeveless, hooded garment with front and back panels connected by a wide strip of fabric.

Desert Fathers pioneer monks of the early Church who often went into the desert to live a solitary life.

Discipline lengths of knotted rope or leather, meant as a penitential tool.

Diurnal book containing the day hours of the Divine Office.

Divine Office the Opus Dei, or the official prayers of the Catholic Church spanning the entire day, comprising eight set times of prayer.

Donate a brother who is not a professed member of the community.

Doxology a short formula of praise to God, especially one in liturgical use.

Ember Days three days of a specified week during each season of the year set aside for prayer and fasting.

Excitator one who excites, especially one whose business it is to rouse others from sleep.

Ferial day day of the week on which there is no feast day, an ordinary day.

Gamelles interlocking steel dishes.

Garth a small piece of enclosed land, usually beside a house or other building, now short for cloister garth.

Gilet thick vest worn under the habit in cold weather.

Gregorian chant official music of the Catholic Church, made up of a four-line staff and square notes called "punctums." The music originated in early Jewish and early Christian Latin chant, to which St. Gregory the Great (540–604) contributed.

Habit the long-sleeved, ankle-length loose outer garment worn by monks and nuns, in this case, made of thick white wool.

Hatch a small enclosure within a wall with doors that open on both sides, allowing objects to be placed and removed from either side.

Hebdomadary a member of a religious group who takes his or her weekly turn in performing sacred Offices.

Hermit in this context, one who from religious motives lives a solitary life, originally one of the early Christian recluses.

Horarium a timed program or plan.

Hours of the Divine Office prescribed set prayers said at appointed times of the day.

Invitatory an invitation to prayer in religious worship, sung only at Matins, the beginning of the liturgical day.

Lanthorn variant of "lantern." A transparent case containing and protecting a light.

Marriage Tribunal an ecclesiastical court determining the validity of marriages. Catholic marriages can be annulled for various reasons, including insanity, fear, conditional consent, lack of sexual consummation, and various other conditions opposed to an essential property of marriage.

Matins the longest of the hours (see **Divine Office**), lasting at least two hours; on feast days, when embellished by additional readings, the Office may continue for more than three hours.

Misericord a ten-inch ledge attached to the lower side of the hinged seat in the choir stall; when the seat is turned up, the misericord provides support while standing.

Missal the book containing the service of the Mass for the whole year.

Mitre the official headdress of a bishop, a tall cap having an outline resembling a pointed arch in the front and back.

Monk originally a hermit or solitary, but applying also to members of some religious orders. Monks live apart from the world under the vows of conversion of life (change in lifestyle), stability in the monastery, and obedience. They typically follow a rule and are devoted to the performance of religious duties and the contemplative life.

Night Office in the Carthusian ritual, Night Office consists of Matins and Lauds, which are said before daybreak.

Novice a newcomer to a profession. At this time, the Carthusian novitiate lasted until solemn profession, normally a matter of five years.

Oblate one who has devoted himself and his property to the service of a monastery in which he lives as a lay brother; he does not take vows.

Office of the Blessed Virgin called the "little" Office and always said in cell, a diminutive mirror of the Divine Office.

Oratory a place designed for divine service but not specifically for use by all the faithful. Here, the place for prayer inside each monk's cell.

Passe-partout a three- to four-inch pronged metal key with a wooden handle for cell doors and monastery gates.

Pater and Ave ecclesiastical shorthand for the "Our Father" and "Hail Mary."

Penitential Psalms traditionally, seven psalms form the Penitential Psalms: 6, 31, 37, 50, 101, 129, 142.

Postulant a person asking to be admitted to a religious order; normally the postulancy lasted from three to six months.

Prie-dieu kneeler and book stand, normally one piece and portable; in this case, built into the wall in front of a hinged bench.

Prior the head monk in each Carthusian monastery.

Procurator the monk assigned to manage the temporal affairs of the monastery.

Psalm any one of the sacred songs or hymns of the ancient Hebrews that together form the Book of Psalms, one of the books of the Old Testament.

Psalter songbook containing the psalms for the liturgical year.

Rector the head or master of a university, college, school, or religious institution.

Relic some object, such as a part of the body or clothing, an article of personal use, or the like, that remains as a memorial of a departed saint, martyr, or other holy person, and as such is carefully preserved and held in esteem or veneration.

Rood screen the rood screen surmounted by a crucifix separates the floor of a church into two parts, one part for the clerics, the other part for lay people or lay brothers.

Rosary a string of fifty-five beads divided into five sets (each having ten small and one large bead), carried on the person and used to assist the memory; also a similar set of 165 beads. The small beads represent Aves and the large ones Paters.

Sacristan individual responsible for the church and altar.

Simple profession a vow to remain in a religious order for a specified time, usually three years.

Solemn profession a vow to remain in a religious order until death.

Spiritual adviser a priest designated to advise individuals on spiritual matters, in this case a solemnly professed priest or monk.

Stile a narrow, spiraled, wooden ladder erected over a fence to allow passage over or through a fence to one person at a time, while forming a barrier to the passage of livestock.

Tabula the notice board; by extension, the cloistered area around the board.

Vestry a room in a church where the Sacristan keeps vestments and liturgical objects.

Vicar one who takes the place of or acts as the representative of another in the performance of ecclesiastical or religious functions; here, the second in command in a Carthusian monastery.

INDEX

PublicAffairs is a publishing house founded in 1997. It is a tribute to the standards, values, and flair of three persons who have served as mentors to countless reporters, writers, editors, and book people of all kinds, including me.

I. F. Stone, proprietor of *I. F. Stone's Weekly*, combined a commitment to the First Amendment with entrepreneurial zeal and reporting skill and became one of the great independent journalists in American history. At the age of eighty, Izzy published *The Trial of Socrates*, which was a national bestseller. He wrote the book after he taught himself ancient Greek.

Benjamin C. Bradlee was for nearly thirty years the charismatic editorial leader of *The Washington Post*. It was Ben who gave the *Post* the range and courage to pursue such historic issues as Watergate. He supported his reporters with a tenacity that made them fearless, and it is no accident that so many became authors of influential, best-selling books.

Robert L. Bernstein, the chief executive of Random House for more than a quarter century, guided one of the nation's premier publishing houses. Bob was personally responsible for many books of political dissent and argument that challenged tyranny around the globe. He is also the founder and was the longtime chair of Human Rights Watch, one of the most respected human rights organizations in the world.

. . .

For fifty years, the banner of Public Affairs Press was carried by its owner Morris B. Schnapper, who published Gandhi, Nasser, Toynbee, Truman, and about 1,500 other authors. In 1983 Schnapper was described by *The Washington Post* as "a redoubtable gadfly." His legacy will endure in the books to come.

Peter Osnos, *Founder and Editor-at-Large*